STEPHEN JOLLY

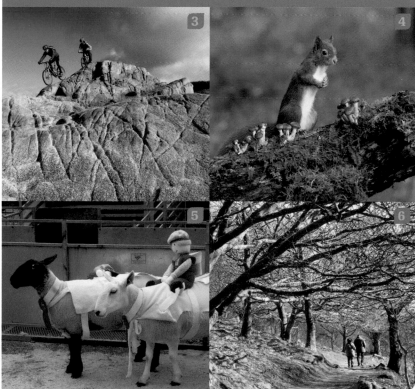

1 Caerlaverock Castle. 2 Auchenmalg shore. 3 Mountain biking at 7stanes Kirroughtree. 4 Red squirrels attract many visitors to Eskrigg Nature Reserve. 5 Local events in Moffat include the annual sheep races up the High Street! 6 Taking it Slow on the Jubilee Path between Kippford and Rockcliffe.

ALAN IRVING

FORESTRY COMMISSION SCOTLAND

DG/DF (SLOW BRITAIN)

DG/DF (SLOW BRITAIN)

200 MILES OF COAST

Rocky beaches, craggy cliffs, sandy bays, tidal mudflats, fishing villages and harbourside towns – these are just some of the scenes to be found along Dumfries and Galloway's 200 miles of coastline, from the eastern end of the Solway Firth to the Mull of Galloway, Scotland's most southerly point.

SLOW TRAVEL

Dumfries
& Galloway

Local, characterful guides to Britain's special places

Donald Greig
& Darren Flint

EDITION 1

Bradt Travel Guides Ltd, UK
The Globe Pequot Press Inc, USA

Bradt

Dumfries & Galloway

Slow down and feel the pressures of daily life ease away. Dumfries and Galloway regularly comes in the list of top regions for quality of life. Plenty of outdoor space, lots of activities to enjoy, and beautiful scenery make this one of the best places in the country to unwind.

1 Portpatrick's picturesque seafront. 2 Painted cottages in Kirkcudbright. 3 Cruggleton Castle on its rocky promontory. 4 'The Seat', an unusual resting place on the southwest Machars, looking out to Luce Bay. 5 The Solway Firth at Powfoot. 6 The iconic Mull of Galloway Lighthouse. 7 Walking around Brighouse Bay. 8 Boats moored in the Isle of Whithorn's pleasant harbour. 9 Traditional stake net fishing at Auchencairn Bay.

WILDLIFE & WILD LANDSCAPES

Travelling around the region you will be met by an ongoing succession of memorable views encompassing a broad range of habitats. The diversity of wildlife is what attracts many visitors and includes both common and rare species.

6

1 The dawn sky at WWT Caerlaverock Wetland Centre. 2 The nuthatch can be found at Eskrigg Nature Reserve and throughout the region. 3 Wild goats roam In Galloway Forest Park's Goat Park on the Queen's Way. 4 The region is a good place to see the rare natterjack toad. 5 Red deer can be spotted in Dumfries and Galloway's wild landscapes. 6 The peaceful waters of Loch Ken. 7 The Devil's Beef Tub in the Moffat Hills. 8 The Grey Mare's Tail is the fifth highest waterfall in the UK. 9 The Knocktinkle viewpoint on the road to Gatehouse from Laurieston shows off the Galloway moors and hill country to superb effect.

7

8

9

RURAL LIFE

Centuries of agriculture have shaped the landscape across the region, from well-grazed pastureland to dry stone dykes. A Slower, more rural way of life continues to be the norm; for many, this is one of the chief attractions of living here.

1 Nestled in the beautiful hills and moorland of Upper Eskdale lies the village of Eskdalemuir. **2** Successful foraging is an art form, one to be learned with the region's resident forager. **3** Belted Galloway cows are fondly known as 'Belties'.

AUTHORS

Donald Greig spent many years working as a travel and wildlife publisher for companies in the UK and Australia before returning to Scotland to settle in Dumfries and Galloway. He has written for a range of national publications, including *Scotland on Sunday* and *Independent on Sunday* newspapers, *Wanderlust*, the UK's leading travel magazine, and *The List* magazine, the Scottish equivalent of *Time Out*. Between 2007 and 2014  he was Managing Director of Bradt Travel Guides, a job which he hopes prepared him adequately for writing this guide.

Darren Flint worked across the UK and Australia before settling as a relative newcomer in Dumfries and Galloway and being hooked from the outset. After a career in tourism development and then conservation with the Royal Society for the Protection of Birds (RSPB), he completed a Masters in Environmental Conservation from UCL. An avid naturalist with a fascination for Lepidoptera, he likes nothing better than donning  his boots and uncovering those hidden corners we all dream about. He is the project officer for a community environmental venture at Castle Loch in Lochmaben.

Donald and Darren are opening a B&B in Moffat and would be delighted to meet any readers of this guide: Summerlea House, Eastgate, Moffat DG10 9AB ✐ 01683 221471 ⏁ www.moffatbedandbreakfast.co.uk

DEDICATION

To Mum, Dad and Isla; simple pleasures and happy days in this special place.
Donald
To Grace; enjoy happy adventures and slow travels.
Darren

Reprinted September 2016   First edition published April 2015
Bradt Travel Guides Ltd
IDC House, The Vale, Chalfont St Peter, Bucks SL9 9RZ, England
www.bradtguides.com
Print edition published in the USA by The Globe Pequot Press Inc,
PO Box 480, Guilford, Connecticut 06437-0480

Project Managers: Anna Moores and Katie Wilding
Cover research: Pepi Bluck, Perfect Picture
Series Design: Pepi Bluck, Perfect Picture

ISBN: 978 1 84162 861 5 (print)
e-ISBN: 978 1 78477 118 8 (e-pub)
e-ISBN: 978 1 78477 218 5 (mobi)
British Library Cataloguing in Publication Data
A catalogue record for this book is available from the British Library
Photographs
© individual photographers credited beside images & also those from image libraries
credited as follows: Alamy.com (A), Donald Greig and Darren Flint (DG/DF (Slow Britain)),
Dreamstime.com (D), Shutterstock.com (S)

Front cover Portpatrick (Doug Simpson/A)
Back cover Belted Galloway cattle (Ewan Chesser/S)
Title page Devorgilla Bridge, Dumfries (stocksolutions/S)

Maps David McCutcheon FBCart.S and Liezel Bohdanowicz

Typeset from the authors' disc by Pepi Bluck, Perfect Picture
Production managed by Jellyfish Print Solutions; printed in India
Digital conversion by www.dataworks.co.in

AUTHORS' STORY

For several years before writing this guide we had been contemplating a move but couldn't decide to where. All we knew was that we wanted to live somewhere 'more rural'; and for me (Donald), it would ideally be in my home country of Scotland. It was only when we stopped off in Dumfries and Galloway that everything fell into place. We had been exploring the Ardnamurchan peninsula and were heading south again and needed somewhere to stay. At the last minute we booked a room at somewhere called Craigadam near Castle Douglas, where a quick overnight stay turned into a three-day exploration and a trip down memory lane, for I had spent several happy childhood holidays in the Stewartry. We couldn't believe that here was a part of the world which, despite its comparative proximity to so many major urban centres, still felt like somewhere that offered a gentler, 'Slower' (in every sense of the word) pace of life. And so to Dumfries and Galloway we moved eight months later, a homecoming for me and a step into a new country for Darren.

A note on 'I' & 'we'

With two of us involved in researching and writing this book, you will find references in the text to both 'I' and 'we'. Wherever 'I' is used, it is a comment from Donald.

ACKNOWLEDGEMENTS

We have met hundreds of people across Dumfries and Galloway in the course of writing this guide, too many to be able to thank everyone individually here. To everyone who has supported us and with whom we have come into contact, including those who have signed up to our Slow Britain Facebook and Twitter accounts, we say a heartfelt thank you. Your generosity of time and spirit has made all the difference.

We would also like to thank the many contributors who have written pieces for this guide. Their expertise and insights bring greater depth of understanding and enjoyment of the region.

Thank you, too, to everyone who entered the photographic competition which was held as part of the development of the guide and congratulations to those whose pictures were selected to be included.

To the following people we owe a particular debt for their support: Cathy Agnew, Robin Baird and Derek Pennycook, Paula McDonald, Russell Murray and family, Celia and Richard Pickup, and Alison Smith.

Finally, we would like to thank the staff at Bradt for their patience and support, particularly Anna Moores, Katie Wilding and Rachel Fielding.

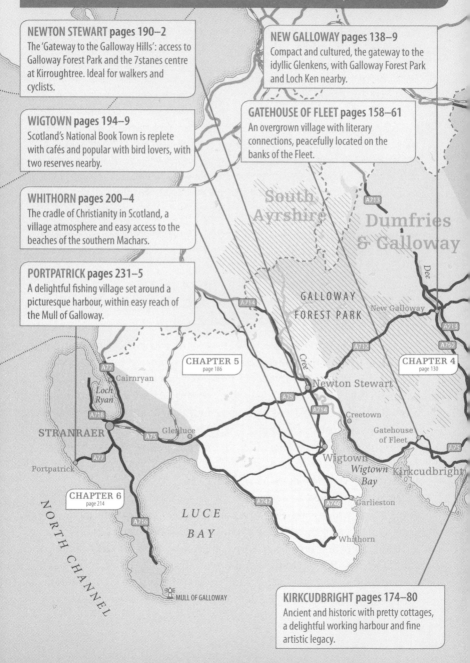

NEWTON STEWART pages 190–2
The 'Gateway to the Galloway Hills': access to Galloway Forest Park and the 7stanes centre at Kirroughtree. Ideal for walkers and cyclists.

NEW GALLOWAY pages 138–9
Compact and cultured, the gateway to the idyllic Glenkens, with Galloway Forest Park and Loch Ken nearby.

WIGTOWN pages 194–9
Scotland's National Book Town is replete with cafés and popular with bird lovers, with two reserves nearby.

GATEHOUSE OF FLEET pages 158–61
An overgrown village with literary connections, peacefully located on the banks of the Fleet.

WHITHORN pages 200–4
The cradle of Christianity in Scotland, a village atmosphere and easy access to the beaches of the southern Machars.

PORTPATRICK pages 231–5
A delightful fishing village set around a picturesque harbour, within easy reach of the Mull of Galloway.

KIRKCUDBRIGHT pages 174–80
Ancient and historic with pretty cottages, a delightful working harbour and fine artistic legacy.

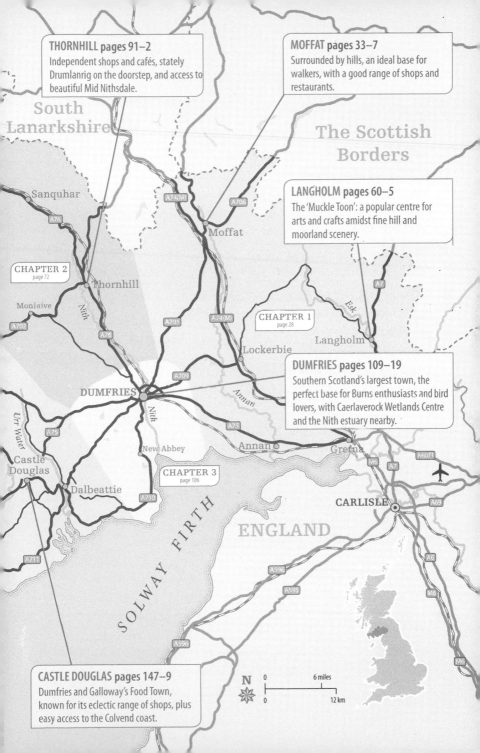

THORNHILL pages 91–2
Independent shops and cafés, stately Drumlanrig on the doorstep, and access to beautiful Mid Nithsdale.

MOFFAT pages 33–7
Surrounded by hills, an ideal base for walkers, with a good range of shops and restaurants.

South Lanarkshire

The Scottish Borders

LANGHOLM pages 60–5
The 'Muckle Toon': a popular centre for arts and crafts amidst fine hill and moorland scenery.

Sanquhar

A74(M)

A708

A76

Moffat

A7

CHAPTER 2
page 72

Thornhill

Nith

Moniaive

A792

A76

A701

A74(M)

Esk

CHAPTER 1
page 28

Lockerbie

Langholm

DUMFRIES pages 109–19
Southern Scotland's largest town, the perfect base for Burns enthusiasts and bird lovers, with Caerlaverock Wetlands Centre and the Nith estuary nearby.

A709

DUMFRIES

Nith

Annan

A75

A75

Urr Water

New Abbey

Annan

Gretna

M6

A7

A6071

Castle Douglas

CHAPTER 3
page 106

Dalbeattie

A710

S O L W A Y   F I R T H

CARLISLE

A69

A75

ENGLAND

A6

A711

A596

A595

M6

CASTLE DOUGLAS pages 147–9
Dumfries and Galloway's Food Town, known for its eclectic range of shops, plus easy access to the Colvend coast.

A596

N

0 — 6 miles

0 — 12 km

CONTENTS

DUMFRIES & GALLOWAY ONLINE

For additional online content, articles, photos and more on Dumfries and Galloway, why not
visit ✑ www.bradtguides.com/d&g and ✑ www.slowbritain.co.uk.

GOING SLOW IN
DUMFRIES & GALLOWAY

Often described as 'Scotland's forgotten corner', Dumfries and Galloway is one of the country's most under-explored areas. The reason is almost completely due to the quirks of geography and perceived isolation. Bordered to the south and west by coastline and to the north by wild moorland and hill country, the region has for centuries been seen as a remote rural outpost. The easiest access point has traditionally been from the east and that hasn't changed today. The M74 cuts across the eastern corner and follows, out of necessity, the north–south travel route of old, for the Annan Valley and Solway Plain offer the most viable place for a major roadway. This means many travellers enter and leave Dumfries and Galloway in less than an hour heading for points north or south with ne'er a moment's thought for what lies east or west. And, it has to be said, the motorway route gives little away: the flatlands around Carlisle stretch up past the eastern end of the Solway Firth and the region presents a distinctly demure face. There are few geographical features of note other than at the northern boundary where the Moffat Hills loom large to the east and the Lowther Hills to the west. What can be seen of those hills gives just a hint of the wilderness that awaits those who slow down and make time for a diversion, for Dumfries and Galloway is home to some of the most glorious scenery of the Scottish Lowlands, scenery which for this particular Scot, even after all these years, can still fill me to bursting every time I see it.

Dumfries and Galloway is a large region, by road almost 120 miles from Langholm in the east to Portpatrick in the west, and over 55 miles at its deepest point from Kirkconnel in the north to Kirkcudbright in the south. What's more, it is sparsely populated. Out of Scotland's 32 unitary authorities, it is the third largest by area but only the twelfth largest by population, with a population density of just 60 people per

THE SLOW MINDSET

Hilary Bradt, Founder, Bradt Travel Guides

We shall not cease from exploration
And the end of all our exploring
Will be to arrive where we started
And know the place for the first time.

T S Eliot, 'Little Gidding', *Four Quartets*

This series evolved, slowly, from a Bradt editorial meeting when we started to explore ideas for guides to our favourite country – Great Britain. We wanted to get away from the usual 'top sights' formula and encourage our authors to bring out the nuances and local differences that make up a sense of place – such things as food, building styles, nature, geology, or local people and what makes them tick. Our aim was to create a series that celebrates the present, focusing on sustainable tourism, rather than taking a nostalgic wallow in the past.

So without our realising it at the time, we had defined 'Slow Travel', or at least our concept of it. For the beauty of the Slow movement is that there is no fixed definition; we adapt the philosophy to fit our individual needs and aspirations. Thus Carl Honoré, author of *In Praise of Slow*, writes: 'The Slow Movement is a cultural revolution against the notion that faster is always better. It's not about doing everything at a snail's pace, it's about seeking to do everything at the right speed. Savouring the hours and minutes rather than just counting them. Doing everything as well as possible, instead of as fast as possible. It's about quality over quantity in everything from work to food to parenting.' And travel.

So take time to explore. Don't rush it, get to know an area – and the people who live there – and you'll be as delighted as the authors by what you find.

square mile. This compares with the Scottish average of 168, the UK average of 660 and English average of 1,072. Beyond the main towns of Dumfries, Stranraer and Annan, all other settlements have a population of less than 4,500.

Our advice is not to attempt to cover all of the region in one go. Any one of the six areas into which this book is divided offers sufficient breadth and depth of interest to fill a Slow week or more. And despite its size, once you're here, if you do want to cover more ground the trans-regional A75 offers quick and convenient access to most points on a road which, even on a bank holiday weekend, rarely feels busy.

While researching this book, we have been told time and again by accommodation owners that a significant number of their guests originally stopped for just one night on their way northwards but, having once had a taste of the area, have returned, often repeatedly, for longer. And therein lies the nub of it. As many friends who have come to stay have proclaimed: 'I never knew that this was here!' But what is the 'this' that they refer to?

Certainly the grandeur and variety of scenery combined with sense of space and a distinctly slower pace of life rank highly. A day spent in the Dumfriesshire Dales or Galloway Uplands soon confirms – if confirmation were needed – that, while the north of Scotland undoubtedly has majestic mountains, you don't have to travel those extra four or five hours (if coming from the south) to find summits that impress. What's more, you can be on a pristine sandy beach in the morning and at Scotland's highest village (and micro-brewery) by the afternoon. And speaking of travel times, it's worth pointing out that it takes less than an hour longer (according to the AA website) to get here from London than it would to Penzance. For those already in Scotland, it's even better. Glasgow and Edinburgh are only a couple of hours away, and even Aberdeen is less than five hours' drive. Distance, therefore, is not the obstacle that some may perceive it to be.

Individuality and authenticity are what make Dumfries and Galloway so appealing. A history which encompasses so many events and people that have been central to the development of a nation; a landscape that is more varied than you would find in most other parts of the country, from upland peaks to sandy beaches; an economy still based largely on agriculture (farming accounts for around 70% of the area), centuries of

---

FEEDBACK REQUEST & UPDATES WEBSITE

Dumfries and Galloway is full of people who have specialist knowledge on their particular part of the region or specific subject, and although we've done our very best to check our facts, we welcome feedback from our readers. If you spot an omission or error, or if you come across a new attraction or a story that you think should be shared, please get in touch, either directly with the authors (details on ♂ www.slowbritain.co.uk) or via Bradt: ♪ 01753 893444 or ✉ info@bradtguides.com.

Contact can also be made via the Facebook page that accompanies this guide: ♂ www. facebook.com/slowbritain. We would love to hear about your travels around Dumfries and Galloway.

Finally, you can add a review of the book to ♂ www.bradtguides.com or on Amazon.

sheep, dairy and beef farming having shaped the landscape; and closely related, a commitment to locally grown produce, which here is a tradition that has never faltered and in recent years has enjoyed even more support than ever. One of the most iconic sights of the region is the distinctive Belted Galloway cattle, completely black except for a white stripe around the middle, set against a background of lush green hills.

For those who are familiar with Dumfries and Galloway (especially those readers who are resident), we hope that you find much in this book to enjoy and perhaps a story or two that will take you by surprise. For those who are just discovering the area, we welcome you to a part of the world which, in this day of mass-market living, remains true to itself and is resolutely and irresistibly real, a sure hallmark of the best of 'Slow'.

SOME PRACTICAL MATTERS

The unitary authority of Dumfries and Galloway is very much an artificial construct. With a region of this size, what happens in its easternmost reaches may have no bearing at all on what is going on in the west. Like most parts of the UK, there are a multitude of ways in which the region could be broken down: geographic features, historic names, regional divisions past and present are all used depending on who you speak to, personal preference and what it is they're telling you. In the end we have opted for a mix of all of the above which we believe is logical in terms of either travelling around the region or basing yourself in just one area, combined with the dictates of geography, how the region is viewed by local people and how you might come to view it yourself. Our aim has been to make sense of it in a way which is easy to get to grips with for first-time visitors but which has a familiarity to it for repeat visitors and those who live here.

Broadly speaking, we have broken Dumfriesshire down into its three component valleys: Annandale, Eskdale and Nithsdale, and with chapters progressing from north to south. Nithsdale itself is split into two chapters to allow greater space for coverage of Dumfries. For Galloway we have taken the old, fondly remembered district of the Stewartry as one chapter, with the rest of the area broken down into its naturally occurring geographical divisions of the Machars (and Moors) and the Rhins. These areas all have their own distinct identities and each of them offers more than enough for a Slow holiday in its own right.

MAPS

Each chapter begins with a map complete with numbered stopping points that correspond to the numbers found within the text. These include all the main towns and sights, plus a few of the more unusual or remote features. To avoid overcrowding the maps we have included a grid reference in the text for some places. The ♀ symbol on these maps indicates that there is a walk in that area. There are also sketch maps for some of these featured walks and there is a map for Dumfries town centre.

The county stretches over a large area and it takes nine 1:50,000 OS Landranger maps to cover every corner (numbers 71, 76, 77, 78, 79, 82, 83, 84 and 85). To make life easier we have taken to using the online OS Custom Made service, which allows you to create a personalised map based on a precise area of your choice. See ⌀ www. ordnancesurvey.co.uk.

ACCOMMODATION

On pages 244–50 we've listed some accommodation ideas for each area. Each was chosen because it has a special quality, be that its location,

A NOTE ON BEACHES, THE COAST & TIDES

The Solway Firth and the Dumfries and Galloway coastline in general is an enchanting stretch of water. From its shores for much of its length are views of the peaks of the Lake District and Cumbria coast and, further west, of the Isle of Man. There is a good choice of beaches: sandy, rocky or simply muddy and estuarine – they all offer something different. Be aware though that the Solway tides run fast with a tidal rise of over 20 feet, while in some places the tidal bore reaches three to four feet and travels at six to seven knots. If you are in an area such as the estuary flats of the eastern end of the region or the merse further west, keep an eye open and don't take chances. If you're looking for somewhere to swim, generally speaking the more sheltered bays and coves of the Kirkcudbright coast are the most popular. For walking and simply enjoying the sea air, there are also some stunning stretches of sand on the west coast of the Machars and the eastern Rhins. Specific beaches have been identified in the text and the website of the Solway Firth Partnership (⌀ www.solwayfirthpartnership.co.uk) has an excellent guide which details beaches with a 'Family Star Rating' and 'Adventurers Rating'. It also has links to tide times for specific locations.

An annual booklet on Solway Tides is available from many newsagents and post offices for a small cost.

character or service. For further details and additional listings, go to
⊘ www.bradtguides.com/D&Gsleeps. The hotels, B&Bs and self-
catering options are indicated by 🏠 under the heading for the area in
which they are located. Campsites and caravan parks are indicated by 🛆.

FOOD & DRINK

Recommendations are very much our personal take on the places we
have enjoyed, perhaps offering an interesting menu or local specialities,
something quirky, a cracking view, an opportunity to meet local people,
or simply where there were no other options in that remote location.
Places come and go, old favourites continue to entertain, others
disappear, and new ventures start up. One of the joys of Slow travel is
that you will find your own special spots; if you are happy to share the
secret, please do tell us about your finds.

ONLINE CONTENT

Printed guidebooks can, alas, never be infinite in length. Happily however,
web pages offer almost limitless additional space for authors so that none
of their research goes to waste. Throughout the guide you will spot the
symbol 🖑 in the text. This indicates that **additional information** on a
specific subject or attraction can be found online at ⊘ www.slowbritain.
co.uk, the website set up by the authors to accompany this guide. On the
same website you will also find details of updates and/or reader feedback
as it reaches us, plus photographs from across the region.

GETTING AROUND DUMFRIES & GALLOWAY

There is no denying that travelling around the area by public transport
can be tricky, particularly when trying to get to some of the more out-of -
the-way places.

Train

There are three train lines, each running north–south. In the east of the
region the main **national West Coast line** runs through Annandale but
has only one station, at Lockerbie. Some trains from the south do stop
at Lockerbie *en route* to Glasgow or Edinburgh, but others only stop at
Carlisle where you have to change to catch a local train.

The **Nithsdale line** is particularly scenic. From Carlisle, the route
passes along the eastern end of the Solway to Gretna and Annan,

and then on into Nithsdale, to Dumfries and north through the Nith Valley to Glasgow via Kirkconnel and Sanquhar, the only station on the Southern Upland Way walking route (pages 14–15). Bikes can be taken on the train to Sanquhar to tie in with the Southern Upland Cycleway (page 15).

Also scenic is the **western line from Stranraer** which cuts up the eastern edge of the Rhins into Ayrshire and on to Glasgow. There are particularly good views on the return journey across the moors at Glenwhilly, down over the Main Water of Luce Viaduct, of Glenluce Abbey and of the Mull of Galloway. On the clearest of days, you can even see the Isle of Man.

Michael Pearson's excellent book *Iron Roads to Burns Country* offers lots of details and stories of these routes.

Significant chunks of the region, notably the Stewartry and the Machars, have no trains at all having lost their lines in the Beeching cuts of the 1960s.

Bus

Bus services offer more options with most places you could wish to visit having a service or two, although frequency can vary widely and even the more popular routes peter out in the evening and on Sunday. We advise not to head off on a day trip by bus without first doing a bit of planning to make sure you can get back. Do double check the timetables and perhaps carry a local taxi number with you, although be warned, mobile phone signal can be very patchy in places.

We have outlined key transport options at the start of each chapter. For the more adventurous we are told that hitching a lift still has some success in the more remote areas. Local public transport information is provided by South West of Scotland Transport Partnership ◌ www.swestrans.org.uk, or alternatively the traveline ◌ 0871 200 22 33 ◌ www.traveline.org.uk.

Car

If you are driving, watch your speed (this is a Slow guide after all)! On the main trunk roads, which are often quiet in comparison with many other areas of the UK, it is tempting to put your foot down but the local police are exceptionally diligent and are regularly spotted with mobile speed cameras. Note that unlike England, Scotland doesn't offer the choice of a speed awareness course instead of a fine.

KNOW THE CODE BEFORE YOU GO

Everyone has the right to be on most land and inland water providing they act responsibly. Your access rights and responsibilities are explained fully in the Scottish Outdoor Access Code (www.outdooraccess-scotland.com).

The key things are to:
* **Take responsibility for your own actions**
* **Respect the interests of other people**
* **Care for the environment**

Walking

The area is a delight for walking. Most of the countryside, from mountain to forest and moorland to seashore, is accessible with observance of the Country Code.

For any keen walkers from the English side of the border, using a Scottish OS map for the first time can be a confusing affair. Where are all the dashed lines indicating footpaths and bridleways? The right to roam means there is no need for these symbols, but it can make it a little harder to determine routes that have been used before or to know if you are likely to end up at an impasse a few miles in. While contentious at the time of finding its way on to the statute book, few landowners we spoke to had any issues of note. That said, avoiding walking close to sheep during lambing is appreciated and if you do find a lone lamb please leave it alone as the mother won't be far away. Needless to say, at any time of year if there is livestock around dogs must be kept on the lead.

Local bookshops hold a wealth of walking information as does a Google search for any area you happen to be visiting. Over the years we have taken to using a highlighter to add routes of interest to our OS maps. There are numerous quality walking books to the area: Pocket Mountains' *Dumfries & Galloway 40 Coast & Country Walks* is a handy little guide with a fine selection of routes all clearly presented. The classic Pathfinder Guide series also nicely covers the area. Dumfries and Galloway Council produces a fine selection of free walking and cycling booklets, plus they can be downloaded from www.dumgal.gov.uk (look under 'Environment' and then 'Outdoor Access and Paths').

A number of long-distance routes cross the area. The most famous is the **Southern Upland Way** (www.southernuplandway.gov.uk) running 212 miles from Portpatrick in the west across to Cocksburnpath on the east coast. The **Annandale Way** (⌀ www.annandaleway.org), established in 2009, is a 55-mile long-distance walking route which runs from the source of the Annan at Annanhead at the evocatively named Devil's Beef Tub down to Annan on the Solway Coast. The new walk in the region is the **Mull of Galloway Trail** (⌀ www.mullofgallowaytrail. co.uk), which runs from the Mull to Stranraer and continues north as the Loch Ryan Coastal Path for a total distance of 35 miles to Glenapp in South Ayrshire where it links with the Ayrshire Coastal Path.

Cycling

The many miles of quiet lanes and forest tracks offer cycling opportunities for all levels of ability, from a simple ride out along the estuary flats through to something more hair-raising like an extreme black grade mountain bike run. Linking Sunderland and Inverness, **National Cycle Route 7** (NCR7) passes right through Dumfries and Galloway taking in Gretna, Dumfries, Castle Douglas and Newton Stewart before crossing Glen Trool Forest on its way north. The Newton Stewart via Glasgow to Inverness section also forms part of **EuroVelo 1 Route**, which starts in Portugal and follows the Atlantic seaboard through France and Ireland. In the east the **NCR74** links Gretna to Lockerbie and Moffat on its 74-mile route northwards to Douglas (⌀ www.sustrans.org.uk). A **Southern Upland Cycleway** is currently in development. Mainly on quiet roads, it is a signed route following the Southern Upland Way from Portpatrick in the west, running across to Moffat and eventually reaching the east coast. Currently there is a signed route from Glenluce to Sanquhar and

A NOTE ON OPENING HOURS

Specific opening hours are always subject to change, especially in an area where there are many 'lifestyle' businesses. Normal opening hours are as you would expect, Monday to Friday 09.00–17.30, although many businesses, including museums, keep seasonal hours and close for lunch (usually, but not always, 13.00 to 14.00). Some villages and smaller towns still have half-day closing for banks, post offices and more traditional shops, which is usually a Wednesday. Most tourist attractions are open on Saturday, but it is advisable to check in advance, and many close or work on reduced hours out of high season. Where this is the case we have stated so in the text as 'seasonal opening'. If you visit out of season, please check opening hours before setting out.

a website in the making (⊘ www.southernuplandway.gov.uk/cms). The area also offers some fine mountain biking and is home to a number of the world famous **7stanes trails** (⊘ www.7stanesmountainbiking.com), the series of seven mountain biking trail centres which span the south of Scotland.

TOURIST INFORMATION & ADDITIONAL RESOURCES

Information offices Information centres are found across the region, some run locally and others by VisitScotland ⊘ www.visitscotland.com/travel/information/centres and its regional division ⊘ www.visitdumfriesandgalloway.co.uk. Details of information centres are given at the start of each chapter.

Local/online For up-to-the-minute news and information about what's going on in the region, *Dumfries and Galloway! What's Going On?* is a superb community-based local resource with a huge following of people who regularly feed in updates and pictures from all across the region. Check its website ⊘ www.dgwgo.com but also follow its very active Facebook page ⊘ www.facebook.com/DGWGO.

Local newspapers One distinctive delight of this region is the plethora of regional newspapers that are still available from local newsagents. Look out for the *Annandale Observer, Annandale Herald, Moffat News, The Galloway News, Dumfries & Galloway Standard*, and *Stranraer & Wigtownshire Free Press*, to name but a few.

Local magazines The award-winning glossy magazine *Dumfries & Galloway Life* comes out monthly and is available from newsagents or by subscription. Covering everything from arts and business to community and wildlife, it's a good source of insider knowledge on the area.

MAKING THE MOST OF SLOW DUMFRIES & GALLOWAY

Getting the most out of Dumfries and Galloway is a matter of taking time to discover and understand what makes the region tick, from habitats and wildlife through to the local economy and culture. Covered below is a selection of topics which begin to lift the lid on the area.

Visitors are advised also to consult the Dumfries and Galloway **calendar of events** which appears on ⊘ www.bradtguides.com/ d&gcalendar and ⊘ www.slowbritain.co.uk. There are many events held throughout the year, too many to list here, but of particular note is the annual **Spring Fling** arts festival, 'Scotland's Premier Art and Craft Open Studio Event' (⊘ www.spring-fling.co.uk), which takes place primarily in May across the region but which is fast expanding to become a year-round event. Also to be noted is the **Big Burns Supper** (⌀ www.bigburnssupper.com), a stonkingly good musical and arts bash which burst on to the scene in 2012 and is held each year in Dumfries over the course of seven to ten days at the end of January.

❧ HABITATS & WILDLIFE

Dumfries and Galloway is fortunate in having within its boundaries a broad range of habitats. It is also fortunate that it is a region recognised for its biodiversity and for its scenic value. As such, there are a number of designated areas of note, including three out of Scotland's 40 National Scenic Areas: the Nith Estuary, East Stewartry Coast and Fleet Valley. Much of the Stewartry is also included in the Galloway and Southern Ayrshire Biosphere, the country's first UNESCO Biosphere.

Land use across the region is split primarily into farming and forestry, both mainstays of the rural economy and both increasingly embracing and integrating tourism in the need and desire for diversification and community engagement. The main private landowner is the Duke of Buccleuch (pronounced Buc-clue), said to be Europe's second-largest

PINE MARTENS IN DUMFRIES & GALLOWAY

One of the most recent developments in the area is the return of pine martens, which have begun to recolonise southern Scotland and are now believed to be in Annandale and Eskdale. According to Scottish Natural Heritage: 'a small number of pine martens were re-introduced to the Galloway Forest in the early 1980s, but the new arrivals are not thought to have spread from this group – which has remained in isolation. These new groups of pine martens have most likely originated from a combination of natural spread and deliberate releases.'

private landowner after the Queen (strictly speaking the land is held in trust). He has two Dumfries and Galloway estates, one at Langholm, and the other, Drumlanrig, near Thornhill (pages 88–90).

Sustainable power has been in use in Dumfries and Galloway since the development of its hydroelectric scheme in the 1930s (page 131). More recently (and controversially), wind farms have been established at many locations and you don't have to travel far to spot them in the surrounding hills.

The region's habitats are classified by the Dumfries and Galloway Environmental Resources Centre (DGERC; ♂ www.dgerc.org.uk), the local records centre, as coastal and marine, farmland, grassland, urban, wetlands, woodland and upland. In conjunction with Scottish Natural Heritage (♂ www.snh.gov.uk), DGERC produces an excellent booklet *Welcome to Wildlife in Dumfries and Galloway*, which describes various habitat types, where to find examples of them in the region, and what wildlife you can expect to see. Most of the sites are also covered in this guide.

One initiative which has recently started is the opportunity to join a nocturnal wildlife tour, run by Wildlife Tours ♂ wildlifetours.co.uk. Explore the Galloway countryside in the black of night with an infrared camera, picking out deer in the fields, birds nesting in hedgerows, badgers snuffling, even mice scurrying. This is a unique experience which offers a new perspective on the landscape, often locating wildlife within feet of where you stand. If you're really lucky you might spot owls or a pine marten.

Birdwatchers will find plenty of interest in the region, not least at the various sites of the Royal Society for the Protection of Birds (referred to as RSPB throughout), all of which are detailed in the text.

Wild Seasons Dumfries and Galloway holds nature-based events throughout the year. Their Wild Spring Festival is Scotland's largest and longest running wildlife festival; see ♂ www.wildseasons.co.uk.

The Belted Galloway

The south of Scotland in general has a reputation for producing good-quality livestock with some notable native breeds. Galloway cattle are known for their hardiness, with the distinctive Belted Galloway being the most popularly celebrated sub-species. Since the 1920s Belties have been exported all over the world and herds are found today in the USA, Canada,

Australia, New Zealand, Africa and mainland Europe. Even if you've never had much interest in cattle, it is difficult not to take a certain delight in this spectacular looking breed. More information on Galloway cattle is available from the eponymous society at ⊘ www.gallowaycattlesociety. co.uk and information specifically on Belties can be found at ⊘ www. beltedgalloways.co.uk. For the story of one of the renowned early breeders of Belted Galloway, Miss Flora Stuart, see pages 206–7.

SAVOURING THE TASTES OF DUMFRIES & GALLOWAY

One of the most noticeable things about the high streets of Dumfries and Galloway is that many still have an independent butcher. This is in keeping with the region's reputation for locally produced meat, but it nonetheless comes as a pleasant surprise in a day when for many people a pre-packed joint from a supermarket is the only option. Greengrocers, too, are not uncommon, and every town has at least one baker. This is very much a part of the world where individuality and distinctiveness hasn't been

THE ECCLEFECHAN TART

Ecclefechan in the east of the region is known partly for its tart, a fruity concoction with a pastry base that is perfect for afternoon tea or dessert. We have been lucky in enjoying the support of Café Ariete in Moffat (pages 36–7), where Mum Vivienne produces a scrumptious Ecclefechan tart to her own recipe, a version of which she has kindly allowed to be reproduced here.

Quantities given suit a medium-sized nine-inch flan tin

9oz sweet shortcrust pastry (made with 9oz plain flour)
Line the flan tin with the pastry. There should be no need to bake blind.

4½ oz butter, melted
7 oz soft brown sugar
18 oz mixed dried fruit (eg: cherries, currants, raisins, sultanas, peel)
2 oz walnut halves
2 eggs, beaten
2 tbsp white wine vinegar

Mix all the ingredients together and pour into the pastry case.
Bake for 35–40 minutes at 356°F/180°C.

The tart freezes well.

completely lost in town centres. Castle Douglas in particular is celebrated for its range of independent shops and is the region's official 'Food Town'. It even has its own high street brewery.

Local specialities suggest the region has a sweet tooth and include Moffat Toffee (available from the eponymous shop in Moffat), Cream o' Galloway ice cream, Galloway Lodge Preserves range of marmalades, jams and jellies, and chocolate from the Cocoabean Company. Locally produced meat and locally caught fish are both widely available, the latter notably from smokehouses in the west of the region.

Farmers' markets are the place to go for a good cross-section of local producers. Markets are held regularly in Moffat, Langholm, Lockerbie, Dumfries, Creetown and Wigtown. Up-to-date details of where and when are posted on the Dumfries and Galloway Farmers' and Community Markets website ⊘ www.dgmarkets.org. Regular stalls at the markets cover an impressively wide spectrum of foods and crafts, from fudge,

WILD FOOD: THE ULTIMATE IN SLOW FOOD?

Wild food guide, chef, consultant and advocate Mark Williams of Galloway Wild Foods (⊘ www.gallowaywildfoods.com) believes foraging to be the ultimate expression of the Slow food movement. Connect with Mark on Twitter (@markwildfood) or via the Galloway Wild Foods Facebook page.

Practised mindfully, foraging delivers good, clean, fair food for everybody. To find, identify, sustainably harvest, process, cook and eat wild ingredients is profoundly connecting with the land and seasons, affording a deep intimacy with one's food.

Local, organic, sustainable, healthy gastronomy is entwined in the very roots of wild foods and Galloway is the best place in the UK to learn about and gather it.

The warming influence of the Gulf Stream and the shelter from Atlantic storms afforded by Ireland, means southwest Scotland enjoys a warmer, gentler climate than comparable areas on similar latitudes. This allows a vast range of species to thrive

year round. I gather over 300 varieties of plant, fungi, seaweed and shellfish within 20 minutes' walk of my home in the Fleet Valley near Gatehouse of Fleet.

As a 'peninsula of peninsulas', Galloway boasts a huge variety of coastal habitats – from tidal estuaries of saltmarsh to rocky shores and opulent beaches – all fine hunting grounds for coastal foragers.

Inland, habitats become even more diverse – a patchwork of farmland framed by bountiful hedgerows, vast deciduous and coniferous forests rich in diverse fungi, upland moors full of aromatic herbs.

With our right to roam and responsibly gather leaves, seeds and fungi for personal beer, chillies and cheese to artists, jewellers and soap-makers. There are also a couple of surprising producers (surprising for this part of the world, that is), one is a winery ⊘ www.glebehousewinery.co.uk and the other a tea grower (page 170).

FORAGING

Dumfries and Galloway has its own resident forager, Mark Williams, who works closely with a number of local restaurants and also runs courses (see box below). Here are some of his tips for foraging in the area.

Plants

Most people are familiar with the common hedgerow fruits of autumn, but that is just one small corner of the wild larder. Succulent winter coastal herbs, vibrant spring shoots and aromatic summer flowers make up an endlessly varied palette for food lovers. Inspiration is round

use enshrined in Scottish law, the largely unspoiled wild delights of southwest Scotland are there for all to enjoy for free.

Inspired by the sheer abundance of delicious, healthy and free wild ingredients around me, I started posting discoveries and recipes from my own wild food journey on my website. This labour of love has grown into a vast free wild food guide, providing in-depth information and recipes, as well as an examination of the broader issues around how foraging can fit into our modern world.

As Scotland's only full-time foraging tutor, I strongly believe that wild food should not be commodified, but be available free to all through improved education, access and land use practices. Galloway is now firmly on the foraging map for chefs, foragers, bushcrafters, herbalists and Slow food

lovers from all over Europe. I can be working with Michelin-starred chefs one day, and primary school children the next – and the joy of my job is that I am teaching them the same things!

Galloway Wild Foods offers a wide variety of scheduled guided walks and foraging events throughout the year at locations across Galloway, but also throughout Scotland and northern England. Some are simple three-hour walks with wild tasters and a wild cook-in afterwards, others are full days exploring multiple habitats and enjoying a ten-course wild tasting menu with foraged cocktails.

The best way to learn is often through private tuition for groups of friends and family. These can be tailored to the precise needs and interests of the group and are always memorable, fun and inspiring.

every corner and I make everything from aromatised wines, to pickles, confectionery and cakes from Galloway's astonishing range of plants. My favourite thing though is to nibble the flavours of special times and places as I move through the breathtaking, edible landscape.

Fungi

Nothing captures the would-be forager-gastronome's imagination quite like wild mushrooms. The striking forms, poetic names (amethyst deceiver, angel wings, horn of plenty anyone?), wide range of flavours and medicinal uses are only half the pleasure: the 'thrill of the hunt' is like a wild treasure trail, an intimate dance with nature. Many people are paralysed by the fear of poisoning themselves, but this is easily overcome by following a few simple rules and joining me on one of my guided fungi forays.

Seaweeds

Marine algae are the richest largely untapped food resource in the world. As there are no poisonous seaweeds, the challenge is in getting to know the most rewarding species (you need to get the tides right for this) and learning how to process and use them in the kitchen. Of the 300 or so species available around the Galloway Coast, my favourites include laver (also known as 'nori'), sugar kelp and pepper dulse (an extraordinary little seaweed that tastes somewhere between truffle and lobster!). I know of no savoury dish that can't be improved by the judicious addition of seaweed.

Shellfish

The Solway Coast is rich in a wide variety of shellfish, most of which can be benignly harvested for personal consumption. While the cockle fisheries are currently closed (though I doubt anybody would object to you gathering a few for your tea), spoot (also known as 'razor') clams, mussels, shrimps and winkles are there for all to mindfully gather.

SOME HISTORICAL PERSPECTIVES

Towards the end of 2014, Dumfries and Galloway was the location of the discovery of a spectacular hoard of Viking treasure from the 9th or 10th century, described as the largest to have been found in modern times. At the time of writing details of the exact location hadn't been released but it is hoped that items from the discovery will be displayed in due course.

There are many historical references throughout this book, one or two of which may require some further explanation, which is given below.

REIVERS & THE 'DEBATABLE LANDS'

Although much of Dumfries and Galloway's southern boundary is demarcated by water, the eastern part, at the southern end of Annandale and Eskdale, is a land boundary with neighbouring England, where over the centuries two warring nations came face to face. This has been a vital geographical pinch point in the development of not just Dumfries and Galloway, but of Scotland as a whole, and the skirmishes that played out here in times past were particularly persistent and violent. From the 13th to early 17th centuries the area from the Solway near Carlisle northeast through Canonbie and up to Langholm belonged to neither England nor Scotland and was known as the 'Debatable Lands'.

The people who lived on either side of the border were in a permanent state of turmoil, with their lands often pillaged by armies travelling north or south. Deprived of their livelihood, the practice of 'reiving' took hold and was passed down through the generations. 'Reiver' comes from the early English for 'rob' and has given rise to the modern 'ruffian'. Both Scottish and English would undertake daring raids into each other's lands, most commonly in winter when long hours of darkness provided cover, to steal cattle and generally wreak havoc.

"The skirmishes that played out here in times past were particularly persistent and violent."

Reiving was an accepted way of life based on tribal affiliations rather than nationality, for raids between clans were just as common as cross-border incursions. It was only with the Union of the Crowns in 1603, on the accession of James VI of Scotland to the throne of England, that order began to be restored.

Visitors to the northern end of Annandale might wish to head for the Devil's Beef Tub (pages 38), a scenic spot with reiving associations. If you visit the Langholm area in southern Eskdale, we have included a walk 'In the footsteps of the Border Reivers' (pages 62–3) and would also recommend 'The Reiver Trail', details of which can be found at ◬ www. thereivertrail.com.

ROBERT THE BRUCE (1274–1329)

No historical perspective of Dumfries and Galloway is complete without mention of Robert the Bruce, Scotland's warrior king who led the Scots in the Wars of Independence, famously defeating a much larger English army at Bannockburn in 1314. Bruce was descended from the Lords of Annandale and is associated with many places in southwest Scotland, all of which have been drawn together by the Robert the Bruce Commemoration Trust into four Bruce trails across the region. Details of the trails are given in a booklet which is available from visitor information centres or which can be accessed online at ⚭ www.brucetrust.co.uk.

COVENANTERS & THE 'KILLING TIMES'

When James VI (James I of England and Ireland) died in 1625, he left to his son, Charles I, a Scottish church divided. During his reign he had attempted to re-establish episcopacy in Scotland, a policy which was resisted by the Presbyterians. On acceding to the throne, Charles I took up where his father had left off and in 1637 at St Giles Cathedral in Edinburgh a new liturgy was read publicly for the first time, effectively bringing the Church of England to Scotland. The resulting riot led eventually to the widespread signing in 1638 of the National Covenant which demanded a Scottish Parliament and General Assembly free from the interference of the monarch. Those who signed the Covenant became known as Covenanters. Thus started a tumultuous period of extreme repression that lasted until the accession of William and Mary in 1689.

During this period, southern Scotland, and the southwest in particular, was strongly Covenanter and over 300 ministers in the Lowlands left their churches, many choosing to hold open-air services in the hills, gatherings which became known as Conventicles. Such services were particularly risky for it was an offence punishable by death to preach from anything other than the Book of Common Prayer drawn up by Charles's Commission in 1637.

The appointment of John Graham of Claverhouse (known as either 'Bonnie Dundee' or 'Bluidy Clavers' depending on which side you stood) in 1681 to bring the southwest to heel marked the start of a particularly brutal campaign in which dissidents were tracked down and executed. In total 82 people were killed in Dumfries and Galloway by Claverhouse and his supporter, Sir Robert Grierson of Lag, Steward Depute of Kirkcudbright, in a period which has become known as the 'Killing Times'.

Today in many of the churchyards across the region you will come across Covenanter graves, some of which have been identified in the text of this guide. Many churches also still hold Conventicles once a year, to which all are welcome.

COMMON RIDINGS

The tradition of Common Ridings stems from the 13th and 14th centuries when local townspeople would ride out to patrol the boundaries of their town to protect it against marauding invaders, be they from across the border or simply from neighbouring clans, and to ensure that their rights – to fishing and common land, for instance – were not threatened.

The oldest Common Riding in Dumfries and Galloway is Langholm's, which has taken place continuously every year since 1759. (Annan's first took place in 1680 but has not been held continuously.) Others are held at Lockerbie and Sanquhar, while the Dumfries ride-outs (as they are called) are part of the annual Guid Nychburris ('Good Neighbours') festival, marking the anniversary of the town's elevation to royal burgh in 1186.

At every Common Riding there are annually selected key players: the cornet, cornet's lass and standard bearer, all of whom also travel to Common Ridings of other towns as well as taking part in their own. Common Ridings tend to be held around the same date in the summer for each town each year, a day in which 100 or more riders plus many more followers and spectators congregate to start the proceedings off early in the morning, when riders are wished 'safe oot, safe in'. Once the riders return there are festivities throughout the rest of the day, with everything from horse races to musical parades.

FURTHER READING

In the course of researching this guide we have dipped into many books. Listed below is a small selection which we gratefully acknowledge (dates refer to editions we have used). Any of these make for interesting reading, but we would particularly recommend Haig Gordon's two books, *The Kirkcudbrightshire Companion* and *The Wigtownshire Companion* for their depth of coverage, insights and entertaining text. Both are available from local bookshops. There is also an equally good *Dumfriesshire Companion* website & www.dumfriesshirecompanion.com.

We have included in the list below possibly the most famous work by local author S R Crockett (1859–1914). To mark the centenary of his death, in 2014 Ayton Publishing released his Galloway works in 32 volumes. All are available from ⬦ www.aytonpublishing.co.uk.

The Antiquities of Scotland (vol 1) Francis Grose, published 1797 and available as a print-on-demand title from Gale ECCO Print Editions via Amazon

The Buildings of Scotland: Dumfries and Galloway John Gifford, Penguin Books 1996

The Galloway Highlands Dane Love, Carn Publishing 2014

The House of Elrig Gavin Maxwell, Longmans Green & Co Ltd 1965

The Kirkcudbrightshire Companion Haig Gordon, Galloway Publishing 2008

The Queen's Scotland: Glasgow, Kyle and Galloway ed. Theo Lang, Hodder and Stoughton 1953

The Queen's Scotland: The Border Counties ed. Theo Lang, Hodder and Stoughton 1957

The Raiders S R Crockett, T Fisher Unwin 1902

The Solway Firth Brian Blake, Robert Hale Ltd 1966

The Wigtownshire Companion Haig Gordon, Galloway Publishing 2008

40 Years of Pioneering Publishing

In 1974, Hilary Bradt took a road less travelled and published her first travel guide, written whilst floating down the Amazon.

40 years on and a string of awards later, Bradt has a list of 200 titles, including travel literature, Slow Travel guides and wildlife guides. And our pioneering spirit remains as strong as ever – we're happy to say there are still plenty of roads less travelled to explore!

Bradt...take the road less travelled

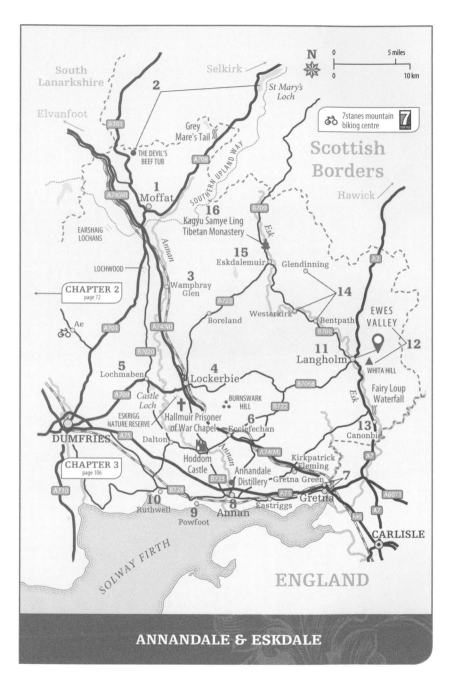

N 0   5 miles

0   10 km

South Lanarkshire

Selkirk

2

St Mary's Loch

🚴 7stanes mountain biking centre **7** stanes

Elvanfoot

Grey Mare's Tail

Scottish Borders

THE DEVIL'S BEEF TUB

A701

A708

SOUTHERN UPLAND WAY

Hawick

A74(M)

1

Moffat

16

Kagyu Samye Ling Tibetan Monastery

B709

Esk

EARSHAIG LOCHANS

Annan

15

Eskdalemuir

Glendinning

A7

LOCHWOOD

3

Wamphray Glen

CHAPTER 2 page 72

B723

14

Westerkirk

Bentpath

EWES VALLEY

Ae

A701

A74(M)

Boreland

B709

🚴

11

Langholm

12

B7020

WHITA HILL

5

Lochmaben

4

Lockerbie

Fairy Loup Waterfall

A709

Castle Loch

BURNSWARK HILL

B7068

Esk

DUMFRIES

ESKRIGG NATURE RESERVE

Hallmuir Prisoner of War Chapel

B722

6

Ecclefechan

13

Canonbie

A75

Dalton

Annan

A74(M)

A7

CHAPTER 3 page 106

Hoddom Castle

Kirkpatrick Fleming

A710

B724

B723

Annandale Distillery

Gretna Green

7

A6071

10

Ruthwell

9

Powfoot

8

Annan

Eastriggs

A75

Gretna

A6

A7

CARLISLE

SOLWAY FIRTH

ENGLAND

1
ANNANDALE & ESKDALE

Annandale and Eskdale account for the entire eastern end of Dumfries and Galloway, abutting South Lanarkshire to the north, the Scottish Borders to the east, the border with England to the southeast, and sloping down to the shores of the Solway Firth directly to the south. Residents of the area are quietly proud of it but feel a frustration that, of the millions who pass through on the A74(M) motorway each year, more don't stop to visit. It's a shame as there is much here to discover and enjoy, far more than may at first meet the eye. In fact, it's an ideal area for exploring slowly.

This is a sizeable area: 31 miles from **Moffat** in the north down to **Gretna** at the border with England, and just under 18 miles from **Lockerbie** eastwards to **Langholm**. The rivers **Esk** and **Annan** rise in the north and flow southwards to empty at the eastern end of the **Solway**. They cut a clear line along the valley bottoms, running through forests and between steep hills, past communities on their banks that have developed over centuries. Spending time in this area is a delight for anyone who loves the outdoors. For **walkers** in particular there is a pack of routes to choose from, whether undertaking all or part of a long-distance trail, or simply devising a shorter loop for a bit of fresh air. **Fishing** is also popular, with a good choice of beats on a selection of rivers. More information about fishing on the River Annan can be found at ⏁ www.riverannan.org and ⏁ www.fishpal.com. **Birdwatching, canoeing, horseriding** and even **carriage driving** can all be enjoyed by expert and novice alike.

You can encounter a wealth of history on the ground, from early **prehistoric stone circles** through **Roman forts**, to memorials to more recent events such as the Lockerbie disaster. There are also connections with **Robert the Bruce**, William Wallace, the Covenanters and the Jacobite Rebellions. The last few hundred years have given rise to numerous famous sons and daughters, including the engineer **Thomas Telford** and philosopher **Thomas Carlyle**. Although **Robert Burns** neither came from, nor lived in, this particular part of Dumfries and Galloway, he did visit and there are one or two places hereabouts that will be of interest to Burns enthusiasts. For romantics incurable or otherwise, **Gretna Green** tells the story of elopements past and marriages present; this small village immediately north of the border is (in)famous worldwide thanks to the historic differences in marriage law between Scotland and England.

The people, communities and economic activities of Annandale and Eskdale are diverse – to say the least – and range from farmers caretaking the land in serene valleys and on isolated hilltops to retired academics running exotic gardens, incomers from the south who have escaped to set up B&Bs, and community trusts who have acquired lochs and raised funds to develop wildlife centres. There's even a Buddhist monastery in the hills, the first to be established in the West. The work of Forestry Commission Scotland is also much in evidence, for conifer plantations make up 27% of land use in the Annan catchment alone.

GETTING AROUND

Annandale is bisected by the A74(M) motorway from Moffat in the north to Gretna in the south, with the A7 heading off northeast through Eskdale, passing through the town of Langholm and on to the Scottish Borders. The two valleys can feel a world apart, separated by river valleys and rolling hills in the south, and craggier hills, isolated moorland and forestry plantations with more circuitous secondary roads in the north. If you're travelling any points between Gretna and Moffat, we recommend following the route of the old main road, now the B7076. With barely any traffic, it is a gentler option than the speed of the A74(M) and so very spacious for a B road.

PUBLIC TRANSPORT

The region's public transport is adequate but isn't viable for reaching the more remote parts. If you're happy to move from centre to centre, then the bus network is fine but there's nothing in the way of an integrated public transport system, and getting around is generally easier by car. The main west coast **train service** runs through the area, but there is only one station, at Lockerbie, served by infrequent Virgin services and the more frequent First TransPennine Express. While this is useful for arriving and departing from points further afield, with no other stops within Annandale or Eskdale, wider travel needs to be linked in with local buses. Scotrail services between Glasgow and Newcastle pass along the Solway Coast upon departing Dumfries, with stations at Annan and Gretna Green.

The Annandale local **bus services**, plus the longer distance inter-regional routes, use the county town of Dumfries as the main hub, with services fanning out through the area. Moffat is well served by the frequent daytime X74 and 101 Stagecoach services. Lochmaben/ Lockerbie are also well served, with Stagecoach/Houstons 81/381, while along the Solway, the Stagecoach service 79 between Dumfries and Carlisle stops off at Ruthwell, Cummertrees, Annan and Gretna. Stagecoach also operate the 380 service between Lockerbie and Moffat, which is useful for linking with the train services.

The Eskdale bus services for Langholm and on to Eskdalemuir and Kagyu Samye Ling Buddhist Monastery are a bit more hit and miss. The First Group service 95 from Galashiels to Carlisle is the most frequent way for getting into Langholm, but this isn't linked to the rest of Dumfries and Galloway. Other routes operate via Lockerbie, with a weekly Thursday 103 service by Andersons, and a daily, if infrequent, Houstons 112 service to Eskdalemuir with the option to then change at the village church for Andersons 124 service on to Langholm. There is also one bus daily, service 123, between Langholm, Canonbie and Annan.

Local public transport information is provided by South West of Scotland Transport Partnership (⊘ www.swestrans.org.uk), or alternatively the traveline (✆ 0871 200 22 33 ⊘ www.traveline.org.uk). For general observations on public transport, see pages 12–13.

CYCLING

Away from the main A roads, cycling is an enjoyable affair, if a little strenuous over the more hilly sections, particularly for those of us not as fit as we used to be. The lanes are generally very quiet, save for the odd farm vehicle, and are a joy to explore throughout the changing seasons. As part of the Sustrans cycle network, **Route 7** runs from Gretna, along the Solway to Dumfries, before linking in to the **Regional Route 10** up to Moffat over a mix of quiet roads and traffic free sections. The easiest

i TOURIST INFORMATION

VisitScotland Information Centre Gretna Unit 38, Gretna Gateway Outlet Village, Glasgow Rd, Gretna DG16 5GG ✆ 01461 337834 ⊙ all year
Langholm Tourist Information Town Hall, High St ⊘ www.langholm-online.co.uk
⊙ May–Sep Note: scheduled to move premises, but at time of going to press new details were not available. Check for updates on ⊘ www.slowbritain.co.uk.
Moffat Information Point Moffat Woollen Mill, Ladyknowe, Moffat DG10 9EG ⊙ all year

way to cover a lot of distance north–south is to take **Route 74** between Gretna, Lockerbie and Moffat, although this is not the quietest route as it runs parallel to the A74(M) for numerous sections. There are also a number of routes starting from Langholm ⊘ www.cyclelangholm.co.uk.

CYCLE HIRE

Annandale Cycles Caledonian Place, Moffat DG10 9EG ✆ 01683 220033 ⊘ www.annandalecycles.com
MoffatCan Old Church Depot, Annanside, Moffat DG10 9HB ✆ 01683 221847 ⊘ www.moffatcan.org

WALKING

With the flat of the river valleys, wide open beaches on the Solway Firth, and the dramatic hills of the Southern Uplands, the two valleys of Annandale and Eskdale offer routes and distances for all tastes and fitness levels. Every local visitor information centre, along with most libraries, town halls and many shops and post offices in the area, stock a wealth of walking information, including OS maps, leaflets and books. On top of this, a quick search on the internet for the area you are visiting will soon turn up numerous routes of interest.

Dumfries and Galloway Council produces free 'Walking in and around' booklets; those to Moffat, Lockerbie and Lochmaben, and Langholm provide varied walking options.

Two long-distance paths cut through the region. The **Southern Upland Way** passes Beattock and Moffat on its 212-mile route from west coast to east. The full route plus suggestions for shorter day walks are detailed on ⊘ www.southernuplandway.gov.uk. The **Annandale Way** (⊘ www.annandaleway.org) starts its 55-mile journey from the source of the River Annan above Moffat and wends its way southwards to the sea at Annan. The route offers plenty of choice for shorter circular day walks: try the spectacular hills around the Devil's Beef Tub at the route start, the newly opened three-mile loop of Castle Loch, Lochmaben at the halfway point, and Annan to the Solway Estuary at the walk's end.

UPPER ANNANDALE: MOFFAT & THE NORTH

A glance at an OS map reveals a mass of thumbprint contours spiralling from the upper reaches of the Annan, where it rises just north of Moffat, down towards Lockerbie 16 miles south. To the west, stretching over to neighbouring Nithsdale, are the Lowther Hills, empty and bleak in parts, rising only to 2,500 feet, but no less striking for that. To the east, the Moffat Hills reach only a little higher, to almost 2,700 feet, but are also not without drama. This area was historically of great strategic importance, for whoever controlled Upper Annandale controlled access to the north and south; today it is dotted with sites of Roman forts and the remains of medieval castles.

Moffat is the only town of any size, and a fine, handsome town it is too. It makes a good base from which to explore the area with plenty of accommodation options, access to the surrounding countryside, and lots of information to hand. The River Annan rises just north of Moffat and runs almost due south along the centre of a corridor lined by hills which has been the main travel route for centuries. The joy of this area, though, lies not just in this central river valley but in the hidden places on either side.

1 MOFFAT

🏠 **Annandale Arms** (page 244), **No. 29 Well Street** (page 245), **Limetree House Guest House** (page 245), **Cauldholm B&B** (page 245) ▲ **Moffat Camping and Caravan Site** (page 245)

Moffat quickly charms most visitors. With its mix of quirky shops and cafés, village atmosphere, friendly locals, range of architecture and its setting in – and proximity to – some of the grandest scenery of the Southern Uplands, it's a place that you want to be. It's also a place of independent character, a former royal burgh and Victorian spa town, and it features in the *Guinness Book of Records*, or at least one of its buildings does: at only 20 feet wide by 162 feet long, **The Famous Star Hotel** on the

High Street is the narrowest hotel in the world. Moffat's other claims to fame are **Chapel Street**, said to be the shortest street in Scotland (though given a run for its money by the miserly named Ebenezer Place in Wick, in the far north of the country), and **Scotland's oldest pharmacy**, Thomas Hetherington, on the High Street, established in 1844.

The town's most famous son is **Air Chief Marshall Hugh Dowding** (1882–1970) of Battle of Britain fame, who was born in Moffat and whose ashes were laid to rest beneath the Battle of Britain window at Westminster Abbey. There is a memorial in his honour in Station Park. If you're interested in World War II history, especially aviation, take a walk down The Glebe, a quiet residential cul-de-sac off the main southern road into town, for the unexpected sight of a full-size replica **Spitfire** (an MK IX Supermarine Spitfire PT 462 to be precise) in the unlikely setting of the front garden of a private house. The owner is a Spitfire enthusiast and had this built having flown the original in Florida during a flying course. A noticeboard in the garden at the bottom of the drive gives more information.

Another local man to make a very distinctive mark was **John Loudon McAdam** (1756–1836), whose family home was in the Stewartry (page 135). The name may well ring a bell, though it's not so much the man you may know of but rather the process he invented. McAdam was a Scottish engineer who became pre-occupied with improving roads. The 'macadamisation' of roads resulted in a harder, more durable surface and did much for travel and communication. When tar was added to the process, the description became 'tarmacadamise', leaving us with the abbreviated 'tarmac'. The basic method introduced by McAdam still informs road building today. McAdam is buried in Moffat for he died here on his way back home to London having been in Scotland for his annual summer visit. His grave can be found in the cemetery on Holm Street, at the southern end of the High Street, where he lies next to his grandmother, who spent the final years of her life in the Moffat area.

"The 'macadamisation' of roads resulted in a harder, more durable surface and did much for travel and communication."

The town's population of 2,500 swells in the summer with a mix of walkers passing through and coach tours stopping off to let passengers stretch their legs and indulge in a spot of shopping at the large

THE WALKERS' TOWN

Moffat sits in the midst of glorious walking country, a perfect base from which to reach the highest ground in the south of Scotland: Hart Fell (2,652 feet); Ettrick Pen (2,269 feet); Loch Fell (2,256 feet); and Queensberry (2,285 feet). In 2008, Moffat became the first town in Scotland to become part of the 'Walkers are Welcome' scheme (⊘ www.walkersarewelcome.org.uk), a UK-wide network of towns and villages which encourage walkers to visit. It's also the starting point of the 55-mile **Annandale Way**, which runs southwards to Annan, and the midpoint of the **Southern Upland Way**, Britain's first official long-distance footpath which runs for 212 miles from Portpatrick on the west coast of Dumfries and Galloway to Cockburnspath on the east coast of the Scottish Borders. The section from Moffat to Cockburnspath has also been dubbed the **Sir Walter Scott Way** due to the connections of the places on the route with Scott's life and work. Moffat's local website has more details, see ⊘ www.visitmoffat.co.uk.

Edinburgh Woollen Mill complex. Entertainment for kids can be found in **Station Park** at the bottom of town, where there is a putting green and a boating/pedalo lake. Also down this end of town is the community-run **Moffat Museum** (Harthope House, Churchgate, DG10 9EG ✆ 01683 220868 ⊘ www.moffatmuseum.co.uk ☉ seasonal), with uncluttered and informative displays which include a Roman brooch found in the nearby hills in 1787 and the oldest longbow discovered in Britain. Passing the late 19th-century **St Andrew's Church**, just around the corner from here is the **old churchyard** at the bottom of the High Street, with the last remaining wall of the pre-Reformation church (c1600). What is obvious when walking around the site is the varying heights of the ground. In 1747, the churchyard was covered in an extra four feet of soil to create more space for burials.

The wide main street is pleasantly browsable and lends itself to a gentle amble up one side and down the other, but do watch out when crossing over as it's easy to forget that traffic runs in both directions on both sides of the road. For a local delicacy, try the **Moffat Toffee Shop** on the High Street.

Just off the High Street, **Well Street** has a range of more specialised shops starting with the excellent butcher on the corner, through the independent Moffat Books, Lothlorien antiques centre with **Toy Museum** upstairs, traditional delicatessen and ending with the funky **Carole's Milk Bar** (page 37).

Moffat's original wealth came from its busy sheep market, in memory of which stands the Moffat ram – more formally known as the **Colvin fountain** – atop its cairn of piled-up stones in the middle of the High Street. Businessman William Colvin presented the statue of the blackface ram to Moffat in 1875, partly in memory of James Hogg, 'the Ettrick Shepherd', who was known to drink in the town. Noted for its peculiar lack of ears, the ram was sculpted by one William Brodie, who is perhaps better known for the diminutive Greyfriars Bobby in Edinburgh.

Wool was overtaken by tourism following the discovery of the health-inducing sulphurous waters of the well in the nearby hills. Rachel Whitford, a bishop's daughter, was walking in the hills east of Moffat in 1633 when she quenched her thirst with a drink from a spring. She recognised the tang as sulphur – a taste of 'stale eggs whipped up with Lucifer-matches' – and thus an industry was born. By the start of the 18th century Moffat was attracting the celebrities of the day, including Robert Burns, and in 1881 a railway branch line was opened from Beattock to Moffat to cope with the increasing numbers of people coming to take the waters.

You can still walk up to **Moffat Well** today, where the smell is as eggy as ever even after all these years. The old **Bath House**, now the Town Hall, can be seen on the High Street. Waters were pumped down here from the well, such was the demand.

¶ FOOD & DRINK

Annandale Arms High St, DG10 9HF ℘ 01683 220013 ◊ www.annandalearmshotel.co.uk. Offers a good range of locally sourced food in its pleasant restaurant, with a menu including the likes of poacher's pie, Cullen skink, Dumfriesshire lamb, raspberry cranachan and the oh-so-tempting pear, chocolate and ginger crumble.

Brodies 1–2 Altrive Pl, Holm St, DG10 9EB ℘ 01683 222870 ◊ www.brodiesofmoffat. co.uk. Good food in a smart friendly and relaxed setting, with a particularly comfy sofa next to the fire, perfect for pre-dinner drinks. Try the double-baked cheese soufflé and the Annandale hogget (a young sheep between one and two years old).

Buccleuch Arms High St, DG10 9ET ℘ 01683 220003 ◊ www.buccleucharmshotel.com. Where wholesome pub food (scampi, ham hock, steak pie, etc) hits the spot.

Café Ariete 10 High St, DG10 9HF ℘ 01683 220313. Warm and welcoming café with an eye-catching sculpture of a ram (*ariete* means ram in Italian) – christened Ramsey – made from old books hanging from the ceiling. The sunglasses finish him off perfectly. This is a family affair: Mitch Murray and his son Russell are usually on hand, while Mum Vivienne is responsible for the wickedly tempting range of cakes. Take-away food is also offered; give them a call to place your order.

Carole's Milk Bar 38-40 Well St, DG10 9DP ✐ 01683 222716. Has the air of a 1950s American diner. Good for coffee and snacks, soups and sandwiches, cakes and scones. Free board games to play and vintage record album covers on the wall.

Claudios Burnside Rd, DG10 9DX ✐ 01683 220958 ⊘ www.claudiosmoffat.co.uk. Serves tasty authentic Italian food in an upmarket trattoria-style setting. Originally opened by Claudio Capriglione and his wife in 1996, it is now run by their children, chef Claudia and Davide front of house.

The Green Frog Hammerlands, DG10 9QL ✐ 01683 221220 ⊘ www.thegreenfrogmoffat. co.uk. A fun café a short way out of the centre with shop, duck pond, fly and bait fishing, and lots of parking.

Harvest Time 24 Well St, DG10 9DP ✐ 01683 221177. Delicatessen and wholefoods shop packed with local goodies and more besides.

Limetree Restaurant Hartfell House, Hartfell Crescent, DG10 9AL ✐ 01683 220153 ⊘ www.hartfellhouse.co.uk. Fine dining, where chef Matt Seddon keeps it all seasonal and local.

THE MOFFAT HILLS

The scenery around Moffat is among the most dramatic in the region. Here, too, is a good selection of **birdlife**: peregrine, merlin and golden plover may be spotted, to name a few.

Our suggested tours focus on the north and east of the region and make use of the key road routes to immerse you in the surrounding countryside, areas which sit just inside the boundaries of Dumfries and Galloway and which also stray into the neighbouring Scottish Borders region. Unfortunately, public transport isn't really an option for these routes, so driving is the best bet, or cycling if you're a very fit, regular cyclist. During the summer the 502 Harrier, bus operated by Telford's (⊘ www.telfordscoaches.com) runs from Moffat over to Hawick in the Borders. It only goes on a Tuesday afternoon from July to September, but for walkers it's an option if you want to catch the bus on its way out of Moffat, get off at the Grey Mare's Tail and walk back. It's a long walk though, so don't underestimate it. (Note: local services can be subject to change – and funding cuts – so do check online before setting out.)

Immediately to the west of Moffat are the Lowther Hills, most of which are covered in the Nithsdale chapter. However, **Earshaig Lochans** and **Lochwood** are both within close reach of Moffat 👆

2 The Devil's Beef Tub to St Mary's Loch

The A701 climbs up out of Moffat to the north and winds its way around the hillside offering superb views across the valley before reaching the edge of the cavernous and carnivorously named Devil's Beef Tub, a huge hollow in the hills, the headwater of the River Annan and the watershed between the Annan and Tweed rivers. Celebrated as one of the most impressive landmarks of the Southern Uplands and possibly the most famous of Dumfries and Galloway's geological features, it is surrounded by four hills and is the site of some rare mountain plants and the occasional cluster of ash and hazel trees, a reminder of the forests that once thrived here.

The name was gained from its reputation as a place the Border Reivers would hide their stolen cattle. From the road it's a long drop down, 1,351 feet to be precise, and in winter the weather up here is usually several degrees colder and harsher than it is just five miles back down the valley in Moffat. In times past this was a particularly treacherous spot and in the Holm Street graveyard in Moffat (the same one in which McAdam is buried) are the graves of James McGeorge and John Goodfellow, the guard and the driver of a Royal Mail Coach, who lost their lives here in a snowstorm in 1831. Despite the warnings and the bad weather, they tried in vain to get the mail through Moffat to Tweedshaws and perished for their troubles. A cairn known locally as the 'Postie Stone' marks the spot where they died a mile or so beyond the Beef Tub, while another memorial, to the **Covenanters**, is located a few hundred yards before the view point itself, commemorating one John Hunter, a Covenanter who was shot by Douglas Dragoons on the hillside opposite in 1685.

Continue northwards from the Devil's Beef Tub and you pass in a layby on the left a cairn marking the source of the **River Tweed**. From here it flows eastwards for 97 miles through the Scottish Borders region to Berwick-upon-Tweed on the east coast. 'Annan, Tweed and Clyde rise a' oot o' ae hillside' goes an old Borders saying, since the rivers Annan and Clyde also rise here on Tweedsmuir, the former flowing south and the latter draining northwest.

At this point we stray out of Dumfries and Galloway into the Scottish Borders region to complete a circular route. Keep heading northwards for another seven or eight miles to Tweedsmuir before taking the road to the right signposted St Mary's Loch and you can enjoy a much longer circuit through splendid scenery and past the reservoirs of **Talla** and **Megget Water** before dropping down to **St Mary's Loch**, a tranquil spot popular with dinghy sailors in the midst of the hills. Turn right at the loch and the A708 takes you back into Dumfries and Galloway and back to Moffat through a dramatic landscape as the road runs down to the valley floor, passing the mighty **Grey Mare's Tail** (♀ NT185148; National Trust for Scotland), a 200-foot waterfall, the fifth highest in the UK. You can stop for a short walk here for views of the falls, or alternatively climb up the side of them on a steep path that leads up to isolated **Loch Skeen** at the top.

3 Wamphray Glen

Eight miles south of Moffat lies Wamphray Glen, once a popular spot with spa visitors seeking the picturesque in remote corners and now part of the Crown's Applegirth Estate. Wamphray Water flows down from the hills into the River Annan, running over several waterfalls and through a wooded glen. A **walking route** is shown on a sign at

CHARIOTS OF FIRE, BORELAND STYLE

A few miles over the hill from Wamphray lies **Boreland**, home to one of the area's more unusual enterprises. Award-winning carriage driver Amanda Saville has been riding horses since the age of two and now spends her time running an equine business called Chariots of Fire (Boreland DG11 2LL ⚭ www.chariots.org. uk) and a registered riding charity, Sports Driving Unlimited. She's a charismatic soul and with her husband, John, and friend Liza it's difficult not to get swept along by their combined enthusiasm for what they do. There are several strands to what's on offer, at the heart of which is carriage driving: the sort where you attach a carriage to a horse, or several horses, and set off on the road, or in the indoor arena if it's wet. Or, in Amanda's case, for a spot of competitive stunt driving through rings of fire with a bit of carriage jumping (yes, really, the carriages are actually jumped) thrown in for good measure.

This is a great place to go for a real Slow experience. Chickens, ducks, guinea fowl, peacocks, pigs, cows and Dutch Zwartbles sheep provide diversion for younger (and overgrown) kids, and anyone of any riding ability can come for a lesson or just for a pleasure drive with the team (four ponies), from novices who would like to try something completely different to experienced drivers. For newcomers Amanda suggests a day-drive experience, in which you try your hand at driving for an hour, then stop for coffee, then go on a pleasure drive with her or one of the staff. What better or slower way to see some of the countryside than from the comfort of a horse-drawn carriage, clip-clopping along at a measured pace between the beech hedgerows, absorbing the sights and sounds of this attractive corner of the region? 🖐

the junction of the Old Carlisle Road from Moffat with the Boreland road (♀ NT121962), and you can park here or up the hill at Wamphray Parish Church (♀ NT131965). The main attraction is the walk through the woods along the river and the three cascades known as The Pot, The Washing Pan and Dubbs Cauldron.

Passing the old mill beyond the falls the route climbs up to **Wamphray Parish Church**, where amongst the fine 19th-century funerary monuments is one to Dr John Rogerson of Wamphray, who after studying medicine in Edinburgh joined many other Scots in travelling to Russia to pursue his career. Rogerson ended up becoming physician to the sexually voracious Catherine the Great, at which time he also acquired a responsibility he might not have foreseen, namely checking all of her lovers for venereal disease. His gravestone commemorates his service to 'His Majesty the Emperor of Russia' and not to Catherine herself, for he remained in Russia after Catherine's death and served succeeding emperors up to and including Alexander I.

"Dr John Rogerson of Wamphray joined many other Scots in travelling to Russia to pursue his career."

MID ANNANDALE

Mid Annandale's attractions are diverse, with less emphasis on walking the hills (though the countryside here is no less walkable) and more on the local communities and the histories that have shaped them. The area is the location of a number of historic towns, and also of the village of **Ae**, a place as diminutive as its name (the smallest place name in English in the UK), sitting on the edge of the much larger Ae Forest. (Ae is pronounced as in the vowel 'A'.) Built in 1947 by the Forestry Commission, the village was home to the workers involved in planting some 25,000 acres of conifers after World War II, making this one of the largest forests in the UK. If you pass this way, you'll notice the anomalous sight of a totem pole on one side of the road. Carved in 2006 by chainsaw sculptor Peter Bowsher ('Chainsaw Pete', from Moffat), it's a work of art depicting scenes from the natural world and different aspects of local life.

The **7stanes mountain biking centre** (♀ NX985896) at Ae has trails for all abilities, plus walks varying from short circuits to longer hikes.

4 LOCKERBIE

⌂ **Nether Boreland B&B** (page 245)

Lockerbie is the first sizeable town north of the Scotland–England border and is on the main road and rail routes between London and both Glasgow and Edinburgh. From the motorway there is little to see of the town other than the large grey mass of the Steven's Croft Power Station: not an auspicious start you may think, but notable for the fact that it is the UK's largest wood-fired biomass station. Lockerbie isn't a major tourist town as such, but it is not without interest, partly for history both distant and recent, partly for sporting prowess, and partly simply for its spirit. There is no tourist information centre here, but details of what's going on can be found in the Town Hall on the High Street.

FROM PICKLEBALL TO CURLING: LOCKERBIE'S SPORTING CHANCE

It was when visiting Lockerbie Town Hall that we met caretaker George Burnett, who along with his wife, Pat, has a unique claim to fame. As regular visitors to the US for many years, they came across the game of **Pickleball**, which they have since brought back to the UK, making Lockerbie the first place in the country where it was played. Described as something like a cross between tennis, badminton and table tennis, players use over-sized table tennis paddles to hit a small ball with holes in it back and forth across a three-foot-high net on a badminton court. The large rear hall upstairs at Lockerbie Town Hall has a couple of courts marked out on it and there's a weekly game on a Tuesday evening from 18.30 to 20.30 at which anyone is welcome, or Wednesday 15.00 to 16.00 specifically for beginners. George and Pat's imported sport created so much interest that they were filmed for Border TV news, footage of which can be found on the ITV website.

Pickleball is only one of Lockerbie's sporting achievements, though, for the town has for many years been associated with the Scottish sport of **curling** and in recent times local curlers David Murdoch, Claire Hamilton and Anna Sloan did themselves proud by bringing home a silver and two bronze medals from the 2014 Sochi Winter Olympics. Lockerbie's ice rink – on which curling is played – is at the northwestern edge of town and is worth a visit either to watch a game or take part. It's a bit like bowls on ice, the aim of the game being to slide your stone down the ice rink with just the right strength of push so that it comes to rest in the centre of the 'house' (target area). More information about curling in general can be found on the website of the Royal Caledonian Curling Club (⌽ www.royalcaledoniancurlingclub.org) and times of sessions at Lockerbie if you want to go along are posted on the Lockerbie Ice Rink website (⌽ www.lockerbieicerink.co.uk).

41

In the 1950s Lockerbie was the eighth richest town in Scotland. Today it's a more modest place but its history is worn proudly and also with a cheeky wink: the quirky **sheep sculptures** on the High Street never fail to bring a smile to my face (and also had our dog very excited – and confused – the first time he spotted them) and are a tribute to the great Lamb Fairs of days past. People would flock (no pun intended) to Lockerbie from miles around for the livestock sale, the money from which allowed the town to buy Lamb Hill to the east and also to build the Scottish Baronial **Town Hall** with its slightly fanciful clock tower at a cost of £10,000. It is said that at the market's height, up to 70,000 lambs would be waiting to be sold on Lamb Hill. Now that would have been quite something.

Lockerbie's more recent history has been dominated by the tragic bombing on 21 December 1988 of Pan Am flight 103 as it passed overhead, which killed all 259 people on board and 11 residents on the ground. The victims of that horrendous event are remembered in a number of memorials, all of which are detailed on the website of the **Dryfesdale Lodge Visitors Centre** (⊘ www.dryfesdalelodge.org.uk). At the lodge itself, west of Lockerbie on the A709, is a remembrance garden and exhibition. There is also a striking **stained glass window** showing the flags of the nations of all those killed in the main hall on the first floor of the Town Hall on the High Street, which at the time of

CHEWING OVER A BIT OF HISTORY

The Jardines' early stronghold was Spedlins Tower, built in 1500 and which still stands on a loop of the Annan, opposite where Jardine Hall once stood. Although in private hands today it has a tale attached which is worth telling. The story goes that the Jardines moved from here in the late 17th century to escape the bogle (ghost) of an unfortunate miller, James Porteous, who fell victim to the poor memory of the first baronet, Sir Alexander Jardine (whose portrait, incidentally, hangs today in Annan Museum, pages 56–7). Porteous suffered the baronet's displeasure for apparently setting fire to a mill and was locked away in the tower dungeon. Off rode Sir Alexander to Edinburgh with the key in his pocket, completely forgetting about the poor man. When he remembered he sent a messenger back post-haste but it was too late and the miller had died of starvation. Time likes to embellish a tale, and it is reported that in the throes of his terrible hunger the miller had gnawed off his own hands and feet. To this day it is said that if you poke a stick into the dungeon at Spedlins it will come back chewed.

writing is only open in the mornings. The main hall itself is kept locked, but if you go upstairs to the office (to the right at the top of the stairs) there is usually someone there who can let you in. East of Lockerbie, at **Tundergarth Church** (♀ NT175808), the Watch Room has also been refurbished as a memorial. The nose of the Pan Am plane came down in the field immediately opposite the church. There is a visitor's book full of heartfelt messages written to lost loved ones and it is difficult not to be moved at this quiet, solemn spot.

"Lockerbie lies within the parish of Dryfesdale, a name taken from the Dryfe Water."

Lockerbie lies within the parish of Dryfesdale, a name taken from the Dryfe Water, which rises east of Moffat to the north and flows southwest to join the River Annan. **Dryfesdale Parish Church** now sits within Lockerbie itself on Townhead Street, but it never used to. The original church was up the Dryfe Valley, but the river changed course one night and washed it away. A second church was built, but it too fell victim to the elements. And so the third, current church was located right in the town itself and built high with a raised entrance, where it has stood since 1898.

In the graveyard are stones of well-known local families, notably the **Jardines**, whose seat, Jardine Hall (now demolished), used to stand northwest of Lockerbie. It was William Jardine (1784–1843) who with James Matheson founded the incredibly successful conglomerate Jardine Matheson in Canton in 1832. One of the original Hong Kong based *hongs* (trading houses) from the days of Imperial China, the company is still in operation today and still controlled by Jardines's descendants. William Jardine himself is commemorated in the old cemetery in the nearby town of Lochmaben (pages 45–6).

Collectors and secondhand enthusiasts will want to have a rummage at **Cobwebs Antiques** (30 Townhead St, DG11 2AE ✆ 01576 207009 ⚲ www.cobwebsoflockerbie.co.uk). It's a veritable treasure trove packed to the gunnels. If you're lucky, owner Irene Henderson will be there as she, too, is a veritable treasure trove, of local history. From her we learned of the Grahams, who set up the poor house in nearby Ecclefechan (pages 47–8), before the village grew to house the workers for Hoddom Castle (pages 48–9), to where they would walk each day. Thank you, Irene; you are a joy for authors researching guidebooks and the lamp we bought fits the spot perfectly.

FOOD & DRINK

On the B7076, five miles north of town, is the café of the **Lockerbie Lorry Park** (lorry not obligatory). We learned about it by chance from someone to whom we once gave a lift. So enthusiastic was she about the fry-ups cooked here that we had to give it a go. She was right. What's more, it's an excellent place not just for a fry-up (complete with haggis and tattie scones) but also for a range of good home-cooked food and unashamedly indulgent desserts such as bread and butter pudding, jam roly-poly, homemade apple pie, banoffee pie and trifle. Truckers and farmers are regulars, and we've even spotted the local undertaker here (not on official business), all being looked after by the cheery ladies behind the counter. **Café 91** 91–93 High St, DG11 2DA ✆ 01576 202379. The main retreat for teas, coffees, scones and lunches. If you're in the area at Christmas time, it's worth popping in for the exuberant decorations alone!

Eskrigg Nature Reserve

Just southwest of Lockerbie on the A709 Dumfries Road, opposite the Dryfesdale Lodge Centre; parking available in the cemetery car park

Established and run by the Lockerbie Wildlife Trust, Eskrigg Nature Reserve is a fine example of a community-based habitat restoration and wildlife project. The history of the reserve makes for interesting reading and can be found at ⌂ www.lockerbie-wildlife-trust.co.uk. There's a whole ecosystem to explore here, but for many visitors the key attraction is the healthy population of red squirrels that is supported by the Scots pines. We saw 14 of them on one visit.

Hallmuir Prisoner of War Chapel

📍 NY128793

A mile and a half southwest of Lockerbie on the Dalton Road is a utilitarian, white-painted corrugated iron building with blue windows. Slightly forlorn, it looks like a pre-fab storage hut and you'd be forgiven for never giving it a second glance. It's more than it seems, though, for this is a chapel, the last remaining building of a World War II prisoner of war camp. The history of Ukrainian expatriation to the UK during World War II is well documented. The men who came to Hallmuir were just a few of the 8,500 former soldiers of the Ukrainian Galicia Division, previously part of the German army and subsequently interned by the British in Austria when Germany surrendered to the Allies, then moved to Italy, whence to Scotland in 1947 rather than leaving them to be handed over to the Russians.

Many of the Ukrainians who came to Scotland during World War II chose to stay when the war ended and the chapel is a unique memorial to them and their descendants. The interior is both vivid and moving, a small outpost of the Ukrainian Orthodox Church in lowland Scotland.

5 LOCHMABEN & THE ROYAL FOUR TOWNS

Lochmaben has long held a place at the heart of Scottish history, renowned as the home of the Lords of Annandale, ancestors of Robert the Bruce (1274–1329). Bruce was brought up in this area; his family is said to have lived in a castle which stood on Castle Hill, though there is little left to see (the site is now the second green of the local golf course). Ruins of a second castle, believed to have been built by Edward I of England in the early 14th century and once the strongest fortress in the Scottish Borders, can be seen on a peninsula in nearby **Castle Loch**.

THE POWER OF COMMUNITY

Darren Flint, co-author of this guide, is also Project Officer for the Castle Loch Lochmaben Community Trust.

After standing empty for a number of years a little white cottage on the side of Castle Loch came on to the market, not overly unusual you may think in this area of plentiful little white cottages. However, what made this spot special was it came with 280 acres of loch, surrounding woodlands and fishing rights. This isn't something that happens every day and the residents of the town of Lochmaben, which nestles up to the northern edge of the loch, and the surrounding Royal Four Towns, were mobilised into action and seized the opportunity to purchase this for future generations. After much form-filling, hoop-jumping and consultation, the fundraising and acquisition of the loch was completed in early 2014.

Castle Loch is now managed by Castle Loch Lochmaben Community Trust (CLLCT)

with the support of a stalwart team of volunteers. Thanks to their efforts, there is now a good path offering a three-mile circular walk around the loch taking in the best of the history and habitats, with plenty of opportunities to enjoy the wildlife. Castle Loch took the top award for Community Project of the year 2014 in the 'People Awards' run by Dumfries and Galloway Life magazine.

Each season offers something different, be it the annual migration of pink-footed geese to the loch in winter, returning sand martins and the grand courtship of the great crested grebe in spring, the summer darting of numerous dragonfly species, or the year-round flash of iridescent blue from a kingfisher and opportunity to see otter and red squirrel.

The wide main street preserves part of the medieval layout. At its head is the small but elegant **Town Hall**, complete with regal statue of Bruce on a plinth outside, plus a statue of one Reverend William Graham in a recess above the door. Graham oversaw the enlargement of the Town Hall in 1869 and, from the satisfied look on his face, he was obviously happy with the results.

Lochmaben today is very much a local town with a strong community presence, a shining example of which is the acquisition of **Castle Loch** thanks to the efforts of the Community Trust (see box, page 45). This is one of three lochs that surround the town, the other two being Kirk and Mill lochs, slightly to the north.

"The Royal Four Towns of Greenhill, Heck, Hightae and Smallholm are notable for their protected status which dates back to the time of Robert the Bruce. It is said that Bruce granted lands and privileges to the 'King's kindly tenants'."

Dinghy sailors can take to the waters on Castle Loch through the Annandale Sailing Club and fishing is also allowed by permit, which can be bought at the post office and also at Halleaths Caravan Park. Until fairly recently Castle Loch was one of only two places in Scotland where the vendace, Britain's rarest freshwater fish, could be found. Sadly it is now believed to be extinct in these waters. Visit ⊘ www. castleloch.org.uk for more information about Castle Loch and all the things to see and do at the site. Further information on fishing is available from Castle Loch Fisheries (⊘ www.castlelochfisheries.co.uk).

There is a wealth of information about the town available at ⊘ www. lochmaben.org.uk, including places to eat and stay, though it is easy enough to find things out once you're here by asking the friendly townsfolk or popping into the Town Hall, where copies of local information leaflets are available.

In the area around Lochmaben are the Royal Four Towns of **Greenhill**, **Heck**, **Hightae** and **Smallholm**, notable for their protected status which dates back to the time of Robert the Bruce. It is said that Bruce granted lands and privileges to the 'King's kindly tenants', conferring upon them a preferential position, to provide garrisons and food supplies for Lochmaben Castle, and since then the good citizens have enjoyed the protection of successive kings and parliaments against local officials and landowners.

Corncockle 🖐

A couple of miles north of Lochmaben is Corncockle, site of Corncockle quarry, where in the 19th century the first dinosaur quadruped fossil footprints in Britain were discovered by local man Reverend Dr Henry Duncan of Savings Bank Museum fame (page 59). A keen geologist, he subsequently presented a paper on his discovery to the Royal Society in Edinburgh.

ᵘᵘ FOOD & DRINK

There are numerous pubs, cafés and shops in Lochmaben serving everything from cooked meals to snacks. At nearby Hightae, the **Hightae Inn** (High Rd, DG11 1JS ✐ 01387 811711 ⊘ www.hightaeinn.co.uk) serves quality local food and is always popular. Booking is essential.

6 ECCLEFECHAN & AROUND 🖐

The shortened version of Ecclefechan's name is bandied around freely and more than once we've heard the joke told of someone running late who 'missed the 'Fechan bus', so don't be surprised if you come across variations on this theme during a visit to the area. This strange name is derived from the Celtic for 'small church' and dates from pre-Roman times.

Ecclefechan has survived good times and bad and made a not insignificant contribution to history as the birth- and burial place of philosopher and essayist **Thomas Carlyle** (1795–1881), whose description of economics as 'the dismal science' may ring true with many in today's economically vexing times. **Carlyle's Birthplace** (DG11 3DG ✐ 0844 493 2247 ⊘ www.nts.org.uk ⊙ seasonal; National Trust for Scotland), with its modest three rooms, is on the High Street.

Visitors to the village are encouraged to linger with a series of **six information noticeboards** dotted down the main street, from the park at the top, near the statue of Carlyle, down the High Street to the last one at the village hall. The noticeboards focus not just on Ecclefechan's famous son, but also on the history and development of the village in general, and through that history tell something of the wider story of the area. This is a good place to visit on a sunny day when you can take your time and saunter down the High Street, ponder the statue of Carlyle, absorb the history and perhaps stop for a spot of lunch at the **Cressfield Hotel** (Townfoot, DG11 3DR ✐ 01576 300 281 ⊘ www.cressfieldhotel.co.uk) or **Ecclefechan Hotel** (High St, DG11 3DF ✐ 01576 300213).

Ecclefechan Church is now closed but the **graveyard** next to it is not. As well as being the final resting place of Carlyle, it is also where one **Archibald Arnott** is buried. Born at nearby Kirkconnel Hall, Arnott was the physician who attended Napoleon Bonaparte during his confinement to St Helena and was the only doctor that Napoleon would countenance in his dying days.

Burnswark Hill

♀ NY185788

Directly north from Ecclefechan is a detour worth taking up to the Roman fort on Burnswark Hill. It's about three miles from the village centre and can be walked or driven. At the summit are the ramparts of an Iron Age fort, with Roman siege camps to the north and south. The view from up here is terrific, a sweeping panorama taking in the eastern end of the Solway Firth with the mountains of Cumbria to one side and Criffel to the other. A pleasant circular walk taking in Burnswark can be started in Ecclefechan or from Tundergarth Church near Lockerbie.

Hoddom Castle & around

⋏ Hoddom Castle Caravan Park (page 249)

Head southwest from Ecclefechan to find **Hoddom Castle** (♀ NY156730). Built 1437–84 it was initially called the Castle of Hoddom Staines ('staines' means stones) as it was constructed from an older castle of the same name that stood on the opposite side of the river and which was said to have been the home of a branch of the family of Robert the Bruce at the start of the 14th century. It was a Herries property from around 1449, Herries being one of the old Galloway families which are still in the area. The castle today is partly ruined and partly used as a centre for the surrounding caravan park.

A couple of interesting diversions on foot can be taken from here (leave your car in the parking area just above the gates into Hoddom Castle). The first is a visit to the **cemetery** on the banks of the Annan, which you can see from the bridge if you look downstream and which can be reached along the riverbank. The graveyard is on the site of a monastery built for St Kentigern (or Mungo) in the 7th century. There is little left to be seen of the monastery complex, but look out for the ghoulish skull and crossbones motif which adorns many of the gravestones, part of a tradition of 18th-century folk art in which heraldic emblems were often combined with symbols of mortality and immortality, such as coffins, hourglasses and, of course, skull and crossbones.

This is an exceptionally peaceful spot in which to while away an hour or two, with a well-placed bench on the riverbank perfectly sited for a picnic. If here early in the morning or at dusk sit quietly and watch for ripples and disturbance at the water's edge and you might be lucky enough to see an otter. The river is a good spot for **salmon fishing**, too, and this is one of the most beautiful stretches on the Annan where you can cast your line. (Permits can be bought at Hoddom Castle; see the Fish Annan page of ✑ www.fishpal.

"The river is a good spot for salmon fishing and this is one of the most beautiful stretches on the Annan where you can cast your line."

com.) Keep an eye open for kingfishers and also look out for passing female goosander ducks with their red heads and long serrated beaks. We have seen them flying back and forth along this straight stretch of the Annan and under the handsome stone bridge.

The other option is to set out from Hoddom in the opposite direction, along the Dalton Road from the car park and then turn left up stone steps and carry on up the hill to reach **Repentance Tower** at the top, from where you get 360° views. The tower dates from around 1560 and various stories explain its name, but all conclude with a similar message that it was built to atone for some act of treachery.

Dalton Pottery
Meikle Dyke, DG11 1DU ♀ NY108737 ✐ 01387 840236 ✑ www.daltonpottery.co.uk
☉ daily in summer 10.00–17.00, weekends only Nov–Mar

From Hoddom it's a short hop westwards to the delightful Dalton Pottery in the village of Dalton. Geoff and Jenny Finch moved here many years ago having hit upon the perfect spot to bring up their young family and to set up their business. Jenny is a potter and, after years of successfully selling to major high street retail brands, decided to go it alone and open her studio to the public. All ages are welcome and everything from adult classes to mug painting for children is offered, and there is a small gift shop and a tea room. Jenny wanted to create an environment in which children would be at ease and parents wouldn't have to worry about things getting broken. This she has done with notable success.

LOWER ANNANDALE

From Gretna Green westwards to Ruthwell, the landscape shelves gently down to the shores of the Firth. The River Sark runs immediately south of Gretna, its winding course demarcating the border between England and Scotland for several miles before it empties into the eastern end of the Solway. The flatlands of the **Solway Plain** are in stark contrast to the hills and rugged coastline which characterise so much of the rest of Dumfries and Galloway. The appeal here is in the sudden and unexpected views across the Solway, the stories of centuries past, the enormous contribution of the area to World War I and II, and a few social quirks and anomalies thrown in for good measure.

7 GRETNA & GRETNA GREEN 🖐

There are few who haven't heard of Gretna and many who, regardless of whether they have been here or not, will offer an opinion. It is certainly a place which inspires love (literally) or loathing. The divide stems primarily from the whole razzmatazz that surrounds the Gretna marriage industry. There is a tale worth telling here though, one of legal precedent, thwarted love, scandal and intrigue.

First we should clear up the confusion between Gretna and Gretna Green, for they are two separate places, albeit right next door to each other. Gretna Green is the small hamlet known for its history of

RINGING THE SWANS AT GRETNA

In 2013, the Famous Blacksmiths Shop celebrated its 300th anniversary. To mark the occasion, the shop teamed up with WWT Caerlaverock Wetlands (pages 122–3) in a scientific project with a romantic twist. Caerlaverock is particularly known for its wintering populations of barnacle geese and whooper swans and so two swans, a male and a female, were fitted with darvic rings which had been blessed over the anvil in a traditional Gretna marriage ceremony. (Darvic rings are the coloured plastic ones, which can be read from a distance through binoculars or a scope.) Whoopers mate for life and live for up to 26 years and it is hoped that this pair will provide scientists with lots of new information about their migration behaviour between Caerlaverock and Iceland. You can keep an eye open for them as the swans have special codes on their rings: on the male's yellow leg ring are the initials GGS for Gretna Green Scotland and on the female's red leg ring are the intials FBS for Famous Blacksmiths Shop.

marriages, whereas neighbouring Gretna is, like the town of Eastriggs (pages 52–3) a little further along the Solway, a planned town that was built during World War I.

For centuries the main coaching route ran right past the Famous Blacksmiths Shop in Gretna. The Scotland–England border lies immediately south and the blacksmith's was the first place you came to. This was the fortuitous circumstance which led to its becoming world famous, for when the 1754 marriage act was introduced in England, making it illegal for those under 21 to wed without parental consent, the blacksmith of the day spotted an opportunity and, taking advantage of the liberal laws in Scotland, offered to conduct weddings over his anvil for any couples who were struggling to wed across the border. (Unlike in England, where marriages were only legal if conducted by a minister, in Scotland the ceremony could be officiated by just about anyone so long as it was in front of two witnesses.) Needless to say, the idea took off and spawned a tradition that, despite fluctuations over the centuries, is as strong as ever.

"Gretna and Gretna Green are two separate places, albeit right next door to each other."

These days the **Famous Blacksmiths Shop** (♀ NY321685) is open for business as usual and you don't have to be getting married to have a look around. Whatever day you visit there's a good chance you may witness (not officially, you understand) a wedding taking place, for these days the blacksmith's hosts weddings in the sort of numbers – around 1,000 each year – that would make traditional churches weep with envy. The cottage also houses a museum and exhibition with a range of fascinating items, including letters from forlorn maidens beseeching the blacksmith priests to find them a husband, for these self-made businessmen-ministers were also regarded as matchmakers by girls from far and wide. It really is a piece of living history. There's also a tea room, gift shop and speciality foodhall with an enticing range of goodies, all usually bustling with a coachload or two (or more) of visitors from all around the world.

It didn't take long for other local businesses to cotton on to their potential as wedding venues. **Gretna Hall**, just across the motorway and built originally in 1710 as a manor house for the Johnstone family, offered a more refined and genteel retreat in which couples could wed. Today it is still offering the same service and operates as a smart hotel.

And just around the corner from it can be found the **Old Toll Bar**, which in 1830 found itself the first house in Scotland when the main route north was diverted. It was too good an opportunity to be missed and the toll keeper was soon pulling in passing couples for a quick service which he would perform himself, for a small fee of course.

FOOD & DRINK

In addition to the tea room at Gretna Green, fine food (sourced locally) and afternoon teas are available to non-residents at both **Smith's Hotel** (Gretna Green DG16 5EA ☎ 01461 337007 ⬙ www.smithsgretnagreen.com) and **Gretna Hall Hotel** (Gretna Green DG16 5DY ☎ 01461 338257 ⬙ www.gretnahallhotel.com).

Bruce's Cave
📍 NY265705

On the subject of traditions and myths, while you're in this area you might want to pop up to **Kirkpatrick Fleming** a few miles northwest of Gretna to take a peek at Bruce's Cave, the spot to where the great leader is said to have retreated in the winter of 1306 after defeat by the English. The cave is on the Cove Estate, where the main house (now holiday apartments) is surrounded by its own caravan site. Sir Walter Scott first told the tale of Bruce in his cave in *Tales of a Grandfather* in 1828. While he was here, it is said Bruce watched a spider spinning a web. Time and again it failed, falling and then starting again, and thus Bruce was inspired to rally once more before going on to succeed against all the odds at the Battle of Bannockburn. From this episode comes the saying 'If at first you don't succeed, try, try and try again'.

The cave makes for a fun trip, with a short walk down through the woods to a walkway and platform attached to the hillside high above the Kirtle Water.

WEST OF GRETNA

Heading west from Gretna, glimpses of the Solway to the south reveal ever-changing views of ever-changing waters and sands stretching across the estuary to Cumbria. Through the village of Rigg with its curious village hall (Mansfield Hall) and on to **Eastriggs**, thereby giving rise to an anomaly that we haven't yet been able to get to the bottom off. Specifically, why is Eastriggs west of Rigg? If you know, we'd be delighted to hear. Eastriggs is known as the Commonwealth Village for it was built

THE WORST RAILWAY DISASTER IN BRITAIN

Dumfries and Galloway holds the unenviable distinction of being the location of three of the worst transport disasters which have ever occurred in Britain: the Lockerbie bombing in 1988, the sinking of the passenger ferry MV *Princess Victoria* off the west coast in January 1953 (page 225) and the tragic Quintinshill rail disaster just north of Gretna Green on 22 May 1915. The circumstances which led to Quintinshill were a mix of signaller error and 'failure to operate rule 55' which required safeguards to be put in place should a train be stationary on a running line. As a result, a southbound troop train travelling at high speed and carrying a Royal Scots battalion headed for Gallipoli ran into a stationary passenger train at Quintinshill. The resulting carnage was compounded shortly

after when a northbound express ploughed into the wreckage, spilling hot coals across the carriages and starting a fire.

In all, 227 people were killed and 246 injured. The disaster accounted for 42% of the casualties suffered by the Royal Scots during World War I. George Meakin and James Tinsley, both signalmen on duty at Quintinshill at the time, were tried for involuntary manslaughter and found guilty in what proved to be a controversial verdict. Both had an unblemished record and both would have to live with their conscience. Tinsley was sentenced to three years penal servitude and Meakin to 18 months, but both were released after just 12 months.

A display about the Quintinshill disaster is included in the Devil's Porridge exhibition at Eastriggs (see below).

to house workers who were brought in from all over the Commonwealth to the nearby munitions factory (see *The Devil's Porridge*, below). In recognition, the streets are named after different countries, regions and cities of the Commonwealth, thus you might see Delhi Road, Brisbane Way or Vancouver Road for instance. Australia, New Zealand, Canada, India and South Africa are all represented.

The Devil's Porridge

Near Stanfield Farm, Annan Rd, Eastriggs DG12 6TF ♀ NY246664 ✆ 01461 700021
🖰 www.devilsporridge.org.uk ⊙ seasonal hours & closed 22 Dec to 19 Jan

During World War I reports were brought back from the front that Britain was losing the war due to lack of ammunition. Following the shell and ammunition crisis of June 1915, Lloyd George, then Minister for Munitions in Asquith's coalition government, resolved to do something and set about a project that was to see the construction of the biggest factory on earth.

A site was needed and the stretch of land along the Solway at Eastriggs fitted the bill. There was nothing here, it was close to mainline transport connections and ships could come up the Solway and dock at Annan. So in September 1915 work began, progressing at an urgent pace. Nine months later production started and by September 1916, each week the factory was shipping out 800 tons of cordyte, a highly explosive mix of nitro-glycerin and nitro-cotton to be used as propellant in munitions.

The construction of the factory was an immense achievement in every sense. Not only was the site enormous, stretching for nine miles from Dornock to Longtown and two miles wide, but the running of such a factory was a complex operation, not least in eradicating as far as possible any fire risk. Workers, the majority of them women, were inspected every time they entered the factory by the 'women police', who paid particular attention to bodices to make sure there were no buttons that could drop off and cause an explosion in the highly volatile propellant mix. There were 125 miles of rail track on the site and fireless steam engines were used, specially constructed with composite wheels to ensure there were no sparks from the rails.

Around 30,000 people worked here and so a whole social infrastructure had to be created too, with every social, religious and educational need taken care of. Churches and schools were built, and so too were cinemas and dance halls. And, of course, housing. There was no way the surrounding towns could absorb such a huge influx of people and so two purpose-built settlements were created, one at Eastriggs which until that time had been only a single farmhouse, and the other at Gretna (as opposed to Gretna Green; page 50).

The architects of these towns were Courtney Crickner and Raymond Unwin, both of them keen supporters of the Garden City movement that had been pioneered by the Cadbury Bournville settlement in Birmingham and Port Sunlight near Liverpool. The towns they created were the most modern in Scotland and after the war attracted the attention of the US government, who had become aware of the limitations of their own public housing and the detrimental effect it had on their war effort. Congress voted to allocate US$50 million to create better living conditions and US architects subsequently looked to the UK for inspiration, including to the developments on the Solway.

The Devil's Porridge presents a fascinating story engagingly presented and well worth a visit. As for where the name comes from, it's thanks to

Arthur Conan Doyle of *Sherlock Holmes* fame. During the war he visited the factory and observed the women workers kneading by hand the mix of nitric acid and cotton waste in large vats. It was this mixture that he subsequently termed 'The Devil's Porridge'.

The exhibition also includes a section on the Quintinshill railway disaster of 22 May 1915 (see box, page 53).

8 ANNAN 👆

🏠 **Waterside Rooms** (page 245)

Annan's fortunes have waxed and waned since the town was made a Burgh of Barony by the Bruces in the 13th century. Industries have come and gone, from shipbuilding and the bustling work of a busy port to whisky distilling and, in more recent times, nuclear power at the local Chapelcross Power Station, which is now partially decommissioned. Despite such fluctuations in its fortunes, an air of determined survival adheres to Annan's High Street with its attractive red sandstone buildings, several decorated with carved stone ornaments, which tell of more prosperous times and of another local industry, quarrying. What's more, there is at least one reason for this welcoming town to be optimistic, namely the redevelopment of the historic Annandale Distillery (pages 56–7).

"Annan's fortunes have waxed and waned since the town was made a Burgh of Barony in the 13th century."

The broad curve of the High Street is dominated by the 19th-century Scottish baronial tower of the **Town Hall**, inside which, fixed to the east wall of the council chamber, is the **Brus Stane** (Bruce Stone), which is believed to have been part of the original motte and bailey castle of the Bruce Lords in the 12th–14th centuries. The story behind the stone's positioning here in the Town Hall was recorded in *The Glasgow Herald* of 20 June 1927, which reported: 'Some years ago, it [the stone] was found at Brendon, North Devon, by the late Dr George Neilson, Glasgow, and its possessor, Miss Halliday, Brendon, generously restored it to the burgh of Annan.' No-one knows how the stone found its way to Devon, but it returned to Annan in 1925, travelling in the car of Mr Thomas Dykes, antiquarian and provost of Annan. Today access to view the stone is by appointment only at the Town Hall. If you do visit, look out, too, for paintings by local artist William Ewart Lockhart (1846–1900) whose work *The Jubilee Celebration in Westminster Abbey, June 21, 1887* was commissioned by Queen Victoria and now hangs in the Royal Collection. Other works by Lockhart can be viewed in Annan's museum. Also notable on the High Street is the B-listed **Annan Observer Building**.

Annan Museum (Bank St, DG12 6AA ✐ seasonal numbers available on website ✆ www.annan.org.uk ☉ seasonally excluding Sun) is a good place to get to grips with the history not just of the town but also of East Dumfriesshire in general. Temporary exhibitions are staged downstairs and there's a permanent exhibition upstairs, where you'll find everything from an engaging video of local fishermen explaining the different types of nets and talking about characters past and present, to portraits of

ANNANDALE DISTILLERY – A SPIRIT REBORN

Northfield, Annan DG12 5LL ♀ NY195683 ✆ www.annandaledistillery.com ☉ daily all year with 45 minute tours starting on the hour between 10.00 & 16.00

One of the most ambitious tourism stories of recent years in Dumfries and Galloway is the rebirth of the old Annandale Distillery and its transformation into a 21st-century whisky-making centre and visitor attraction. To celebrate its opening, Professor David Thomson, who has been the driving force behind the project, and Linny Oliphant, Visitor Experience Manager, have kindly contributed the text below to this guide.

Born 1836, fell into a deep sleep 1918, wakened from slumber 2007, restoration of natural beauty begins in 2011 ... 'A sleeping beauty awakens' is how the re-development of the historic Annandale Distillery has been described. A long-term ambition for Dumfries-born Professor David Thomson, a consumer psychologist, and Teresa Church, a nutritionist, they describe their special project as a 'labour of love'. Thomson and Church are owners of MMR Research Worldwide, a global sensory and consumer research company, so this is something of a departure from their normal area of work, but one which is fuelled by their passion for David's home region and a fascination with whisky production in the area.

The formidable Annandale Distillery spans three whisky-making eras and a period when it was used in farming. Originally owned by George Donald, an exciseman from Elgin in its first whisky era c1830–83, the tenancy was then passed to John Gardner, the son of a former mayor of Liverpool in 1883, and finally Johnnie Walker acquired it in 1893. From 1924 to 2007 it was owned by the Robinson family, who were producing the then famous 'Provost' brand of porridge oats from their mills in Annan with the distillery maltings, kiln and mash house converted into a grain-drying plant and the bonded warehouses used for housing cattle.

Now the impressive listed building has been painstakingly refurbished and is entering its the local gentry, old photos of the area and an exceptional Bronze Age sword in remarkable condition. Among many other exhibits are displays relating to the RAF presence during World War II, the development and decommissioning of Chapelcross, and a glass case full of items from the Common Riding tradition.

If you go down to the water at Whinnyrigg (⊙ NY209648) (take Seafield Road south of the town) you'll not only get a good view across to Cumbria but you'll also see nets in the water. Fishing along the Solway is mostly with haaf nets and other forms of 'fixed engines' – nets secured to the shore or seabed. Haaf nets consist of a single net

fourth whisky era. 'The transformation has been quite spectacular. I feel I know some of the beautiful stones here personally' explains Thomson, referencing the impressive sandstone reclaimed from outbuildings attached to the walled garden at the nearby Castle Milk Estate.

Annandale Distillery produces two styles of whisky honouring two of Scotland's most iconic figures, both with strong ties to the Annandale area. The smoky, peaty 'Man O' Sword' is the 'single malt whisky of kings' inspired by Scotland's most famous warrior king and 7th Earl of Annandale, Robert the Bruce, while the non-smoky 'Man O' Words' pays tribute to the national bard, Robert Burns.

Tours start under the Charles Doig-designed malt kiln and visitors can see the handcrafted wash backs and mash tuns and the vibrant copper stills hand-built by Forsyth's of Rothes. A viewing platform enables a peek into the mill room which houses the malt bins, conveyors and Porteous Mill, which has come from the now demolished Caperdonich

Distillery in Rothes. Outside, the historic site of the old still room was excavated by archaeologists from Glasgow University.

The project incorporates local cultural knowledge, too, for Annandale Distillery's branding is a tribute to Annan's rich maritime history and shipbuilding heritage, with the 'A' of Annandale in the image of a billowing sail.

Between 1830 and 1930 over 2.5 million people emigrated from Scotland, many of them leaving from Annan and the other Solway ports. 'We want to create a sense of belonging that links Annandale Distillery with local people, with whisky enthusiasts around the world and with people of Scottish heritage living anywhere on this planet' says Thomson.

Visitors are offered different tour options and can meet Distillery Manager, Malcolm Rennie, formerly of Kilchoman Distillery, Islay. Local craftsmanship is displayed in the woodwork and furniture which has been made by Kirkcudbright master craftsman, Ian Cameron-Smith. There are also coffee and gift shops.

mounted on a wooden frame which is carried into the water and held there by the fisherman.

This historic spot has been much used over the centuries for crossing the Solway, notably just to the east at Bowness Wath ('wath' means ford), which was used by cattle drovers crossing between Bowness in Cumbria and Annan up until 1863. In the 19th century the Solway Viaduct was built, forming a safer crossing point until falling into disuse and then being demolished in 1934. The viaduct was a lifeline for local workers who had a habit of running across it for last orders at the pub, since closing time was half an hour later in England than in Scotland.

The Annan shore makes for an interesting walk and there's a circular loop of around five miles called the **Annan Shore Walk**, which is signposted starting from Annan Town Hall and takes in Whinnyrig, Summergate and Waterfoot. Along the way you pass information boards and points of interest for local fishing methods, the Solway Viaduct and the grassland and sand flats of the Annan Merse, a Site of Special Scientific Interest (SSSI) with populations of wading birds. Full details can be found online at the local community website, Annan Online (www.annan.org.uk).

FOOD & DRINK

Café Royal 95 High St, DG12 6DG 01461 202865. Reputedly the favourite restaurant of local lass Ashley Jensen, who came to fame in the TV programme *Extras*. It has a reputation for serving a smashing fish supper and, as well as offering the usual take-outs, it has a seating area inside and garden tables at the back.
Del Amitri 95 High St, DG12 6DG 01461 201999 www.del-amitri.co.uk. Located above the Café Royal. Since opening in 2007 it has received an AA rosette and also entered the Michelin guide with a two-knife-and-fork rating. Del Amitri has also been reviewed favourably by the food critics of Scotland's two major nationals: *Scotland on Sunday* and *The Herald*. Praise indeed. The menu changes monthly to offer the best seasonal produce, with local meat, game and fish appearing often.

WEST OF ANNAN

West of Annan the A75 sweeps northwest towards Dumfries veering away from the Solway and crossing gentle hills that shelve down to the water. The more interesting option is to stay south of the A75 on the B724 and take a couple of diversions, one right down to the shoreline at Powfoot and the other to Ruthwell, an unassuming wee place with a couple of unexpected attractions.

9 Powfoot 🖐

For a complete change and something of a surprise, make your way to Powfoot, just under four miles west of Annan. You'll know you're almost there when you reach a brightly decorated bus stop that guarantees blue sky and bobbing boats even on the most dreich day. Turn down the road here to reach the pretty settlement on the shore of the Solway, red cottages nestled around the most English of greens, built at the turn of the 20th century as a holiday village.

Enjoy the gigantic sky and views of the Cumbrian mountains, and take a walk out over the sands but be aware of the tide times and do not venture out too far at the cusp of low tide. The Solway is notorious for its racing, treacherous tides. Look out for a strange circular structure about 600 yards from shore; this is all that remains of a tidal swimming pool.

This is a good spot for birdlife, too. We stood here at dusk one evening mesmerised by a huge flock of wheeling birds above the sands, behaviour which according to Mike Youdale of the Wildfowl and Wetlands Trust (WWT) is typical of knot.

10 Ruthwell

Four miles west of Powfoot brings you to Ruthwell, famous for two things, both connected with one man, Reverend Dr Henry Duncan (of Corncockle quadruped fossil prints fame; page 47). The first is the **Ruthwell Cross**, an 18-foot-high stone Anglo-Saxon preaching cross which is thought to date from the 8th century and is in remarkable condition. It is one of Scotland's rarest treasures. Carved with scenes from the New Testament, the cross was deliberately broken in 1642 so it could be more easily hidden – and protected – during the Reformation. Duncan restored it in 1818 and it was later installed in a specially built apse at Ruthwell Church, where it can still be viewed today. The church is kept locked but a sign is posted with directions of where to collect the key from a nearby house.

Duncan is remembered as a man of vision and compassion and it is these qualities which led him to establish the world's first savings bank, the Ruthwell Parish Bank, in 1810 in the building which now houses the **Savings Bank Museum.** He also founded a couple of local newspapers, through which he encouraged the local population to start saving. Talk about a canny Scot!

ESKDALE

Eskdale is more sparsely populated and remote than neighbouring Annandale and it tends to look as much to the Scottish Borders region and south to Carlisle as it does to the rest of Dumfries and Galloway due to its geography and associated road and transport connections. Public transport is a trickier option here and driving is the best way to get around, especially once you venture up into the hills. The scenery is inspiring and the attractions are varied, from the old mill town of **Langholm** in the south, now reinventing itself as a cultural centre for arts, crafts and theatre, to the village of **Eskdalemuir** (one of the wettest in Britain, but don't let that put you off) set in glorious countryside, and the nearby **Kagyu Samye Ling Buddhist Monastery**. It is difficult to spend time in Eskdale and not feel drawn in by its beauty, sense of community, self-sufficiency and welcoming people. We have been here in all weather conditions and have never been disappointed.

11 LANGHOLM
🏠 **Eskdale Hotel** (page 244)

Langholm sits snugly in the valley of the Esk at the confluence of the River Esk, Ewes Water and Wauchope Water, its white stone buildings bearing testament to the quarries of days past on neighbouring Whita Hill and its watery geography demanding such a proliferation of bridges that one enthusiastic guidebook writer in the 1950s declared 'So many bridges, so many waterways! Why, at first glance this Muckle Town of Langholm seems like a little Venice.' Comparisons with La Serenissima aside, Langholm nonetheless holds its own as a place of culture, cuisine and curiosity, all of the best possible local sort. It is also the home of renowned local artist Julie Dumbarton who attracts an international following to her courses. See ⊘ www.juliedumbarton.com for more details.

'Please Slow Down Here Comes Langholm' declares a road sign as you enter the town from the south and well may the good townsfolk want to reduce the speed of the traffic that passes along its main street. The sign is particularly apt, though, for Langholm bears all the hallmarks of a genuinely 'Slow' town: shops selling local produce (including handmade chocolates no less), cafés serving home-cooked fare, a burgeoning arts and cultural scene with galleries and craft shops displaying the work of local artists, and a friendly visitor information centre staffed by volunteers.

This is a great base from which to **walk** in the surrounding hills, to spot the local fauna and flora, or to **fish** the beats of the Esk. Nearby **Canonbie** to the south of the town (page 67) also makes a good base if you want to explore the area and sits on a particularly pretty stretch of the Esk with good fishing and fine riverside walks down to the border with England.

Historically, Langholm was the site of the highly significant Battle of Arkinholm in 1455, when supporters of James II defeated the Black Douglases who had controlled the area for so long, and thus ended a civil war. It was after this time that many local families came to prominence, names that are still heard today across the area: Scott, Beattie, Irvine, Glendinning, Maxwell and Armstrong.

Once known as the 'Muckle Toon' (the 'big town'), in the 19th century Langholm had a reputation internationally for the tweed woven in its mills, an industry which, at its peak around 1890, employed some 1,200 people. Sadly, the last mill, Reid and Taylor, closed in 2013 when operations were moved south to Yorkshire under new owners.

The town is closely associated with the great engineer **Thomas Telford** (1757–1834), born in the tiny settlement of Glendinning (see box, page 68) to the northwest and who at a young age was apprenticed to a local stonemason. Telford left a bequest to the Langholm Subscription Library (as it was then), the interest on which was used to buy a fine collection of books. Some of them can still be seen in the Langholm Library (accessed from the Market Place at the back of the town hall and not to be confused with the public library on Charles Street), leather-bound volumes with 'Langholm Library Telford Legacy' tooled on the spines. Today they are stored upstairs in a newly created, temperature-controlled space, but they used to be kept in a splendid barrel-vaulted room on the first floor which has since been put to alternative use: the addition of a false ceiling has improved the acoustics no end and it is now used by the **town pipe band** for practising on weekend afternoons. Listen out for them and if you're here on a sunny day you may find them outside in the car park around the back.

Outside the library door stands a statue of **Admiral Sir Pulteney Malcolm**, one of Langholm's many famous sons and daughters, all of whom are detailed on a noticeboard towards the northern end of the High Street. Several Malcolms made the grade for their contribution

Langholm circular walk: in the footsteps of the Border Reivers

Landranger map 79, Explorer maps 323/324; start: Kilngreen car park ♀ NY364848; 6 miles/2½ hours (including breaks); moderate

The 'Muckle Toon' has many fine walks, with numerous circular routes all beginning from this walk's start point. This moderate route on hard surfaced tracks and grass hill paths with some steep sections provides a fine mix of habitats, history and upland views. Kilngreen car park is just north of the town centre (A7), on the edge of the River Esk and is accessible by buses 95/103/124. There are lots of refreshment options in Langholm.

From 1 **the car park** head away from the town, upstream along Ewes Water, and cross at Ewes Bridge. By the pillars at the estate entrance and sawmill go left through the wooden gates and follow the path left around the field edge, **Langholm Castle** ruins stand in the centre of this field. Follow the path along the bank of the River Esk, pass the elegant **Duchess Bridge**, cast in 1813 and the first cast iron bridge in Scotland, and on past the pheasant-rearing sheds.

The path bends right, then away from the river, and up to 2 **Holmhead Farm** (♀ NY354858). Follow the track around to the left in front of the steading, and on past North Lodge staying on the main woodland track. After about half a mile the woodland opens up and offers views of Potholm Farm and the Eskdale hills.

At the track junction, by the wooden bench, take the left fork down the hill, and pass above Potholm Farm to the 3 **T-junction** (♀ NY355878). Turn sharp right and follow the track as it meanders up the hill. Cross the stile and turn immediately right, following the line of the fence as it climbs up between Wrae Hass and Potholm Hill.

Just before the brow of the ridge, cross the stile on your right, through the field and over the next stile. Follow the old stone dyke (wall) as it climbs **Potholm Hill**, and, on a clear day, enjoy the 360° views along the Ewes and Esk valleys, and down to the Solway Firth and mountains of the Lake District behind.

Continue following the dyke down off the hill, over the ladder stile and alongside a more robust wall. Keep straight ahead when this wall bears sharply left, and continue to the summit

to military and economic life; another, Sir John, is commemorated by the Malcolm Monument on Whita Hill (pages 65–6) above the town. Pulteney and John were just two of the 17 children of parents George and Margaret, who farmed at nearby Burnfoot.

of **4 Castle Hill** (♀ NY361862). As you begin to descend, head for Langholm through the scrubby hawthorn trees that scatter this hillside, pass the footpath marker and join the rough track. Cross the ladder stile and carry on downhill to the road, passing Pathhead and returning to Ewes Bridge and the car park.

Shorter route: if time is tight or you are simply in the mood for a shorter walk, there is a pleasant alternative to the longer route. Follow the first two stages of the above described walking route, as far as the North Lodge, at which point turn a sharp right on to a track that follows along the far side of the wall (instead of continuing straight ahead on the main woodland track of the longer route). Stay on this track, ignoring any side paths, as it passes through attractive woodland, to emerge and continue along a field edge. The path then turns a sharp left between two fields and after about 200m reaches the path, from the longer route, coming off Castle Hill. Having joined the longer route, continue back to the car park in Langholm.

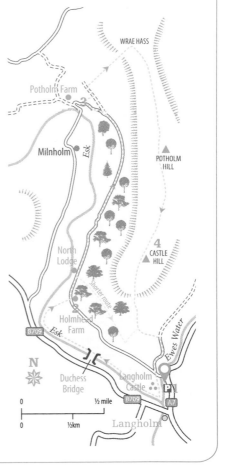

The library was built on land gifted by the Duke of Buccleuch, whose local estate has owned much of the surrounding countryside since the mid 17th century. Today, **The Buccleuch Centre** (DG13 0AW ✆ 01387 381196 ☍ www.buccleuchcentre.com) on the western side of the Esk is one of the main arts and entertainment venues in southern Scotland.

The library has seen much history, for it was also at one time frequented by Chris Grieve, better known as **Hugh MacDiarmid**. His mother was the library caretaker and from 1899 to 1913 the family lived here in a house which has since been gutted. MacDiarmid is also commemorated on Whita Hill (page 65).

Today there is a **visitor information centre** (page 32) downstairs where Margaret Pool and a team of volunteers do a sterling job. Do pop in to see them, and if you plan to visit the MacDiarmid Memorial, pick up a copy of the leaflet which explains what all of the panels mean.

The High Street and river make for a nice circular loop taking in the town's main shops and points of interest as well as showing off the various waters to best advantage. Start at the riverside car park at the northern end of town, make your way along the High Street passing **Abbott's Chocolate Shop** (High St, DG13 0JH ✆ 07742 718248 ⌨ www.abbottschocolates.co.uk) where since 2010 Dennis Cockburn has been producing exquisite confectionery too good to resist. What's more, he also runs workshops where you can try your hand at making your own. Look on the opposite side of the road for the **Royal Bank of Scotland** building, noting the quirky carved heads

"The High Street and river make for a nice circular loop taking in the town's main shops and points of interest."

which can be seen around the door. They represent members of the family of Robert Wallace, the first manager. Continuing along the street you'll come to **Cut the Mustard Gallery** (54–56 High St, DG13 0JH ✆ 01387 381180 ⌨ www.mustardgallery.co.uk), where Lisa Rothwell Young runs silver-making workshops and organises a range of other arts and crafts classes. The gallery itself displays the work of many local sculptors and artists while Lisa's partner, Barry, is a photographer and runs both one-to-one and group courses (⌨ www.barryyoungphotography.co.uk). A short way beyond the gallery is the Eskdale Hotel, in which is housed a small collection of artefacts relating to **the Clan Armstrong**.

At the southern end of the High Street you can cut down either side of the Truly Scrumptious delicatessen to the river, either passing the **Thomas Hope Hospital**, named after another son of the town, or down the intriguingly named **Laird's Entry** on the other side. The story behind the latter is that it was at one time the only way down to the river, and was thus the entry to Rosevale House, home of the banker and lawyer 'laird', John Little. Once down at the river, cross over and take a moment to wander around the church and riverside gardens before strolling back along the bank. The scant remains of **Langholm Castle**, built in the 16th century by one Christopher Armstrong, brother of the notorious reiver Johnnie Armstrong, stand in grounds across the double-arched stone bridge on the western side of the river at the north end of town.

Every summer Langholm comes alive to the sound of pipe bands, cheering crowds and horses cantering through the streets for the annual **Common Riding** or Riding of the Marches. Langholm's is a particularly fine celebration usually held towards the end of July. If you're in the area at the time, we'd recommend it highly as a day of grand tradition and entertainment.

¶ FOOD & DRINK

Eskdale Hotel Market Pl, DG13 0JH ℰ 01387 380357. Conveniently located in the centre of Langholm, serving teas, coffees, soups, sandwiches and fuller meals in the small bar.
Truly Scrumptious 70 High St, DG13 0JH ℰ 01387 380402. Offers a good selection of teas and coffees in fine bone china, along with sandwiches and fuller dishes in a charming vintage tea room and garden, with knick-knacks for sale and old cabinets lining the walls. Homemade soups, fresh breads, meats, teas, everything from oatcakes to flavoured vinegars, quince jelly and Applewood smoked cheddar.

12 WHITA HILL & EWES VALLEY

To the east of Langholm are the **Langholm and Newcastleton hills**, with **Whita Hill** (♀ NY379847) 🖐 the first summit, easily accessed by a road from the northern end of town. They are not the highest hills but the views from up on the moors, one of the few remaining large areas of moorland in southern Scotland, take in the Solway plain and eastern end of the Firth to the south and west and the lovely Ewes Valley to the north. Towards the top of the hill you can park by Jake Harvey's eye-catching **Hugh MacDiarmid memorial**, based on the idea of an open book – obviously so when you see it – and constructed from steel and bronze. To get the most out of it, pick up a leaflet from the tourist information centre in Langholm (page 32), which explains what all the different panels mean. Nearby, at the summit of Whita Hill, is the obelisk of the **Malcolm Monument**, almost 100 feet

THE KIRKTON BELL RINGS OUT

There is another tale attached to this curious churchyard feature which was told by one John Elliot of Langholm in a lecture he gave to a local archaeological society in the 1950s and which is reproduced in a book called *The Ewes Valley* by Brenda L Morrison and R Bruce McCartney, who have kindly given permission for it to be reproduced again here.

Mr Elliot tells us: 'No doubt you have heard the story of the wedding at Kirkstyle which was so tragically interrupted by the ringing of this self-same bell at dark midnight. Perhaps it might be worth telling again.

The fun was getting fast and furious when suddenly there was a toll of the bell. One or two people noticed it, but no-one mentioned it and they went on with the dance. Another sharp toll, at which womenfolk looked at one another a little scared. The men affected to make light of the incident and the merriment was resumed but in a more chastened spirit.

Again came the ominous sound – doubled in number and intensity. This could be ignored no longer. The dancing ceased and the more daring of the men volunteered to venture into the kirkyard – dead of night though it was – and investigate this mysterious ringing of the bell. Just as they entered, however, there was heard a more clamant toll than ever and the men ran helter-skelter back to the house. Do not blame them, for these were the days of Burke and Hare and everything relating to the kirkyard was eerie and regarded with fear and superstition. But

high and erected in 1835 to Major General Sir John Malcolm, 19th-century governor of Bombay and envoy to Persia. If you're up here in the summer, keep an eye open for adders which can sometimes be spotted. We've also seen red grouse among the carpet of ling heather.

North of Langholm follow the A7 and course of Ewes Water along **Ewes Valley**, a strikingly beautiful stretch of countryside surrounded by hills on either side, with wonderfully named hamlets such as Unthank and Fiddleton. This is the main road north to Edinburgh and fairly quickly leaves the Dumfries and Galloway region, but before it does it passes a local curiosity, the bell at Kirkton, three miles north of Langholm. Here in the churchyard of **Ewes Kirk** (♀ NY369908) a bell hangs in the fork of a tree. It has been here for well over 150 years, some reports say 300 years, and hung originally in the first church that stood here, but was later moved to a tree in the churchyard when the church was demolished. That tree had to be felled owing to its condition, so the then minister, Mr Kerr, stored the bell in the vestry for a while but then re-hung it in an adjacent tree. And there it is to this day.

their being safe in the house did not stop that fearsome ringing of the bell.

Consternation reigned and at last the company deemed it an occasion on which the aid of the minister should be invoked. So a deputation set out to the manse, and, rousing the minister, they told him – what he himself could now hear – how the kirk bell was being rung by unseen hands whose could be no other than Auld Nick himself. The minister reproved them for their foolish fears and, greatly to their comfort, volunteered to accompany them to ascertain the cause of this unseemly occurrence. They had got to the brig over the Kirktoun Burn when there was another series of loud and insistent peals. They looked to the minister – but he was down on his knees saying "Let us pray"– after which they betook themselves to the wedding.

All the long dread night that bell kept ringing and once, when day dawned, there was eager anxiety to ascertain the cause. It was then discovered that someone had maliciously tethered the minister's goat to the bell rope hanging loose from the tree, and every movement of the goat straining at the tether caused the bell to toll. Great was the indignation at the Kirkstyle, but the culprit was not discovered until many years later, when a well-set-up man visiting his native valley from America, made the astounding confession that he was the scamp who had done this scandalous thing.'

13 CANONBIE & THE DEBATABLE LANDS

🏠 **Byreburnfoot Country House B&B and Cottages** (page 244)

South of Langholm lies the village of Canonbie, a small settlement of houses strung out along the west bank of the Esk. If you're here in spring, look out for the thousands of daffodils that line the road between here and neighbouring **Rowanburn**. In 2005, the good folk of Canonbie and Rowanburn joined together to plant 36,000 bulbs linking their two communities and creating the 'Marie Curie Roadway of Hope'.

It's a quiet area today, and with a good accommodation option (page 244) makes a pleasant base for exploring the area, for fishing, or for walking the surrounding hills or along the Esk. The quiet, however, belies a lively past. For 300 years Canonbie was at the heart of the so-called Debatable Lands (page 23) until eventually James V lost patience and in 1530 took action, imprisoning various local lairds for their lack of action, notably Johnnie Armstrong of nearby Gilnockie Tower. Just over 20 years later, in 1552, a physical barrier, Scots Dike, between the two countries was built.

THOMAS TELFORD 🌿

From early beginnings at remote Glendinning, Thomas Telford (1757–1834) rose to become one of the greatest engineers the world has known. Telford either worked or advised on an astonishing number and range of projects in a host of countries, including Scotland, England, Ireland, Sweden, Poland, Germany and Austria. It seemed there was no civil engineering challenge to which he couldn't rise, including roads, bridges, aqueducts, churches, manses, canals, harbours and docks. His boundless energy and vision were vital in the dawn of the Industrial Revolution, opening up transport routes, improving trade and industry and advancing his home country at an unprecedented rate. He was also the founder and first president of the Institution of Civil Engineers. In all his time, though, he never forgot where he had come from, often referring back to his early days in Eskdale and ultimately bequeathing part of his estate to the libraries of Langholm and Westerkirk, which are still in use today. Telford's final days were spent in London and he is buried at Westminster Abbey.

Gilnockie Tower, a couple of miles north of Canonbie off the A7 at Hollows, is the only habitable Armstrong Tower still in existence from the original 90 or so pele towers in the area. The tower was home at one time to Johnnie Armstrong, the most feared and respected reiver in the 16th century, who was lured to his death by James V on pretence of a meeting. From the top of the tower you can see into England. Tours of the tower are offered by appointment, see ♂ www.armstrong-clan.co.uk for further details.

If you fancy a walk while in this area, there are a couple of waterfalls popular with locals. The first is the **Fairy Loup Waterfall** (♀ NY5783) at Byreburn, which can be accessed from the east bank of the Esk between Byreburnfoot and Byreburnside. The second is a little further to the east, **Penton Linns Waterfall** (♀ NY3774). From Canonbie take the B6357 towards Newcastleton and at Harelaw take the Penton turning. The falls start at the bridge over Liddel Water, which also marks the Scotland–England border.

14 BENTPATH, WESTERKIRK & GLENDINNING

The B709 runs northwest from Langholm and offers splendid views to the hills to the northeast. The hamlet of **Bentpath** (♀ NY312902) is prettily arranged on either side of a bridge across the River Esk and overlooked by Westerkirk Parish Church on the hillside opposite. The surrounding hills and lanes are those that were known to **Thomas Telford**, who was born a few miles up the single-track road at **Glendinning** (♀ NY299969), where a cairn on the hillside has been erected in his memory. It's an isolated spot and you can't help but wonder about the circumstances that made it possible for a young lad from such a remote backwater to leave such a mark on the world.

Part of Telford's legacy stands in the form of **Westerkirk Library** on the main road out of Bentpath, in front of which is a stone monument to the great man himself. The library was founded in 1791 and is the oldest one still in use in Scotland. Telford left £1,000 towards its maintenance and today it holds over 8,000 books and records going back 200 years. Anyone can visit but opening times are limited and borrowing of books is restricted to those who live in the parishes of Westerkirk and the surrounding villages. Further details are at www.futuremuseum.co.uk.

NORTH ESKDALE

From Bentpath to Eskdalemuir the road winds through a series of valleys and climbs up into the hills. The countryside is dotted with traces of ancient camps, notably **Castle O'er** (♀ NY243928) and **Bessie's Hill**, two Iron Age ring forts which are linked by a six-mile walk. The **Eskdale Prehistoric Trail** takes in these and seven other sites (out of the 60 sites of archaeological importance in the area) and is marked with signposts, starting from Bentpath, running up to Eskdalemuir and then returning down the eastern side of the valley. The trail can be driven or cycled but the sites themselves are accessed on foot.

15 ESKDALEMUIR

Approaching the hamlet of Eskdalemuir from Langholm, look out for two sets of stone circles on the left down towards the river, first the **Girdle Stanes**, dating back perhaps as far as 4000BC, and then the smaller **Loupin Stanes** (♀ NY256966) from around 2500BC, from where there is a delightful view northwards.

"Eskdalemuir stands 600 feet above sea level in an exposed valley of the White Esk."

Eskdalemuir stands 600 feet above sea level in an exposed valley of the White Esk and was the location in days past of the curious Handfasting Fair. Originating from the late 14th century, this was an annual event at which local lads and lassies would clasp hands as a sign that they wished to embark on hands as a sign that they wished to embark on a year's trial marriage. Twelve months on, at the fair the following year, if they still wished to marry then the appropriate ceremony would be arranged. However, if either of the partners had changed their mind, then he or she could walk away with no obligation, unless children were involved in which case they went with the unsatisfied party. The practice died out in the 18th century but was only formally proscribed by an Act of Parliament in 1940.

Eskdalemuir today is known chiefly as the location of the Kagu Samye Ling Monastery (see below) but it also is benefitting from a new community 'hub' and café, which is providing a central gathering point for those who live in this relatively isolated village and its surroundings. Check out what's on if you're going to be in the area (see box, opposite).

16 Kagyu Samye Ling Monastery & Tibetan Centre 🖐

DG13 0QL ♀ NT246002 ✆ 01387 373232 🖉 www.samyeling.org ⊙ temple: daily 06.00–21.00; tea room and shop: 09.00–17.00

Just north of Eskdalemuir unsuspecting visitors are in for perhaps the biggest surprise in the whole of Dumfries and Galloway. Among the hills stands the tall golden stupa of Kagyu Samye Ling Buddhist Monastery established in 1967 and the first in the West. Visitors are welcome to drop in and have a wander around. The temple is open until 21.00, while a stroll around the peace garden and grounds can be taken at any time of the day. The Tibetan Tea Rooms offers many tasty treats and the recently extended shop offers both local and Nepalese items.

"Among the hills stands the tall golden stupa of Kagyu Samye Ling Buddhist Monastery."

Nothing quite prepares you for your first sight of the main temple; there is little hint of it from the road, even though you know it's there. Inside it's a riot of colour: pristine and primary reds, yellows, golds, blues and greens. Every morning 1,000 small water bowls are filled and every afternoon they are emptied and dried. Standing watching from the back of the temple, the silence is broken only by the sharp ring of glass on glass as the bowls are stacked by two volunteers in the half-light of the late afternoon, not a word spoken between them. Visitors are welcome to look in, but please remove shoes and be quiet, especially if there is a class in progress.

🍴 FOOD & DRINK

Eskdalemuir Community Hub and Café The Old School, DG13 0QJ ✆ 01387 373760
⌂ www.eskdalemuir.com. During the 1950s, the school at Eskdalemuir was attended by
around 50 children. That number gradually declined until the school was closed in the 1990s.
Now with the help of Lottery money, the school has been converted into a welcoming and
spacious community hub and café. It's a characterful, bright and airy place which makes
use of old school chairs (look for graffiti from days past on the undersides) and the old roller
blackboard on which menus are chalked up, but which also combines well with the new,
including European oak and American cherry finishings, a toasty wood burning stove, and
a fine array of solar panels out the back. Everything from morning coffee to themed bistro
evenings is offered in the café, and events are held in the same building so do check on the
website (or on the café's Facebook page) to see if anything is on while you're in the area.
Keep an eye open for birds, too. We spotted a dipper in the stream which runs past the door.
The Tibetan Tea Rooms Kagyu Samye Ling Monastery & Tibetan Centre, DG13 0QL
✆ 01387 373758 ⌂ www.samyeling.org. The tea room at the monastery makes for a
relaxing break with a difference thanks to its traditional décor and brightly coloured Tibetan
rugs lining the benches. Teas, coffees, snacks and fuller vegetarian meals are served in a
peaceful atmosphere of good karma.

DUMFRIES & GALLOWAY ONLINE

For additional online content, articles, photos and more on Dumfries and Galloway, why not
visit ⌂ www.bradtguides.com/d&g and ⌂ www.slowbritain.co.uk.

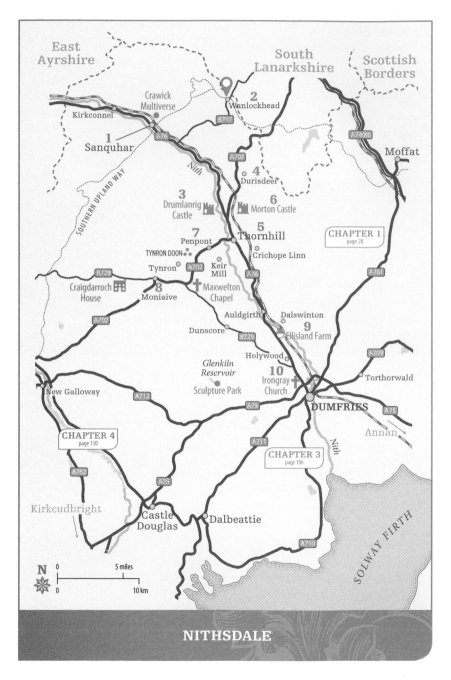

NITHSDALE

2
NITHSDALE

Nithsdale cuts a narrow swathe down the landscape, with the river valley broadening out as you head south towards Dumfries and the Nith estuary. The area is bordered by East Ayrshire and South Lanarkshire to the north, the Glenkens area of Dumfries and Galloway to the west, and Annandale to the east. The River Nith, long known for its excellent salmon and trout fishing, is the longest of the rivers of the Dumfriesshire Dales, running 65 miles from its source in the Carsphairn Hills of East Ayrshire down to the Solway, passing the key towns of **Sanquhar, Thornhill** and **Dumfries** *en route*. The rail line follows the course of the river for much of the way, with stations at Kirkconnel, Sanquhar and Dumfries.

The joy of Nithsdale is in the drama of the valleys and gorges of the Nith, and the magnificence of the passes to the northeast

"The joy of Nithsdale is in the drama of the valleys and gorges of the Nith."

which form two of the main access routes to the area and which are generally regarded as the grandest of the 'southern highlands'. Both Mennock and Dalveen offer breathtaking and moody scenery with high hills dropping sharply to the valleys below. At the top of the Dalveen, the River Clyde rises as not much more than a puddle at the start of its journey to Glasgow. Keep an eye open for wildlife and birds of prey around here. We had a terrific view of a short-eared owl on one trip.

The area is strongly associated with Robert Burns. Afton Water, captured by Burns in his eponymous poem, rises just outside the Dumfries and Galloway boundary in East Ayrshire and joins the Nith at New Cumnock. Burns lived in Nithsdale and travelled its length and breadth during his time as an exciseman, before moving in his final years to Dumfries. Whilst at Ellisland Farm (pages 102–4) he was at his most productive in terms of his body of work, even if this period highlighted how unsuited he was to being a farmer.

To keep chapters to a manageable size and for ease of exploration, this chapter includes all of Upper and Mid Nithsdale, but only the upper part of Lower Nithsdale. Dumfries itself and the Nith estuary are covered separately in *Chapter 3*.

GETTING AROUND

North–south (or vice versa) is the predominant travel direction in Nithsdale. The busy A76 from Ayrshire follows the Nith Valley all the way down to Dumfries at the river's estuary. The other main 'A' road, the A702, strikes out westwards from the small town of Thornhill, passing through numerous pretty villages, heading for the Glenkens (*Chapter 4*). On the quieter, more remote lanes, we also found that hitching and/ or offering a lift still had some success, which turned up many an interesting conversation and friendly chat.

PUBLIC TRANSPORT
Either end of the Nith Valley benefits from having an accessible **train service**, something that much of Dumfries and Galloway doesn't enjoy. **Scotrail** (⌀ www.scotrail.co.uk) runs a frequent service throughout the day Monday to Saturday and a very infrequent one on a Sunday, which takes in Dumfries and Sanquhar along its Newcastle to Glasgow route.

The Nithsdale **bus services** tend to follow the north–south A76, which means that Thornhill and Sanquhar don't fare too badly, with services such as the 236 and 246 operated by Stagecoach Western/Houstons/ DGC Buses/MacEwans (although return tickets issued by one operator might not be accepted by another on the same route – always check when buying). Moniaive is mainly served via Thornhill by the infrequent 202 and 212 services Monday to Saturday, operated by James Robertson and Yules. Sundays are a 'no go' for this journey. Wanlockhead is served Monday to Saturday by the 221 Stagecoach Western/DGC Buses from Kirkconnel and Sanquhar, which is handy for taking a day trip up into the hills or if you want to walk part of the linear Southern Upland Way, just make sure you don't miss the last bus back.

There are also various infrequent services that run around the area once a month or on alternate Fridays, such as the Cairn Valley Community Transport between Castle Douglas and Moniaive. Local public transport information is provided by South West of Scotland

Transport Partnership (⊘ www.swestrans.org.uk), or the traveline (⊘ 0871 200 22 33, ⊘ www.traveline.org.uk).

CYCLING

There are plenty of small quiet lanes and tracks criss-crossing the Nith Valley, which make for pleasant, if sometimes quite hilly cycling. Consulting the OS map for the area soon reveals numerous options for routes between the key towns and villages that avoid the busier trunk roads. The **Kirkpatrick Macmillan Trail** (⊘ www.bikemap.net) was developed in 1990 to mark the 150th anniversary of the invention of the pedal bicycle at the Nithsdale hamlet of Keir Mill and runs from just north of Dumfries up to Keir Mill itself. To work the legs a little harder the trip to Wanlockhead has one steep route up along the B797, taking in the beautiful Mennock Pass. You will work up a sweat arriving, but can enjoy freewheeling down on your return. See Dumfries and Galloway Council's free *Cycling in and around Nithsdale* booklet for a good selection of cycle routes.

CYCLE HIRE

Rik's Bike Shed Drumlanrig Castle, Thornhill DG3 4AQ ⊘ 01848 330080. Bike hire, and Rik himself is usually on hand to advise on a range of circular trails around the Drumlanrig Estate suitable for all abilities.

WALKING

The Southern Upland Way and **Enterkin Pass** are two of the more famous linear routes which offer fine upland walking, with glorious views to match. The bus service between Sanquhar and Wanlockhead offers the chance to complete a 7½-mile section of the Southern Upland Way

i TOURIST INFORMATION

There are no information centres in this area, but stop and ask any shopkeeper or café owner for advice and you'll be given plenty of information to help you on your way.

Thomas Tosh in Thornhill (page 92) and A'The Airts in Sanquar (page 83), both have helpful staff and carry a good range of local information.

The nearest information centre is the **VisitScotland Information Centre Dumfries** (page 108).

(SUW) and return by bus. Not all walking in the area has to be quite as strenuous though, the views from the valley bottoms, along the River Nith and tributaries such as Mennock Water are a joy. We often randomly pick from any number of village churches to stop off at to have our picnic (you're always guaranteed a bench in a kirkyard), then strike out to explore the village and chat to the residents, who are more than happy to share their knowledge. Or simply wander around the streets of Sanquhar, Thornhill or Moniaive, stopping for a spot of shopping or tea and tray bake. Dumfries and Galloway Council has produced free 'Walking in and around' booklets – Thornhill and Sanquhar, Wanlockhead and Kirkconnel – that provide numerous varied walking options for this chapter.

UPPER NITHSDALE

Entering Upper Nithsdale from East Ayrshire, slag heaps testify to the coal mining days of the past, an industry which sustained Kirkconnel and Sanquhar for many years, and which latterly has lent itself to the development of a new world-class environmental arts attraction for the region in the form of a regenerated former open cast coal mine site. The **Crawick Multiverse** project (pages 82–3) is art on a grand scale and promises to help put this sometimes overlooked area firmly on the tourist map.

In the northern reaches the valley is broad, with the Nith flowing first on one side of the road and then the other, teasing you onwards. Access to Upper Nithsdale from the north is either on the main A76 from East Ayrshire, or on the B740 from South Lanarkshire. The latter is a particularly attractive route, well worth the drive through the **Lowther Hills** for its splendid scenery.

Kirkconnel is the most northerly town in Upper Nithsdale, and is said to be the burial place of St Conal, a shepherd's son who in the 6th century was taken by St Kentigern to the monastery at Hoddom in neighbouring Annandale (page 48) to be prepared for the priesthood. Conal later returned to his home where he administered to his flock, preaching in a church at the foot of Kirkland Hill to the north and baptising converts in the nearby well, where an outdoor service is still held once a year. In the 18th century the **church** was moved closer to the developing town, to the site where it now stands at the northern end of the main street. Next to the gate a **sign** tells the story of local man **Alexander Anderson**, who in the 19th century worked first as a surfaceman with the new Glasgow and Southwestern Railway before becoming known for his poetry in the Scots tongue.

1 SANQUHAR & AROUND 🖐

🏠 **Blackaddie Country House Hotel** (page 245)

The royal burgh of Sanquhar was once a mining town and historic wool centre and is today a popular stopping point on the **Southern Upland Way** with a population of just over 2,000. Crawick Water courses its way down through the hills passing near the wonderful **Crawick Multiverse** (pages 82–3), flowing into the Nith on the edge of town to the north, while Euchan Water tumbles down the **Euchan Falls** before joining from the southwest. **Crawick Mill** was the first large-scale mill in Upper Nithsdale, capitalising on the burgeoning wool trade in the early 19th century. From here carpets known for their quality and durability were sent out around the world, and from Sanquhar itself arose the now internationally famous **Sanquhar**

"Sanquhar is one of Scotland's oldest burghs having been made a royal burgh in 1598 by James VI."

knitwear. Wool was the mainstay of the local economy until the development of the coal industry in the late 19th century, and the First Statistical Account of Scotland shows that in 1793 the sheep to human ratio here was 10:1. By the 19th century Sanquhar's sheep fair was one of the country's most important, notable also for the fact that it was a 'character market' in which stock wasn't actually shown but was traded on the character and reputation of the dealer.

Sanquhar's name is believed to come from 'Saen Caer' meaning 'old fort', thought to be taken from the old Roman fort just north of town. It is one of Scotland's oldest burghs having been made a royal burgh in 1598 by James VI. In the 17th century the town became a centre for the Covenanters when Reverend **Richard Cameron** rode in along with his brother and a handful of supporters and affixed a paper to the town cross which was read aloud and in which he renounced his allegiance to Charles II. This was the first **Sanquhar Declaration** and it cost Cameron his life. The king declared war on him and around a month later Cameron and his men were surprised and killed at the Battle of Airds Moss in Ayrshire. Cameron's name lived on, though, for in 1689 it was adopted by **The Cameronians**, a regiment which lasted 279 years until the defence cuts of the 1960s.

THE POETRY HIGHWAY

Local poet Hugh McMillan lives in Nithsdale and, thanks to a commission from the Wigtown Book Festival (pages 195–6) has written a sequel to the notorious *Gallovidian Encyclopaedia* published in 1824, a hilarious and partly slanderous work which was withdrawn from publication as a result of the furore it caused at the time. His latest poetry collection is *The Other Creatures in the Wood (Mariscat)*. Hugh tells us there is much to celebrate in the cultural life of Nithsdale and he is particularly fond of Upper Nithsdale. He has written the following piece for this guide.

Thomas Carlyle once told Queen Victoria that the most inspirational road in Scotland was the road from Carsluith to Creetown. This is not true. For inspiration and exotic insights into life, that road, lovely though it is when the tide's in and the sun is shining silver on the waters of the Solway and on the battlements of romantic ruined castles, pales into insignificance when compared to the A76 trunk road from Holywood to Kirkconnel.

The A76 actually has a historical poet at each end of it. It passes Ellisland where Burns lived for a while and produced a massive number of songs and poems, and Friars Carse where his poem 'The Whistle' recalls a gigantic drinking competition.

> Six bottles a-piece had well wore out the night,
> When gallant Sir Robert, to finish the fight,
> Turn'd o'er in one bumper a bottle of red,
> And swore 'twas the way that their ancestor did.

At the other terminus we have the railwayman poet Alexander Anderson, born in Kirkconnel in 1845.

> Langsyne, when life was bonnie,
> An' a' the warld was fair,
> The leaves were green wi' simmer,
> For autumn wasna there.
> But listen hoo they rustle,
> Wi' an eerie, weary soun',
> For noo, alas, –'tis winter
> That gangs a twalmonth roun'.

Anderson was a surfaceman who later became Chief Librarian at Edinburgh University. His poems, in Scots and English, are often gently sad reflections on the passage of time, on the dampening of the fire.

> Love, turn thy gentle feet away,
> How can I be thy lover?
> A low wind grieves among the leaves,
> And the time of the rose is over.

Drink, weather and the death of love, all on the A76.

A bendy bus used to operate on this road, before they were outlawed, and the back of the bus, past the so called 'Disney seats' where the bus bent, was generally full of colourful characters who, out of the driver's sight, often engaged in a range of creative activities, though seldom poetry. I have written many poems, or parts of poems, on the bus, though usually in the front part. I find it best when the bus has broken down, and your hand doesn't shake, but sometimes it's enough just to watch and listen, writing it down when things get less dangerous.

> A little crow in his shiny suit
> but he has a voice like something put
> on metal to scratch cars,
> and a good half inch of Vladivar
>
> left between his knees.
> In front, old ladies squeeze
> against their seats like paste.
> He's not out of his face,
>
> it's just that Big Ted
> bounced a brick off his head
> the other day,
> and now his girlfriend wants his DNA.
>
> He takes a swig. Outside, the valley
> where we both were born sways
> in shades of green and brilliant yellows.
> It's summer and it follows
>
> the plot we've long since lost.
> His mobile goes off:
> No Da, I'm sober and I'm dressed.
> Aye. I really am. Honest.
>
> The little box goes dead.
> He sits and gravely nods his head,
> then stares quite sadly up at us,
> as he lobs his bottle up the bus.

'Another Lost Boy on the Cumnock Bus'

It is the blend of the beautiful and the inevitable detritus of living that makes the Upper Nith Valley so appealing. It's a lived in landscape and that's where poetry is best born.

Five years after Cameron's declaration a second one followed on the same spot, this time by Reverend **James Renwick** who had attached himself to the Cameronian sect and in effect picked up where Cameron left off. This second declaration was also to come at the ultimate cost and in 1688 Renwick was captured in Edinburgh and hanged at the age of just 26.

SANQUHAR KNITWEAR

Known for its distinctive pattern and style, Sanquhar knitwear first developed in the 18th century when the local wool trade was gaining traction. It's a specialist art practised by relatively few people, one such being Alison Thomson. She was interviewed by Anne Foley, Manager of the delightful A' The Airts Arts Centre in Sanquhar, who has kindly given permission for her resulting article to be published here.

Alison Thomson has lived in Sanquhar since the 1980s but her interest in the historic Sanquhar pattern began long before that. Alison was raised in Midlothian, where she showed a talent for sewing and knitting from an early age, having learned these skills from her mother. During the war, when there was only low quality wool available she knitted her first scarf for her father, who wore it with great pride. That was when her passion for knitting started. In the 1950s Alison moved to Shetland with her husband Kenneth, who was a minister in the Church of Scotland.

It was while in Shetland that Alison mastered Fair Isle knitting (the technique is very similar to Sanquhar knitting) and witnessed how women in Shetland gained some financial independence through their knitting. Alison became increasingly interested in the history of knitting. As her family grew up, she bought her first knitting machine and started producing jerseys for the family. After a spell on the Scottish mainland,

Alison and family moved to the Orkney island of Sanday. There she became one of the directors of the Isle of Sanday Knitters, where she influenced some of the designs.

When she moved to the Borders in the 1970s Alison set up 'Eildon Designs', supported by a group of hand knitters. A friend showed her a pair of Sanquhar gloves, which she had never seen before, and she started to research the history of the Sanquhar Pattern. She discovered that no-one had developed the pattern into larger items, as the Fair Isle knitters had done, and was inspired to start designing them herself.

It was a happy coincidence when in 1984 her husband was offered a ministerial charge at St Bride's Church in Sanquhar. Alison opened a shop specialising in Sanquhar designs and recruited a group of local ladies to produce garments under her label 'Original Sanquhar Jerseys'. The shop closed when Alison retired but she is still actively producing these lovely high-quality items of knitwear in her home to this day.

A walk down Sanquhar High Street takes in the history of the town. The striking **Tolbooth** at the northern end was designed by renowned architect William Adam and bears its pleasing symmetry proudly thanks to the sweep of the double staircase up the front exterior, black railings (a later addition) adorned in summer with colourful hanging baskets. The Tolbooth was at one time used as a jail, by all accounts one of the most insecure in Scotland. It is said that detainees would regularly break out of an evening to spend the night at home, before returning in the morning, and one man went home for blankets because he was cold!

Inside the Tolbooth is the local **museum** (High St, DG4 6BN ⊘ www. dumgal.gov.uk/museums ☉ closes for lunch) with a good audio-visual introduction to Sanquhar and Upper Nithsdale and displays on many aspects of local life, including the very distinctive Sanquhar knitwear. Midge and Flea, Pheasant's Eye, Fleur de Lys and Rose and Trellis patterns are all shown, and if you fancy a scarf, gloves or any other items for yourself, orders are taken at A' The Airts next door.

Robert Burns is remembered in the town. He was a regular visitor to Sanquhar as he carried out his duties as an exciseman, and he named the town 'Black Joan' in his ballad 'Five Carlins' (Carlin meaning old woman) in which the five Dumfriesshire boroughs are personified as five women, each giving their opinion as to who should be their parliamentary representative at Westminster. Burns was admitted as an honorary burgess of Sanquhar in 1794 and the town today has its own Burns Club known, of course, as The Black Joan.

Take a stroll down the main street with its brightly painted houses and neat gardens. Look out for information plaques (some a little weathered) on the walls and in the entranceways to the old closes that run between the houses. On the right-hand side is **A' The Airts** café and arts centre (page 83), while almost opposite on the left-hand side is the **post office**, believed to be the oldest in the world, in continuous operation since 1712 (spot the date above the door). A little further along stands the stark granite obelisk of the **Cameron Monument**, marking the spot (more or less) of the town cross, where Cameron and Renwick pinned their papers and made their declarations.

Sanquhar Castle (♀ NS785093) has stood a sad ruin (now fenced off) for well over 300 years at the southern end of town, set off to one side in a defensive position at the top of a steep bank that runs down to the river plain. Built originally in the 11th century, Sir William Douglas, the first Duke of Queensberry, bought the estate in 1639 and despite going on to build Drumlanrig (pages 88–90), the castle at Sanquhar remained his favourite home.

Heading south from Sanquhar, the single-track road along the southern side of the Nith follows the line of the hill and offers views back across the river to town and the castle. Rejoining the main road, just past the turning to Wanlockhead is a **picnic area** and toilets on the banks of the Nith, a pleasant spot to stop for a moment. Dippers can be spotted in the water and you can walk alongside the river. Immediately after this, take a look at the **bridge** over the Nith. There are pleasant

"The road runs through mixed deciduous woodland of chestnut, beech, alder and oak."

views up and down the river, birds flitting around (we spotted a green sandpiper here) and a curious story attached. In the stone wall of the bridge can be seen some **grooves**, which according to the plaque on the wall were made around 1870 by a runaway horse that was startled by a passing train and leapt on to the wall before plunging to its death in the Nith below. Also noted is that 'the grooves were perpetuated … as a warning to disobedient youth of future generations'!

The single-track road across the bridge climbs up into the hills. This is a good access point for the splendid scenery of Upper Nithsdale. The road follows Burnsands Burn for a short distance before climbing and passing farmhouses and old stone buildings, communities of just three or four homes with terrific vistas back down the valley. The road runs through mixed deciduous woodland of chestnut, beech, alder and oak. Take your pick of the lanes to follow, but if you head for Penpont (pages 94–6) there are views across the village as you follow Penpont Burn down to the bottom of the valley.

Crawick Multiverse

♀ NS775115 ⌂ www.crawickartlandtrust.org ⊙ check website for opening times & entry charges

Immediately north of Sanquhar, the work of renowned architect and landscape designer Charles Jencks can be viewed in all its glory at the impressive Crawick Multiverse, a major land restoration project completed in 2015 (at the time of publication work was in its final stages). Jencks lives a little further south in Nithsdale (page 102), and the astrological and cosmological themes which characterise his own garden, and much of his work generally, are strongly in evidence here. The site occupies 55 acres and the scale of the work is striking. Virtually all of the materials used in its creation have come from the site itself, including the use of many hundreds of boulders which were unearthed in the early stages, some of which are now used to line the North–South Path, a 450-yard walkway oriented precisely on a north–south axis. Other features include an amphitheatre which uses the shapes and forms of a total eclipse and which is used for events, two galaxy mounds, Andromeda and Milky Way at 82 feet and 49 feet respectively, water-filled lagoons, and scalloped cliffs with Comet Walk above. For 360° views the Belvedere offers a great vantage point, complete with a hand constructed from boulders which points to the North Star. A path around the site connects the four ecologies of grassland, mountains, a water gorge and a desert.

Crawick Multiverse has echoes of both Stonehenge and Glastonbury Tor but is very much a work of our time and of its own location, a unique addition to the Dumfries and Galloway landscape.

¶¶ FOOD & DRINK

A' The Airts 8–12 High St, DG4 6BL ℰ 01659 50514 ⏁ www.all-the-airts.com. 'A vibrant wee arts centre in the heart of Upper Nithsdale' as it describes itself. Friendly and welcoming, it's a great spot to sit and watch the goings-on of the High Street, not to mention enjoy the enticing selection of sandwiches, soups, cakes and other baked goods.

Blackaddie Country House Hotel Blackaddie Rd, DG4 6JJ ℰ 01659 50270 ⏁ www. blackaddiehotel.co.uk. Chef Ian McAndrew bought the hotel in 2007 and since then has been wowing diners (and reviewers) with his talents. McAndrew trained with Anton Mosimann and has been ranked alongside David Adlard, Alastair Little and Gary Rhodes. Bookings are essential for the small, intimate dining room which is also open to non-residents of the hotel. Dishes are all locally sourced as far as possible and McAndrew grows many of his own ingredients in the two acre grounds of the hotel on the banks of the Nith.

Oasis Restaurant Nithsdale Hotel, 1 High St, DG4 6DJ ℰ 01659 501333 ⊘ most evenings & weekends. Recently refurbished, the restaurant is ideal for dinner for two or larger groups and is also a good place for an early evening drink.

2 WANLOCKHEAD ✋

Between Sanquhar and Thornhill, the B797 heads off to the northeast, up the Mennock Pass 6 miles to Wanlockhead, Scotland's highest village at 1,531 feet (and location of Scotland's highest pub and micro-brewery, too).

High above Wanlockhead

❄ OS Landranger map 78, Explorer map 329; start: Museum of Lead Mining (accessible by bus 22), ♀ NS874129; 5 miles/2½ hours (including breaks); moderate

Beginning any walk in Wanlockhead offers the leg-saving bonus of already starting from a lofty position; this means every step upwards opens up ever-growing vistas of hills, moorland and valleys. It also has the added bonus of a difficult refreshment choice upon your return – tea room at the mining museum, or the village inn complete with micro-brewery?

This is a simple route on hard surfaced tracks and grass hill paths, with some steeper sections, but best not attempted in adverse weather as the saddle above the Enterkin Pass when heading over to East Mount Lowther can be very windy. Haggis, our little terrier, sometimes struggles to keep upright when crossing.

From the end of the 1 **Museum of Lead Mining car park**, climb the steps continuing to the road, where you cross and join the marked Southern Upland Way. Continue past the houses and start to climb uphill across open moorland with the hills ahead dominated by the masts and distinctive 'golf ball' radar. The moorland is managed for red grouse, which are abundant in among the heathers; listen out for their tell-tale 'Go-back Go-back' call.

Cross a wooden bridge and follow the path until it meets the tarmac service road, turn right, following the road around the bend and join the grass path found at the end of the 2 **crash barrier**. After a short distance this will once again join the tarmac road, turn right and follow the road until you come to a large 3 **gap in the crash barrier** on your right (♀ NS884109). Go through the gap and walk across the open moorland, there isn't a distinct path, but continue until you reach the track and fence.

Turn right and follow the track down to the saddle (the low point between the two hills). Look off to your left at the saddle, this is the Enterkin Pass, which Daniel Defoe in *A Tour Thro' the*

This is exceptional countryside with steep hills on either side creating a narrow pass all the way up to the top. Sheep roam freely (mind your speed if driving), gulleys drop down, and scree slopes plummet to Mennock Water, the course of which is followed by the road for much of the trip. Pictures of the pass have been mistaken for Glencoe and it comes as a surprise to many that Scotland's highest village should be here and not further north in the Scottish Highlands.

For the energetic, there are walks aplenty to be enjoyed from the village, while the really determined can cycle up and freewheel back down again.

Whole Island of Great Britain (1726) described as: 'Enterkin, the frightfullest pass, and most dangerous that I met with, between that and Penmenmuir in North Wales'.

Keeping the fence close to your left, ascend **Auchenlone (East Mount Lowther)**. This is the steepest section of the walk, but it eventually plateaus out as you approach the summit and the **4 locator post** (♀ NS878100; erected in 1944). Once you have caught your breath, take a moment to enjoy the views, which on a clear day take in the length of the Nith Valley from Sanquhar to your right, all the way down to the Solway Firth to your left and the hills of the Lake District beyond.

Retrace your steps back to the saddle and take the path off to the left passing under the **5 pylons**. Keep following the path, crossing a burn and rejoining the tarmac road. At this point retrace your earlier route back to Wanlockhead.

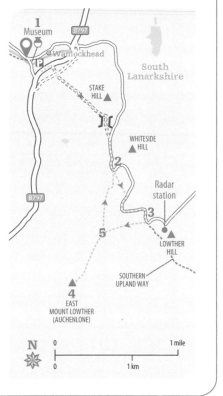

A popular but lengthy walk from Wanlockhead takes in the Enterkin Pass, described by Daniel Defoe in his *A Tour Thro' the Whole Island of Great Britain* (1726) as 'a precipice horrible and terrifying'. It was also famously the location of a 1684 Covenanter ambush of Dragoons.

Robert Burns was a visitor to Wanlockhead in 1789. He made use of the local services of the day and commissioned the blacksmith to make spiked shoes for his horse, Pegasus. In payment he wrote a poem, 'Pegasus at Wanlockhead'. Pegasus is now commemorated, cast in lead, atop the column on the central roundabout at Thornhill (page 92).

THE LIFE OF A LEADMINER'S SON

The following text is taken from historical records and reproduced here with the permission of Wanlockhead Museum Trust.

One of a family of ten, I was born at Wanlockhead, Dumfriesshire, in the year 1861. My boyhood was spent in the midst of comparative poverty, under whose grim shadow so many toilers live and die. Of my parents I say nothing here, except that my love and reverence for their memory remain undimmed to this day. The amount of love and self-sacrifice involved in bringing up a large family on the earnings of the lead miner at that period – from 15 to 17 shillings per week – I leave to the imagination of my readers. In spite of poor environment my boyhood was, on the whole, happy and care-free. My greatest delight was to roam the glens and hills of my nativity. My pet aversion was the school, and to be confined within its four walls when the sun was shining and the birds singing outside was to me the refinement of cruelty. My parents and teachers must have been at their wits' end with me, for, in spite of heavy punishment, I played truant whenever opportunity offered. I was employed as a lead washer at the age of 13, for the magnificent wage of fivepence per day. This was increased at the rate of one penny or twopence yearly, at the discretion of the manager. After working five years at lead washing it came my turn to go underground as a labourer and miner's assistant, where in course of time I became a fully qualified lead miner.

The village itself hunkers down, a scattering of houses randomly arranged, some nestling into the lee of the hills, others more exposed to the breezes that whistle through. It's an appealing place, a welcoming sight after the austere surroundings of the drive up. There's plenty to see and do here, too, not just in Wanlockhead but also in the neighbouring village of Leadhills over the border in South Lanarkshire. Gold was mined here 400 years ago and can still be found today, but the opening of lead mines in the 17th century is the real reason for the village's existence. A community of lead miners once lived here, extracting lead, silver and gold from the surrounding hills in mines owned by the Duke of Buccleuch. Employment and the allure of untold wealth brought in prospectors and workers alike, swelling the population to such an extent that by 1916 the local school had 125 pupils. With the closure of the mines, the numbers dwindled and by 1943 had dropped to just 35, though they swelled again with evacuees during the war.

Hidden Treasures (plus adjoining tea room, page 88) is the collective name of most of the various points of interest in Wanlockhead.

Run by an efficient team of locals, it is based at the **Museum of Lead Mining** in a hollow in the hills at the lower end of the village. Under the Hidden Treasures umbrella comes the museum, a walk into one of the actual mines, access to one of the miner's cottages preserved as it was in the days of the mines, access to the miners' library and a gold panning experience. Also included, though administered separately by the National Trust for Scotland, is the **Beam Engine**, a unique piece of hydraulic pumping equipment which is the only remaining water-bucket engine to be seen in a mine in the country.

There is much to interest and entertain here and, either on its own or combined with a walk in the surrounding hills, a visit to Wanlockhead makes for a good day's outing for all the family. And, of course, there's always a spot of gold panning to have a go at. (Wanlockhead has hosted the World Gold Panning Championships – yes, really, they exist – and regularly hosts the British and Scottish championships.) In addition, there is a **narrow-gauge railway**, completed by famous engineer Robert MacAlpine in 1902 in the days when lead had to be transported across the hills to Elvanfoot to the northwest, from where it was carried on to Leith Docks in Edinburgh. The railway today runs only between Wanlockhead and Leadhills (⌂ www.leadhillsrailway.co.uk ⊙ seasonally at weekends, check online) but is a delightful way to meander through the hills from one village to another. Enthusiasts should look up details of the 'Driver Experience Day'.

To complete the picture of life in the hills, carry on from Wanlockhead to **Leadhills**, a couple of miles down the road just over the border into South Lankarkshire, where you'll find the **oldest subscription library in the world** and the **highest golf course in Britain**, and which was once home to John Taylor who, when he died in 1770, was believed to be 137 years old. His story is told on a board at the cemetery, where his grave can be found. There is an excellent heritage trail around the village, free leaflets for which are available from a dispenser attached to the railings opposite the Hopetoun Hotel. There's also a village shop here if you're in need of any provisions.

¶¶ FOOD & DRINK

Hopetoun Arms 37 Main St, Leadhills ML12 6XP ✆ 01659 74234 ⌂ www.hopetounarms. co.uk. Occupies an 18th-century shooting lodge and was commented on by Dorothy Wordsworth while writing about her travels through the area with her brother and Samuel

Coleridge in 1803. From snacks to hearty fare, coffees to whiskies in front of the fire, it's a welcoming spot.

Museum of Lead Mining Wanlockhead ML12 6UT ✆ 01659 74387 ⬙ www.leadminingmuseum.co.uk. Serves teas, coffees, cakes, soups, scones, sandwiches and daily specials, and there are some interesting historical photographs and documents on the walls to browse with your brew.

The Wanlockhead Inn Garden Dyke, ML12 6UZ ✆ 01659 74535 ⬙ www.wanlockheadinn.co.uk. Scotland's highest pub offers lunches and evening meals. The inn stands on the site of what used to be the Duke of Buccleuch's hunting lodge and if you ask, convivial landlord James McKelvey will show you a picture of what it used to look like. His son Dean started up and runs the Lola Rose Brewery on the same site, Scotland's highest micro-brewery, producing the aptly named 1531 beer with the cracking strapline of 'Beer with Altitude'!

MID NITHSDALE

Mid Nithsdale is home to some of the area's most striking scenery, especially as you head west towards the neighbouring Glenkens area. Here, too, are charming villages and an attractive estate town, **Thornhill**, closely associated with one of the finest stately homes in Britain, **Drumlanrig Castle**. Also connected with Drumlanrig, at Durisdeer, is one of the area's most striking churches and a marble memorial which gives even the best Greek edifices a run for their money. A sense of community and culture pervades, both across the area and also within the individual villages, and there is a thriving arts scene encompassing music and literature in particular. Even just the thought of heading over this way fills us with gleeful anticipation; there is always something going on, the scenery and changing light always reveal a new view, and the people are as friendly as you could wish for.

3 DRUMLANRIG CASTLE

Thornhill DG3 4AQ ⚲ NX852993 ⬙ www.drumlanrigcastle.co.uk ⊙ castle: summer only; estate grounds: all year. Check website for details.

No visit to this part of the world is complete without spending time at Drumlanrig, arguably the jewel in Dumfriesshire's crown and notable not least for the distinctive pink hue of the sandstone from which it is built. In some respects Drumlanrig is something of an anomaly: called a castle, it is actually more of a house (a mansion house, true, but a house nonetheless). The broad façade that greets visitors on the approach up the drive is actually the back, not the front; and despite its mighty appearance, it is not as large as it first appears (though it is by no means small – with 120 rooms, they say there is a window for every day of the year), for it is actually four L-shaped tower houses joined together around a central courtyard, each of which has its own circular staircase within its tower. It was only in later years, as lady's dresses became larger and moving up and down the old staircases became more problematic, that the main staircase within the building was added. One other oddity is that the elegant external staircase by which the house is entered, with sweeping stairs rising up both sides of the building, is not quite symmetrical. If you look at the house from a distance and count the ground floor arches which flank the staircase on either side, you'll see that they don't quite match in number: they are out by half an arch.

Drumlanrig's history is not without its quirks either. Completed in 1689 for the first Duke of Buccleuch, he moved in but spent only one night here. The story goes that the duke was unwell and, despite calling for his servants, the place was so big that no-one heard him and nothing

DRUMLANRIG BY LAND ROVER: AN INSIDER'S VIEW

Brian Hammond usually runs the Land Rover tours of Drumlanrig. He started working on the estate almost 50 years ago under the grandfather of the current duke and is a veritable treasure trove of information about its workings and history, and the people behind the scenes. Spending time with him offers a unique insight into what makes Drumlanrig the place it is today.

Tours last up to half a day, can include a picnic, and are for a minimum of two people and maximum of five. To a degree they are also weather dependent since one of the highlights is a drive up a precipitous dirt track to the top of Par Hill, from where there are spectacular views over Kettleton Dam west back to Drumlanrig, up to Sanquhar to the north, and right down to the Solway to the south. Come in August and the heather is particularly brilliant.

Brian is, by his own admission, proprietorial about Drumlanrig and his enthusiasm is infectious. He offers an occasional 'Hidden Heritage Tour' (⌂ www.drumlanrigcastle. co.uk for details), which ends on the rooftop that Dorothy Wordsworth apparently described along the lines of 'all half-cut onions and upturned cups and saucers' when she visited on 19 August 1803. From this lofty vantage point the description is apt, but the view is a rare one and, if we say so ourselves, can't help but make you feel a little proprietorial, too.

could happen in a hurry. Off he went the next morning back to his small castle at Sanquhar, never to sleep here again.

Drumlanrig today is one of the homes of Richard Scott, tenth Duke of Buccleuch and 12th of Queensberry, Europe's second-largest private landowner after the Queen and one of only five people in the UK to hold two separate dukedoms. Fourteen rooms are open to the public and visitors can only enter as part of a tour. As you would expect, the rooms are sumptuous and filled with priceless works of art and furniture, including paintings by Van Dyck, Holbein and Rembrandt, and a tapestry that was worked on by Mary, Queen of Scots. Family stories abound, including that of the irresponsible fourth duke who brought the estate to its knees through profligate spending, but who was succeeded by his son, the much shrewder fifth duke who married – of necessity, one might imagine, but apparently for love – one of the richest women in Europe.

There is an enormous amount to see and do here, not just in touring the house but also exploring some of the 45 acres of formal gardens (not to mention the 100,000 acres of the estate). The stables have been converted and house a visitor centre and independent shops, as well as a restaurant and a small café. If you want to explore further afield, bike hire is available from Rik's Bike Shed next to the shops (page 75). And if you fancy venturing right out into the wilds, then the best option is to take a Land Rover tour organised and run by the estate (see box, page 89).

4 DURISDEER

📍 NS894038

Tucked away in the lee of the Lowthers on a road that goes nowhere, there can be few spots more peaceful than Durisdeer. Aside from its delightful setting, what makes Durisdeer so remarkable (and yet comparatively unknown) is its church, shaded by mature sycamore trees and positioned beside a collection of pretty cottages and a war memorial.

"Tucked away in the lee of the Lowthers on a road that goes nowhere, there can be few spots more peaceful than Durisdeer."

A **church** is first mentioned here in the 13th century, but the present one was built in stages and dates from 1695 to 1720. One of the first noticeable things is that it is out of proportion with its petite village surroundings, telling something of its importance, for Durisdeer was the parish kirkton for nearby Drumlanrig. The other surprise is the arresting combination of Presbyterian and Baroque, the former in the solid X-plan church with its central pulpit, galleries and box pews with central communion tables, the latter in the exceptional baldacchino in the Queensberry burial vault to the rear of the church. Carved in 1695, it is known simply as the 'Durisdeer marbles' and has been accurately described as a 'riot of swagged fabric, garlands of flowers, urns, barley-sugar columns, cherubs, skulls and pediments, all in gleaming white marble'. It is a sight to behold, a monument not just to James, second Duke of Queensberry and his duchess, Mary, but also to late Baroque ostentation and extravagance.

Beneath the monument lies the burial vault of the Douglas family, among whom is the third duke, whose wife Catherine ('Kitty') was much courted in literary circles and was a friend of Alexander Pope. Something of an eccentric beauty, she was renowned for the grand parties at her London home and gained notoriety for being expelled from the court of George II for taking up the cause of John Gay, who had been refused a licence for *Polly*, the sequel to his immensely successful *Beggar's Opera*. She is buried here at Durisdeer having died in 1777 after a brief illness caused, according to Horace Walpole, by eating too many cherries!

There are some fine funerary monuments in the graveyard, including a sombre memorial to Daniel McMichael, Covenanter, who was shot dead in 1685.

You may wish to plan a visit to Durisdeer on a Sunday, to tie in with the offer of afternoon teas in the church (third Sunday in July to second Sunday in September; check ⊘ www.scotlandchurchestrust.org.uk for more information).

5 THORNHILL & AROUND 🌷

🏠 **Buccleuch & Queensberry Arms Hotel** (page 245), **Trigony House Hotel** (page 245)

Smart, tidy and compact, Thornhill is an exemplary estate town that's clearly comfortable in its own skin. As one guidebook writer of old commented, it's a place that displays a blend 'of dignity and humility – dignity of ducal spaciousness and the humility of well-trained, well-planned obedient streets in which doorways and windows are as regularly spaced as buttons on a waistcoat'. Its poise is, of course, thanks to its long relationship with nearby Drumlanrig and the earls of Queensberry, the third of which founded the town in 1664 as a Burgh of Barony. Their influence is explicit, notably in the **Mercat Cross** at the very centre of town, on top of which slender column is a lead figure of **Pegasus**, the emblem of the dukes of Queensberry, which was cast at Leadhills (page 87). There may have been a Roman settlement here, but the town in its present layout dates from 1714, when it was a staging post on the new road from Dumfries to Glasgow.

The main attraction of Thornhill is its sheer pleasant browsability. It's a place to come for lunch or afternoon tea and a wander around the shops, or somewhere to base yourself to discover the delights of Nithsdale. A walk along West Morton Street will bring you to the **war memorial** and also a memorial to **Joseph Thomson**, Africa explorer, who was born in nearby Penpont in 1858. Thomson is buried in **Morton Cemetery**, further up the street.

¶¶ FOOD & DRINK

Buccleuch and Queensberry Arms Hotel 112 Drumlanrig St, DG3 5LU ✆ 01848 323101 ⏃ www.bqahotel.com. Serves quality restaurant or bar meals. The restaurant has one rosette and the menu is filled with local dishes such as smoked Solway haddock, Auchenbrack estate pheasant, local wild rabbit and Buccleuch rib eye steak. Bar snacks are also available. Restaurant reservations are recommended for Friday and Saturday nights.

Drumlanrig Café & Restaurant 53–54 Drumlanrig St, DG3 5LJ ✆ 01848 330317. Offers everything from breakfasts to pizzas, as well as teas, coffees and sandwiches throughout the day at reasonable prices. Perfect for a relaxed bite to eat.

Thomas Tosh 19 East Morton St, DG3 5LZ ✆ 01848 331553 ⏃ www.thomastosh.com. Fun and friendly, housed in an impressive former parish hall building, with a good selection of teas, coffees, soups, sandwiches and cakes in one half of the building, and an exceedingly good gift shop in the other.

Trigony House Hotel Closeburn DG3 5EZ ✆ 01848 331211 ⏃ www.trignyhotel.co.uk. Just south of Thornhill this hotel is open to non-residents for lunch, afternoon teas (by reservation only) and dinner. It serves 'rustic' food which is regularly reviewed positively by the press.

6 Morton Castle

♥ NX891992; Historic Scotland

Northeast of Thornhill, ruined and isolated Morton Castle stands in one of the most tranquil and romantic locations of any castle in Scotland. It's believed to have been here since at least the 14th century and was a stronghold of the Douglases. However, as part of the negotiations to return the captured David II in 1357, one of the conditions stipulated by the English was that Morton, along with various other castles, be destroyed.

If the weather is warm, this is a great spot for a picnic, sitting on the hill overlooking the artificial loch that surrounds one half of the site. It's also a good place to bring kids, with heritage and nature trails to follow.

Keep an eye open for wildlife here: on one visit we saw a large colony of frogs living in the bottom of the ruined tower and, built into niches in the walls above, two large nests of birch twigs and wool. Whichever birds had opted to nest here had chosen a good site, with dinner trapped in the bottom of the tower below.

Crichope Linn
♀ NX910955

Almost due east of Thornhill, off a small back road between Gatelawbridge and Closeburnmill, a path takes off into the woods signposted for Beattock. About half a mile along this path in the bottom of the valley are the gorge and rapids of Crichope Linn, an impressive waterway that has carved its channel through the rocks over the centuries. Nature lovers have been coming here for a long time, there's some rather neat Victorian graffiti chiselled out of the rocks, and it's believed that Burns may have added his signature, too. In summer this is a lush and beautiful place, otherworldly, but take note and take care, the path is very narrow and in parts almost eroded completely, and it follows a course which at times runs high above the water. It is far from the easiest of walks, not suitable for children while in its present state and you may also wish to keep dogs on a lead. We advise caution: attempt it at your own risk.

Old Dalgarnock Churchyard
♀ NX876936

Nothing remains of the village that once stood at Dalgarnock except its churchyard, sitting in isolation at the end of a driveable dirt track south of Thornhill. Follow the sign for Kirkbog Farm and, when you reach it, continue through the farmyard, past the cottages on the right and down the track straight ahead. Here in a beautiful setting with tall beech trees framing the cemetery gate is one of the most peaceful and poignant churchyards we have visited. Aside from its location and the echoes of the village it once served, it is notable for a monument to the Nithsdale Martyrs and the grave of the persecuted Covenanter James Harkness. If the weather is clement, pack a picnic and relax awhile here, soaking up the silence.

PENPONT, MONIAIVE & THE WEST

There's an other-world feeling about the villages and landscape of the western part of Mid Nithsdale. It's almost Tolkienesque, as if it's part of the 'Shire', a sense reinforced by the place names themselves: Penpont, Moniaive (pronounced *Mon-e-ive*), the water and glen of the Scaur (pronounced Score), *Striding Arches*, Tynron (pronounced Tin-ron) ... This is an area where the mobile library still does the rounds and community spirit is strong.

7 Penpont & around

🏠 **Scaurbridge House** (page 246)

Crossing the Nith Bridge on the A702 as you head west from Thornhill, look out for the ancient cross in a field on the left, the only **Dark Age cross** in the region still in its original position, a late 9th- or early 10th-century Celtic shaft richly decorated on all sides. A little further on, take note of the beehive-like cairn on top of a small hill in a field to your right. This is one of several works by, and references to, the renowned sculptor **Andy Goldsworthy** (see box, opposite) that punctuate this part of Nithsdale.

Goldsworthy lives in **Penpont** a short way on. The village was built originally to house families displaced by new farming methods. Today it is strung out along the road, complete with tea room and village shop on the main street, with a couple of roads leading off and a few houses and a church set back. The **Penpont Heritage Centre** (Marrburn Rd, DG3 4BL ♀ NX847947 ✆ 01848 330700 (answerphone) 🖥 www. penpontheritage.co.uk ☉ seasonal on Sat afternoon or by arrangement) was created by the communities of Penpont, Keir and Tynron, and occupies a 19th-century cottage which was the birthplace in 1858 of the Africa explorer, **Joseph Thomson**, who subsequently lent his name to Thomson's gazelle. (If closed, ask in the tea room at the corner of the cross.)

"The Penpont Heritage Centre occupies a 19th-century cottage which was the birthplace in 1858 of the Africa explorer, Joseph Thomson."

Head south out of the village, towards Keir, and there's a lovely view of Penpont Church up to your left. In the other direction, for an escape into the impressive surrounding countryside, follow Scaur Water up Scaur Glen or, alternatively, take a circular route following Penpont Burn up

ANDY GOLDSWORTHY OBE: COLLABORATING WITH NATURE

Born in Cheshire in 1956, Andy Goldsworthy grew up on the northern side of Leeds before studying at Bradford College of Art and then graduating from Preston Polytechnic. He lived in Yorkshire, Lancashire and Cumbria before moving to Scotland, initially to Langholm (pages 60–5) in 1985 and then, a year later, to Penpont, where he still lives today.

Much of Goldsworthy's work is characterised by its ephemeral and transient state. He likes to work outside with nature, making use of anything he can lay his hands on – literally. 'I like to work with my hands' he says. 'I need the contact and shock of hand on materials.' Those materials consist of ice, leaves, rock, clay, petals, twigs, quarried stone, flowers, mud, thorns, pinecones … to name just a few. Once created, the work is left to weather and allowed to decay, during which time Goldsworthy photographs it in its various states. Thus the decaying work is as relevant as the freshly made one.

Some works, such as a 'rain shadow' in a slate quarry made by lying on his back, arms outstretched during a short burst of rain, are fleeting, disappearing as quickly as they were created. Others have greater longevity, such as *Striding Arches* (page 98) near Goldsworthy's home. 'It's the landscape around my home that is most important to me, and it is to that landscape that I keep returning, and which is the place that I can learn most about nature and my relationship with it' he said in an interview with the BBC. All of his works are innovative, intense and uniquely personal.

Goldsworthy has worked all around the world, from the North Pole to Australia, often on his own but sometimes with others, such as specialist dry stone wallers. 'My work is a very personal and private act but usually made in public places. Sometimes I feel embarrassed but I have to get on with it' he commented in an interview with *The Observer* newspaper in August 2014. In that same interview he reaffirmed his commitment to his adopted home: 'My studio is the fields and farms around where I live. Working with the land is to work alongside its people. The social nature of landscape has a profound effect upon my work… In Scotland I've met with not just tolerance but real engagement. That's what keeps me there.'

Marrburn Road and loop around to come down Scaur Glen. The roads are narrow but the views are breathtaking.

South of Penpont lies **Keir Mill** (♀ NX855935), where in 1839 at **Courthall Smithy** the blacksmith Kirkpatrick Macmillan invented the bicycle. The smithy is a private house now, but it sits by the road with a plaque on its gable wall. A replica of Macmillan's bike can be seen in the lower level of the Loreburne Shopping Centre in Dumfries, while the man himself is buried in Keir churchyard.

Head west from Penpont and you reach **Tynron**, a picture-perfect village in a hollow of the Shinnel Water, clustered around a now sadly deconsecrated church with gargoyles and chimneys. In the graveyard are the graves of a number of Covenanters. From Tynron, there's a path to the mighty **Tynron Doon** (♀ NX819939), 1½ miles away. Conspicuously sited on the summit of a steep-sided spur of Auchengibbert Hill, it was first occupied during the Iron Age and it's easy to see why it was chosen as a strong defensive hilltop position.

"The landscape around here is exquisite and worth exploring to revel in the hills, the views and the peace. Strike off down a random road of your choice and see where it takes you."

The landscape around here is exquisite and worth exploring just for the sake of it, to revel in the hills, the views and the peace. Strike off down a random road of your choice and see where it takes you. Continue over to Moniaive and you'll be met with a panorama across the hills and views down to the village itself; turn around and come back the way you came for a vista northeast towards Durisdeer (pages 90–1), Wanlockhead (pages 83–7) and the Lowthers.

8 Moniaive & around

🏠 **Auchencheyne B&B** (page 246), **Three Glens House** (page 246)

Much has been written about Moniaive over the years, and not without reason. This charming village has a strong community ethos with its own choir, an outstanding (but pricey) eco-lodge accommodation option (page 246), its own chocolatier, and an informative locally run website (⊘ www.moniaive.org). It is rivalled in its ebullient spirit only by neighbouring Penpont, and just as Penpont can lay claim to celebrity residents past and present, so too can Moniaive. Historically, Anna Laurie, subject of one of the most famous of Scottish songs 'Annie Laurie' (also known as 'Maxwelton Braes'), lived in nearby Craigdarroch House (see box, opposite), while today the area is the Scottish home of Alex Kapranos of the band Franz Ferdinand. He bought the house of **James Paterson**, one of the group of artists known as the Glasgow Boys, who spent over 20 years in the area painting the hills of Nithsdale and scenes along the Solway Firth.

Take a stroll down the High Street to soak up some of the village atmosphere and pass **The George Hotel**, one of the oldest inns in

TOWNS & VILLAGES

Community spirit is strong throughout the region and is often reflected in the appearance of well-kept towns and villages. Nowhere is very big, which means that wherever you go it doesn't take long before you find your way around and get talking to the locals.

1 Castle Douglas, the region's Food Town, viewed across Carlingwark Loch. 2 Arts and Crafts style cottages line the road at Parton. 3 The one-time spa town of Moffat has several traditional coaching inns. 4 Wigtown, Scotland's National Book Town, sits above Wig Bay.

1

HISTORY & HERITAGE

From hero kings to literary legends, a rich historical and cultural seam runs across Dumfries and Galloway, with reminders of times past coming in all forms.

2

3

1 The Famous Blacksmith's Shop at Gretna Green. 2 The Wigtown Martyrs monument at Wigtown. 3 The interior of the fascinating Stewartry Museum. 4 Wanlockhead Leadmines. 5 Moat Brae, 'home' of *Peter Pan*. 6 The 'Quorum' sculpture in Galloway Forest Park. 7 Robert Burns, a notable figure in the region's history, has pride of place at the top of Dumfries High Street.

FESTIVALS & EVENTS

Communities across the region celebrate both the past and present in a wide range of events, from the profound to the slightly surreal. Music, art and wildlife all feature strongly, but perhaps the most universally anticipated events are the annual Common Ridings, especially in the east of the region.

1 Langholm's Common Ridings is the oldest in Dumfries and Galloway. 2 A straw effigy marks the site of the annual Wicker Man Festival. 3 Driving through rings of fire at Chariots of Fire in Boreland.

CRAIGDARROCH

Country living at its most gracious is epitomised by the elegant and distinctively pink Craigdarroch, one of Mid Nithsdale's most striking private properties which is open to the public as part of the Historic Houses Association scheme each July (non-members charged). The Sykes family has owned the 2,500-acre estate since 1962, but its origins go back to a strong tower of the 1300s on land which it is believed may have been gifted by Robert the Bruce. Parts of the original tower can still be seen, notably in the massive, thick walls that separate the original structure from the later additions of celebrated Scottish architect William Adam in 1729, and from the Victorian extensions of the mid-1800s.

A visit to Craigdarroch is one of those rare but delightful glimpses into the annals of dynastic and domestic life behind doors which are normally closed to all but a few. The house was owned by one family, the Fergussons, for over 600 years until being sold in the 1920s. A succession of different owners then followed before it became the home of the Sykes. 'It's a very liveable house' says Danish-born Carin Sykes, and visitors do, indeed, get a clear sense of how very liveable it is during a visit. Despite its apparent size from the outside, there are comparatively few rooms, though each of the rooms that visitors see is, of course, a striking expression of architectural refinement and well informed personal taste. With William Adam's involvement and a collection of furniture and paintings from across the centuries, one wouldn't expect it to be anything other.

Carin is usually on hand to meet visitors and to explain the Craigdarroch family histories, which make for fascinating stories. Old photographs, copies of bills, and tales of love affairs lost and marriages gained are all part of the narrative, none more so than that of Anna Laurie, who in 1710 married Alexander Fergusson and subsequently spent her entire married life as mistress of Craigdarroch.

There are too many stories to tell here, but if you get the chance to visit, then ask about the 'Craigdarroch curse' and its origins in the famous Battle of Killicrankie, and also the 17th-century whistle won from one of Anne of Denmark's retinue in a drinking game. Outside, look out for the quirky minister's changing room near the chapel, the wedding stones embedded in the walls of the house, and also the grand trees, notably a particularly fine copper beech and, along the drive, an impressive sequoia.

Scotland where Covenanters gathered in the Killing Times (pages 24–5). Pop into **The Moniaive Chocolatiers** (The Old Post Office, DG3 4HN ✆ 01848 200000 🖱 www.tartanchocolate.co.uk) for a tartan chocolate or two, and then continue along to the **village cross**, erected in 1638. The Tower House (now private) next to the cross was built in 1865 for the local school master. Further along, **Cottage Row** is a beautifully preserved row of traditional cottages, beyond which is Kilneiss House, built as a wedding present for James Patterson. At the end of the street, on a hillside overlooking the village, is a monument to **James Renwick**, who was born in Moniaive and became famous for the second Sanquhar Declaration in 1685 (page 80).

Moniaive sits at the confluence of Dalwhat Water, Cairn Water, Craigdarroch Water and Castlefairn Water. A short circular walk of 1¼ miles along the embankments takes in all four. Head out from Chapel Street, just past the school, and follow a loop to arrive back a little further along Chapel Street.

Anna Laurie's home, **Craigdarroch** (♀ NS741909; see box, page 97) is located beyond Moniaive in a gorgeous setting surrounded by hills a couple of miles along the B729. Anna herself lived between 1682 and 1764, and came originally from nearby **Maxwelton House** (also known as Glencairn Castle) which lies a short distance southeast of Moniaive and Kirkland. It is not open to the public but there is a good view of it from the B729. Quaint **Maxwelton Chapel** (♀ NX825895), built in 1869, lies east of the house in its own grounds, serene and inviting on a rise above a pond with views to the hills.

Seven miles northwest of Moniaive (but feeling a lot further), up a small road that follows the course of Dalwhat Water, *Striding Arches* (♀ NX700973 ⊘ www.stridingarches.com) is no easy jaunt but is worth the effort to experience this remote art installation by renowned landscape artist Andy Goldsworthy (page 95). Wend your way up from the village, continuing on where the road turns into a gravel forestry track. Just as your nerve starts to falter and you convince yourself that you must have taken a wrong turn, you arrive at a small parking area and interpretation boards.

"The surrounding area is grassland of wildflowers, alive at our last visit with butterflies and moths, including ringlet and Scotch argus."

The work, a series of red sandstone self-supporting arches, each around 12-feet-high with a span of 21 feet, stands proud in the landscape, left to the elements to weather and frame the surrounding countryside. Easy walking from the parking area is Byre Arch, an old barn with an arch passing through the wall from inside to out to end on the hillside. The surrounding area is grassland of wildflowers, alive at our last visit with butterflies and moths, including ringlet and Scotch argus. Stone carvings chart the evolution in location names through the ages. If you're feeling energetic, venture further up in to the hills to see the arches at Colt Hill, Benbrach, and Bail Hill.

Southeast of Moniaive the A702 strikes out through the hills and over the moors to St Johns Town of Dalry in the Glenkens area (see *Chapter 4*).

¶¶ FOOD & DRINK

Craigdarroch Arms High St, DG3 4HN ✆ 01848 200205 🖫 www.craigdarrocharmshotel. co.uk. Serves reasonably priced pub fare and there's accommodation on site. Owner Tim O'Sullivan took over a few years ago and offers a warm welcome to guests who arrive from all over the world. 'We had someone who came for two weeks from Australia' says Tim, 'but six weeks later he was still here!'

LOWER NITHSDALE

Rolling hills, wooded valleys and country lanes that meander through leafy dells characterise Lower Nithsdale. For an area which abuts the region's main town, Dumfries, it can come as something of a surprise to discover such bucolic charms in so close a proximity to an urban centre. The main A76 follows the course of the Nith here as it does for much of Nithsdale, and the heavy lorries and traffic can be off-putting, but stick to the minor roads to either side, and you could be in a different world. Garden enthusiasts might like to note that almost all of the Dumfriesshire gardens that are part of the Scotland's Gardens collection are in Lower Nithsdale; check their website for details of opening days 🖫 www.scotlandsgardens.org.

Away from the A76 this is good cycling country: many of the smaller roads run along the bottom of the valleys and avoid particularly steep gradients, and with so few cars on the road it is a pleasure to rely on pedal power. Two fine options are the previously mentioned Kirkpatrick Macmillan Trail from Dumfries to Penpont via Dunscore (page 75); and Dumfries out to Duncow windmill, partly using the Caledonian Cycleway.

Broadly speaking, Lower Nithsdale in the context of this guide is the area from Amisfield to the northeast of Dumfries, up to Auldgirth to the north and then out to the Glenkiln Reservoir and Sculpture Park to the west. Dumfries and the Nith estuary (ie: points south of the A75), both of which are also classed as Nithsdale, are covered in the next chapter.

All of the places mentioned in this section lie to the north and west of Dumfries, with the exception of the village of **Torthorwald** (♀ NY034784), which is immediately to the east. This small village, not much more than a hamlet, is split by the busy A709, the main cut-through from Dumfries to Lockerbie and the motorway north. On the southern side of the road stands the ruined 14th- to 15th-century **Torthorwald Castle**, but the main point of interest is actually on the northern side

"Cruck Cottage, a rare surviving example of a building type that was common in Dumfriesshire from medieval times."

of the road, down the lane which leads off the main road. Here, with gable end to the lane, stands **Cruck Cottage** (♂ www.cruckcottage. co.uk), a rare surviving example of a building type that was common in Dumfriesshire and southern Scotland from medieval times through to the early 19th century. The construction consists of oak 'crucks' or trunks as the main support in a traditional A-frame, with a roof of tie-beams and branch rafters, laid with heather turf and thatched with rye straw. The cottage had been almost derelict when it was gifted by the owner to Solway Heritage in 1990 after which a major restoration was undertaken. The detailed work in maintaining it is impressive and a real testament to the craftsmen involved and the continued support of the Cruck Cottage Heritage Association. The cottage is kept locked but the key can be obtained from one of the villagers.

AULDGIRTH TO DUMFRIES, EAST OF THE NITH

The village of **Auldgirth** on the banks of the Nith marks the upper limit of Lower Nithsdale, where the quiet road from Kirkton meets the rather busier A76 from Dumfries. Both the Nith and the A76 bisect the village, separating the residential area and its inn (see opposite) from the village store, post office and café across the road. If you're heading this way, pop into the shop to meet the energetic Kava, who not only runs it (and the adjoining café) but is also a keen silversmith. His work is based on a fusion of Pakistani and Scottish designs and a small selection is on display in the café.

Dalswinton

Head south of Auldgirth on the east side of the Nith and a couple of miles brings you to the unpretentious estate village of Dalswinton, no more than a row of painted cottages on either side of the road. The surrounding Dalswinton Estate was once home to the Comyns, one of the most powerful families in the country in medieval times, one of whom, John III, Red Comyn, was famously slain by Robert the Bruce in Dumfries in 1306.

Dalswinton House (private) was commissioned in the late 18th century by Patrick Miller, who created an artificial loch in the grounds on which he launched the world's first steamboat in 1788. He was also the landlord and friend of Robert Burns, who took on the farm at Ellisland (pages 102–4).

A little further on from the village stands one of the estate's most intriguing buildings. With its bellcote, spire and red corrugated iron walls and roof, **Dalswinton Barony Church** (♀ NX942850) looks far more New England than Scotland and comes as something of a surprise.

Built in 1881, it's a good example of a 'tin church', of which many were made for use both at home and in the colonies overseas. This was perhaps the original and most ambitious flat-pack assembly ever seen, well before Ikea got involved, for churches were manufactured in kit form and then shipped to the point of order. Inside, the walls are clad in timber pine and the floor

"Dalswinton House was commissioned by Patrick Miller, who created an artificial loch in the grounds on which he launched the world's first steamboat in 1788."

and pews are also of pine. Many such churches have either disappeared altogether or are no longer in use, but services are still held here on the second and fourth Sundays of the month and the Landale family, the owners of Dalswinton, continues to maintain the building. If you would like to look inside, either come along to a service or contact the minister, David Almond (✆ 01387 710572) or the Dalswinton estate office (✆ 01387 740279).

⊺⊺ FOOD & DRINK

Auldgirth Inn Auldgirth DG2 0XG ✆ 01387 740250 ⊘ www.auldgirthinn.co.uk. With its arched windows and crosses on the chimney stack you might think the inn looks more like a monastic retreat than a modern hostelry. You wouldn't be far wrong, for it dates back to the times when monks travelled from the abbey at Melrose in the Scottish Borders to Whithorn (pages 200–4) in the Machars on pilgrimage to the shrine of St Ninian. Today it offers tasty bar meals sourced from local produce, with seasonal specialities throughout the year.

AULDGIRTH TO DUMFRIES, WEST OF THE NITH

Approaching Dumfries from Auldgirth, the connections with Burns grow ever stronger, first at **Ellisland Farm** (see below), a couple of miles south of Auldgirth signposted off the A76, where he lived from 1788 to 1791, and then in Dumfries itself, to where he moved from Ellisland and where he died (see box, page 111). A mile or so south of Ellisland, on a small road off to the left, is **Portrack House** (Holywood DG2 0RW ♀ NX939829) 👆, home of the American architect and landscape designer **Charles Jencks**. The house isn't open to the public, but the garden, known as 'The Garden of Cosmic Speculation', is, on one day a year, as part of Scotland's Gardens.

A couple of miles further on from Portrack, where the minor road rejoins the main A76, is **Holywood**, now virtually a suburb of Dumfries. To the east of the A76 is the late 18th-century church, now private but with access allowed to the graveyard. The bell in the tower is said to be the oldest in Scotland, though alas it is no longer rung. To the west of the A76, in a nondescript field, stand the **Twelve Apostles**, at around 290 feet in diameter notable as the largest stone circle in Scotland, dating from the 3rd or 2nd millennium BC. Access to the field can be gained via a stile over the fence on a minor road off the B729.

9 Ellisland Farm

Holywood Rd, Auldgirth DG2 0RP ♀ NX929838 ✆ 01387 740426 🖰 www.ellislandfarm.co.uk

Burns was offered a choice of three farms by Patrick Miller of Dalswinton (pages 100–1); this was the worst of the three but it was the one he opted for, describing it as 'the poet's choice'. It has often been said that he made a poor farmer but that there was something about the surroundings of Ellisland which brought him poetic inspiration, and for any visitors today with an ounce of romance in their souls, it's easy to see why. Sitting on the banks of the Nith, the charm of the setting could easily outweigh any misgivings about the stony, infertile ground and its suitability as a farm.

"There was something about the surroundings of Ellisland which brought Burns poetic inspiration."

Burns moved to Ellisland at the age of 29. By then his poetry had earned him both fame and money, but he was far from wealthy having already given half of his earnings to his brother to stave off poverty. Farming Ellisland proved useless and it was while living

LITERARY SHENANIGANS
AT ELLISLAND & FRIARS CARSE

While living at Ellisland, Burns was a regular visitor to nearby Friars Carse (now a hotel), which belonged to Robert Riddell of Glenriddell. During one such visit, Burns was introduced to Captain Francis Grose, who at the time was on his second tour of the country while compiling his *Antiquities of Scotland* (a book which has proven invaluable in researching this one). Burns suggested to Grose that he should include in his *Antiquities* the ruinous kirk at Alloway, the village in Ayrshire in which he was born. Grose agreed on condition that Burns supply an account of the witchcraft stones associated with the ruin. This Burns duly did, sending to Grose a prose tale which he then followed up with a rhyming version, *Tam o' Shanter*, which Grose printed. It is said that Burns wrote it in one day while pacing back and forth along the banks of the Nith at Ellisland. Visitors today can follow in his footsteps and take a stroll along the 'Tam o' Shanter Path'.

here that Burns became an exciseman, taking up a position in 1789 in which he was responsible for checking taxes in the ten parishes of Upper Nithsdale. The work was exhausting, often requiring long rides of 30 to 40 miles per day, so in 1790 he took up a new excise role based in Dumfries, to where he moved shortly after.

Whitewashed cottages around a central courtyard are evocative of a bygone era at Ellisland. Only one room in the house in which Burns lived is open to the public, but in the adjacent Old Granary there's a very good audiovisual presentation and interesting displays, including one on excise which contains Burns' own arithmetic book. There's also a collection of fun limited editions of the Robert Bryden 1896 etchings illustrating some of Burns's best-known work, including *The De'ils Awa' Wi' the Exciseman*, *Tam o'Shanter* and *The Haggis*. Other buildings from the time contain a selection of displays, including dioramas and a collection of agriculture and farming instruments.

Burns was in the way of writing poems for friends and while at Ellisland also presented a volume to Robert Riddell, as well as starting a second one to be presented once completed. However, in December 1793 Burns's friendship with the Riddells ended suddenly as the result of a drunken incident at Friars Carse. On Burns's request, the volume of poems was returned. Following Burns's death, both volumes, which have become known as the 'Riddell Manuscripts', were sent to his biographer and, at a later date, were sold to John Gribbell of Philadelphia, an American industrialist and philanthropist. Gribbell then endeared himself to the Scottish people by gifting them the manuscripts, which now form the most significant items in the Burns collection of the National Library of Scotland, to whom they were presented as part of the library's early collection in 1926.

SOUTHWEST FROM AULDGIRTH

Å Barnsoul Caravan Park (page 246), **Glenmidge Camping and Self-catering** (page 246)

Away from the A76, the hills and valleys of Lower Nithsdale come into their own. The pretty village of **Dunscore** sits on a hill with fine views to the north from the parish church of 1823. The area has many associations with the Covenanters and is scattered with communion stones and hillside graves from that time. In the church itself is a memorial to **Jane Haining,** who was born in Dunscore and was the only Scots woman to die in Auschwitz.

From Dunscore head west to explore the countryside, myriad hills and burns making this a delightful area simply to meander around and soak up the scenery. To the west, you could follow the **Glenesslin Burn** on a single-track road up to **Loch Urr** and **Mid Nithsdale**. To the northeast, travel through Dalgonar and up to the quirkily named **Glenmidge**, a lovely spot in a hollow in the hills which we are assured doesn't live up to its name (at least, no more

"Glenmidge, a lovely spot in a hollow in the hills which doesn't live up to its name."

so than any other area) and which offers good camping (page 246).

Alternatively head south, where you will find **Newtonairds Hostas & Garden** (DG2 0JL ♀ NX884801 ✆ 01387 820203 ✍ www.newtonairds-hostasandgarden. co.uk ☉ seasonally for limited hours), where since moving up from Surrey in 2004 James and Carol Coutts have been developing (and re-developing due to repeated winter flooding) the national collection of hostas in the cottagey garden around their 19th-century corner lodge. It's been a labour of love and a process of personal therapy for them both, but the result is impressive.

From Newtonairds continue to **Irongray** (see opposite) on the southern side of Cluden Water, a pretty area with a memorable church and with such a rural feel that it is difficult to believe you're only three miles from Dumfries. For a spot of leafy relief in a watery glade, head west from Irongray to reach the locally known beauty spot of **Routin' Brig** (♀ NX886797), where the high arched bridge surrounded by native woodland crosses the Cairn Water as it tumbles over rocks and drops down the gorge to a pool at the bottom. When the water is low it's a great spot for a paddle. Around four miles further on from here to the southwest lies **Glenkiln Reservoir and Sculpture Park**, an open-air museum established in 1951. Up until recently this was the site of a number of world-class sculptures dotted among the hills, including works by Henry Moore, Jacob Epstein and Auguste Rodin. Alas, in 2013 one of the Moore's, worth an estimated £3 million, was stolen and, at the time of writing still hadn't been recovered (and most probably never will be). As a result all of the sculptures have been removed except Moore's *Glenkiln Cross*. You may also spot his *Reclining Figure*, but on closer inspection will discover that, sadly, it's a replica made of fibreglass. Its setting, however, remains memorable.

10 Irongray Church

Irongray's splendid sandstone and cream-painted church occupies a beautiful setting surrounded by hills. The church was built in 1803 and in the graveyard is the tomb chest of Helen Walker, on whom Sir Walter Scott based Jeanie Deans in *The Heart of Midlothian* (1818). Having refused to lie to save her sister from a charge of infanticide, she walked to London to petition the Duke of Argyll for a reprieve. The inscription on the tomb is written by Scott. At the entrance to the church grounds note the protruding stones over the wall, in-built steps worn smooth in the shape of a shoe from centuries of use.

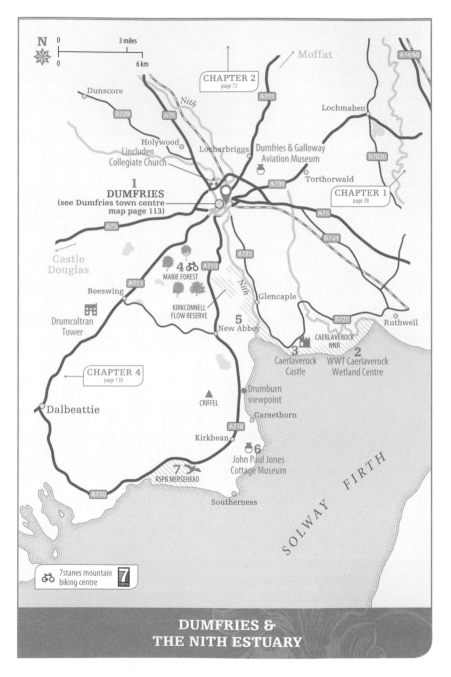

N

0   3 miles
0   6 km

Dunscore

B729

A76

Nith

Moffat

A74(M)

CHAPTER 2
page 72

A701

Lochmaben

Holywood
Lincluden
Collegiate Church

Locharbriggs

Dumfries & Galloway
Aviation Museum

B7020

A709

Torthorwald

1
DUMFRIES
(see Dumfries town centre
map page 113)

CHAPTER 1
page 28

A75

A75

B724

Castle
Douglas

A711

B725

A710

4 🚲
MABIE FOREST

Nith

Glencaple

B725

Ruthwell

Beeswing

KIRKCONNELL
FLOW RESERVE

5
New Abbey

CAERLAVEROCK
NNR

Drumcoltran
Tower

3
Caerlaverock
Castle

2
WWT Caerlaverock
Wetland Centre

CHAPTER 4
page 130

CRIFFEL

Drumburn
viewpoint

Carsethorn

Dalbeattie

A710

Kirkbean

6
John Paul Jones
Cottage Museum

SOLWAY

FIRTH

A718

7 ✈
RSPB MERSEHEAD

Southerness

🚲 7stanes mountain
biking centre

7
7stanes

DUMFRIES &
THE NITH ESTUARY

3
DUMFRIES & THE NITH ESTUARY

At the southern end of the Nith, just before river broadens to estuary, lies Dumfries, southwest Scotland's main town. It's a historic place with a wealth of interest, some fine buildings, riverside parks, and several significant Burns attractions. It's also home to a new major literary attraction still in development related to J M Barrie and *Peter Pan*. The ambitious **Moat Brae** project (pages 104–5) promises to help cement Dumfries's place on the tourist map as it comes to fruition over the coming years. Each year Dumfries also hosts one of Scotland's premier winter music events, the **Big Burns Supper**, to coincide with the bard's birthday on 25 January.

South of Dumfries the river divides the landscape in two, with the flatter wetlands of an internationally important bird reserve on the eastern side and the mighty **Criffel** dominating the west. The eastern strip is enchanting, a place of ever-changing light and colours, mudflats and saltmarshes, where ships from far-flung places once docked and to where enormous colonies of birds – **barnacle geese**, in particular – now return each year. To the west lies a historic abbey, one of the most romantic in Scotland's history, a 7stanes biking forest (pages 124–6) also known for its butterflies, and towards the southernmost reach a quaint waterside village with a fine pub.

GETTING AROUND

The main trunk road, the A75, passes around the north of the town linking the Carlisle to Glasgow A74M motorway over in the east to the towns of Castle Douglas, Newton Stewart and Stranraer in western Dumfries and Galloway. As the A75 passes Dumfries numerous other main roads radiate off northwards to places such as Lockerbie and Moffat; and further afield to Kilmarnock. The town and surrounding roads generally flow freely, although, as with any main town, it is best to avoid rush hour. The Dumfries traffic on the A75 is also noticeably heavier, particularly with haulage lorries, about an hour or so after a ferry has come into Cairnryan.

Dumfries itself is a compact town and not too difficult to navigate. Parking in the town, at the council-owned sites, is free, but you need to display a disc (free from local shops and council offices) and to observe the time limits. Once in the centre all the town's main sites and attractions are within easy walking distance of each other.

PUBLIC TRANSPORT

Scotrail runs a frequent **train service** throughout the day Monday to Saturday and a less frequent one on a Sunday, along its Newcastle, Carlisle to Glasgow route, which stops at Dumfries.

Many of the local and regional **bus services** use Dumfries as their main start/end point. The key routes for sites and attractions along the Nith Estuary are the 6a for Caerlaverock operated by Stagecoach Western/DGC Buses, and the 372 to New Abbey by Houstons Coaches.

Local public transport information is provided by South West of Scotland Transport Partnership ($\mathcal{O}$ www.swestrans.org.uk), alternatively the traveline ($\mathscr{D}$ 0871 200 2233 $\mathcal{O}$ www.traveline.org.uk).

CYCLING

Dumfries has a traffic-free cycle network that connects many of the main places. **Cycle hire** HUBs ($\mathcal{O}$ www.gosmartdumfries.co.uk) have been installed at key locations across the town, and bikes can be hired from one HUB and returned to any other HUB.

The country lanes either side of Dumfries and along the west and east flanks of the Nith estuary offer surprisingly different scenery. The west route, starting at Dock Park or Whitesands, leaves Dumfries using the **National Cycle Route 7** (NCR7; $\mathcal{O}$ www.sustrans.org.uk) taking in lochs at Lochfoot and Beeswing, Mabie Forest, the attractions of

---

i TOURIST INFORMATION

VisitScotland Information Centre Dumfries 64 Whitesands, Dumfries DG1 2RS $\mathscr{D}$ 01387 253862 $\mathcal{O}$ www.visitdumfriesandgalloway.co.uk $\odot$ all year

New Abbey and the National Nature Reserve at Kirkconnell Flow. The eastern route, also leaving Dumfries on the NCR7, offers fine estuary views across to the granite dome of Criffel, historical and wildlife attractions at Caerlaverock, and the drama of the tidal bore at Glencaple. For thrill seekers, the **7stanes** mountain biking at Mabie Forest (⊘ www.7stanesmountainbiking.com/mabie) has trails for all abilities, from graded routes for novices to 'Turn to the Dark Side'.

See Dumfries and Galloway Council's free *Cycling in and around Nithsdale* booklet for a good selection of cycling routes.

WALKING

Walking around Dumfries and the Nith Estuary offers choices of such variety that you can be high up in the hills in the morning, on a riverside or forest walk at lunchtime, before exploring the old streets of Dumfries in the afternoon. Criffel, rising above New Abbey and the Nith Estuary, dominates the skyline, and offers a challenging walk. There are many routes that incorporate Criffel and plenty of information locally, so we have opted to include different routes within this chapter.

Dumfries itself offers a variety of walking options, including trails themed to Burns and the local arts scene, and the town can make an alternative option to the hills if the weather is dreich, but is equally good for a wander on a warm summer's day.

Dumfries and Galloway Council has produced a free booklet, *Walking in and around Dumfries & New Abbey*, which offers a good selection town and country of walking options.

1 DUMFRIES

🏠 **Barr Farmhouse** (page 246), **Glenaldor House** (page 246)

Southern Scotland's largest town straddles the Nith where it twists and turns in its final approach to the Solway a few miles further south. We find Dumfries an eminently likeable place offering a mix of history and every-day functionality, and its rakish charm is supported by deep-rooted local pride. Compact and easy to walk around, it has a population of just under 44,000 (at the last census) and, while it may not be a major tourist centre in the way of Edinburgh or Glasgow, equally it is not without its sights and attractions and comfortably offers enough to keep visitors occupied for a few days, especially anyone with an interest in Burns. It is also the

LADY DEVORGILLA

Few women are as well remembered in Dumfries and Galloway as Devorgilla, Lady of Galloway. Born in 1210, at the age of 13 she was married to John, Baron de Balliol of Barnard Castle in Durham, who in 1263 founded Balliol College in Oxford. Devorgilla was educated, intelligent and took an active role in public life, founding Greyfriars Convent in Dumfries as well as endowing Balliol College after her husband's death with enough money to ensure its future. With John Balliol she became one of the largest landowners in Europe, and on his death she founded and built the abbey at New Abbey (page 127), south of Dumfries, in his memory. Descended on her mother's side from the kings of Scotland, her son John was briefly king, albeit known as 'toom tabbard' or 'puppet king' to Edward I. Her grandson, John's son Edward Balliol, was also king, while another grandson was John III Comyn, 'Red Comyn', who was murdered by Robert the Bruce in 1306.

location of the oldest working theatre in Scotland and the 'home' of *Peter Pan*, for it was here that J M Barrie dreamed up Neverland.

Dumfries has long been known as '**Queen of the South**', a name which is attributed to one David Dunbar, a local poet who, while standing in the general election of 1857, in one of his addresses described the town as such. It stuck and is today not only synonymous with the town, but also with the local football club. The club's unofficial nickname is the 'Doonhamers', which in turn is generally synonymous with folk from Dumfries. Its origins lie in the 19th century, when many people worked away from home, especially the railway workers who were based in Glasgow and talked about going 'doon hame' ('down home'). One particularly notable doonhamer of recent years is Adam Wiles, better known as DJ Calvin Harris.

History has been made in Dumfries, for it was here that Robert the Bruce famously slew his rival, the Red Comyn, in Greyfriars Kirk in 1306, thus blazing the trail to Scottish independence at Bannockburn eight years later. The town's motto, 'A Loreburn' from its coat of arms, dates from those early years when Dumfries was a frequent place of conflict due to its proximity to the Scotland–England border and was regularly subjected to attack. 'A Lore Burn' would ring out the shout, 'to the muddy stream', summoning arms to the town's weakest point on its eastern edge. Today you'll come across the modern spelling, Loreburn, frequently: it's the name of the shopping centre, primary school, housing association … you can't miss it.

The river has been central – both literally and metaphorically – to Dumfries's development and is today still crossed by the massively buttressed Auld Brig, commonly referred to as the **Devorgilla Bridge** after Lady Devorgilla's (see box, opposite) original structure of the 13th century. This was the main link to the kingdom of Galloway, whose lands started immediately west of the Nith. Sitting on the frontier of Scotland's wild southwest, Dumfries was a place where pilgrims stopped on their way to Whithorn (pages 200–4). Partly for them did the good Devorgilla build Greyfriars Monastery on the Dumfries side, where now stands Greyfriars Kirk.

From the late 17th century right through to the mid 20th century, Dumfries was a thriving port, mostly with local coastal trade in crops and livestock. In the 18th century the town established links with the British Colonies in North America and shipping increased, and by 1740 so much tobacco was being imported from Virginia that Dumfries became known as the 'Scottish Liverpool'. John Paul Jones, the 'Father of the American Navy', was born just south of Dumfries (pages 128–9) at the wide mouth of the Nith and it was from here that he sailed to America.

In conjunction with the developing port, Dumfries became one of the most important market towns in southwest Scotland and was on the droving route from the far west (page 226), with great herds of cattle

BURNS IN DUMFRIES

After living at Ellisland (pages 102–4), Robert Burns moved into Dumfries while still working as an exciseman and here he spent the final years of his short life. The town is replete with references to the poet and there is a **Burns Trail** which links all of the relevant points of interest (a leaflet is available from the visitor information centre), many of which are also covered by the walk overleaf. Burns first lived in a flat in the 'wee vennel' as it was known, or Bank Street, before moving to his house in Mill Street (now Burns Street). A

Burns statue stands prominently at the top of the High Street and in addition to the Burns Trail there is a **Burns Walk** along the Nith, from Dumfries to Dalscone, passing the confluence with Cluden Water at Lincluden (page 117). Along the High Street, the **Hole in the Wa'** was one of Burns's regular drinking haunts, though perhaps his favourite was the **Globe Inn Close**, also on the High Street. And near to both is the **Midsteeple**, where in July 1796 Burns's body lay in state before the funeral procession to St Michael's Kirk (page 116).

being brought by boat from Ireland and then across Galloway on foot, before continuing, still on foot, to the major cattle markets in the south. At **Midsteeple** on the High Street a sign gives the droving distances; it's notable that Glasgow and Edinburgh are closer than Portpatrick on the west coast, and it's particularly sobering to see just how far cattle had to be walked to market: Huntingdon 272 miles and London 330 miles.

Dumfries became a busy mill town in the 18th and 19th centuries. The suspension bridge across the Nith was built in 1875 to help workers – mostly girls – reach the tweed mills on the far side of the river. It is said that 1,200 girls used to cross this bridge each day on their way to work, often stopping to stamp their feet all at the same time to hear the noise and feel the bridge sway.

The arrival of the railway in the 19th century marked the start of the decline of the port, but by the early 20th century the town reinvented itself as a centre for car manufacturing with the opening of the Arrol Johnston factory in July 1913. Known as 'The Rubber Works', the factory was part of a company that became the largest car manufacturer in Scotland.

In more recent years Dumfries has become home to a burgeoning and pioneering range of academic institutions at the Crichton University campus, including the Crichton Carbon Centre and the Solway Centre for Environment and Culture, the latter part of Glasgow University's Dumfries campus. Also found on the Crichton Campus is a treat for foodies, Marco Pierre White's restaurant, Wheelers (page 119).

A TOUR OF THE TOWN ON FOOT

Walking the town is by far the best way to get to know it, and given its comparatively small size, it's an easy route that takes in the main sights.

1 Midsteeple on the pedestrianised High Street or **2 Greyfriars Kirk** (officially known as St Bride's Anglican Church) on Church Crescent make for good starting points. The present church dates only from 1868 but stands close to where Devorgilla's Greyfriars Convent stood, before the high altar of which Robert the Bruce slew the Red Comyn in 1306. This was also the site of Maxwell's Castle, more of a fortified town house than a castle and one of the many homes of the Maxwell family. It was bought by the townsfolk who pulled it down in 1720, following which the New Church was built in 1727. That, too, was eventually demolished and replaced by the present church.

Opposite the entrance to Greyfriars stands a **3 statue of Robert Burns,** executed in Carrara marble from a model by Scottish sculptor Amelia Paton Hill, who is believed to have been the first woman sculptor to have a sculpture exhibited in a public space. The statue is a strong work showing Burns seated with a dog at his feet and was unveiled in 1882 by Archibald Primrose who went on to become one of the country's least remembered prime ministers (1894–95).

From Greyfriars, head down **4 Friars Vennel** to **5 Whitesands** on the east bank of the river. This was left as orchards and grazing until the 18th century, when the first line of buildings was erected. The river is broad here and runs fast over the weir when the water's high. In autumn, if the conditions are right, you can see salmon leaping. Where the buses stop, look out for the **'DIY Statue' plinth**: hop up and stand on the indented feet plates, it's your opportunity to be a Dumfries 'Local Hero'!

The **6 Devorgilla 'Old' Bridge** is an impressive span and offers pleasant views up and down the river from its midpoint. On a calm sunny day the bridge reflects in the Nith below just before it cascades down the weir. Sandmartins skim the water, feeding on the wing, the willows on the west bank trail lazily, ducks squabble and seagulls swoop. At the far side is the **7 Old Bridge House** (Mill Rd, DG7 2BE ☉ seasonal) which claims to be the oldest house in Dumfries, with parts of it dating from 1620 when they rebuilt the bridge with houses at either end. Although small, it's worth a visit for its well-presented information boards about the history of Dumfries, of the bridges and of the house itself.

Leaving the museum, turn left and walk along the river to the **8 Robert Burns Centre** (Mill Rd, DG2 7BE ℰ 01387 264808 ◈ www. rbcft.co.uk), housed in an old mill building. In addition to telling the story of the connections between Robert Burns and Dumfries, the centre also houses an intricate scale model of Dumfries in the 1790s, the time that Burns was here, plus a bookshop, café (page 117) and popular **Film Theatre** (art house cinema) which screens movies most evenings.

From the centre, walk up Millbrae and then climb up through the gardens to **9 Dumfries Museum and Camera Obscura** (The Observatory, Rotchell Rd, DG2 7SW ℰ 01387 253374 ◈ www. dumfriesmuseum.com ☉ all year, reduced hours out of season; free

THE HOME OF NEVERLAND

In the northwest corner of central Dumfries, tucked into the bend of the Nith, lies **Moat Brae** (George St, DG1 2EA ℰ 01387 255549 ◈ www.peterpanmoatbrae.org), a Grade B listed building described as a 'five-bay, four-storey Greek revival town house' designed by Scottish architect Walter Newall, who came from nearby New Abbey (page 127) and was the leading architect of the area from the 1820s until his retirement. (The house's slightly strange name comes from the medieval Maxwell Castle which was built in 1300 just around the corner on the site of the present Greyfriars Kirk; page 112.) Newall also designed the Assembly Rooms on George Street (more or less opposite Moat Brae) and remodelled the observatory which is now the museum and camera obscura (see above).

Moat Brae was built in 1824 for a local (merchant) solicitor and Postmaster General but in 1865 was bought by the Gordon family. Their son Stewart attended Dumfries Academy, to where J M Barrie, the author

of *Peter Pan* came to school in 1873 at the age of 13 from his family home in Kirriemuir north of Dundee. The Barrie family were great believers in good education and not only did Dumfries Academy have a particularly good reputation, but Barrie's eldest brother, Alexander, was inspector of schools for Dumfriesshire.

Barrie and Stewart Gordon became instant friends and from the outset Gordon, who called himself Dare Devil Dick, called Barrie Sixteen String Jack. 'He asked me if I would join the pirate crew' wrote Barrie in later years. Together the boys played in the garden at Moat Brae and it was here that Neverland was invented. Barrie later wrote 'I think the five years or so that I spent here were probably the happiest of my life, for indeed I have loved this place' and on being awarded the Freedom of the Burgh of Dumfries in 1924, he reflected that 'when the shades of night began to fall, certain young mathematicians shed their triangles, crept up walls and down trees, and became entry to museum, small charge for the camera obscura) 🖐, the region's largest museum with an extensive collection on local history and pre-history, including the fossil footprints discovered by Dr Henry Duncan at Corncockle Quarry (page 47).

The camera obscura started out as a means of studying the sun but quickly became a tourist attraction. Even today the view on a clear day is impressive, with a surprising degree of detail. The guide offers an enlightening commentary, and if the sun is out and the sky clear you might even be able to spot the northern mountains of the Lake District 30 miles to the south. Do note, though, that the camera obscura doesn't work on a wet day, so choose your time your visit according to the weather report.

pirates in a sort of Odyssey that was long afterwards to become the play of Peter Pan. For our escapades in a certain Dumfries Garden, which is enchanted land to me, were certainly the genesis of that nefarious work'.

Fast forward 70 years and up until 1997 Moat Brae was operating as a nursing home, after which it was left empty and fell into a state of disrepair. Although designated for demolition the building was eventually acquired by the Peter Pan Moat Brae Trust in 2009. Since then there has been a Herculean effort by many people to move the project forward, with a vision to create a centre for children's literature, complete with a Neverland garden to the rear (with Pirate Cave, Skull Rock and Wendy House, of course). An enormous amount has been achieved and at the time of writing the building had been brought to a safe, watertight state, completely stripped back to its basic structure, ready for further development as further funds are released and raised. Funds to date have been contributed by Historic Scotland, the Heritage Lottery Fund and Creative Scotland amongst others, as well as the many private donors. Local resident Joanna Lumley continues to lend her weight as the trust's patron.

The final vision incorporates an exhibition space in the basement, period furnishings on the ground floor, a literary centre on the first floor, and sessions with a creative artist in residence in the attic. It is hoped to open fully in 2017 and to link with a number of strategic partners, including the Scottish Story Telling Centre and Scottish Book Trust. Project Director Cathy Agnew, a driving force behind the development, tells us she would like to create a 'Bank of Stories' in which people can 'deposit' their own stories, either orally or in writing, and other people can 'withdraw' them to listen to or read. What a lovely idea! In the meantime, Moat Brae will continue to hold occasional open days so that people can come and see the most recent developments, and tours can also be arranged for groups by appointment. Keep an eye on the website for details.

Dumfries Museum has a shop (but not a café) and offers plenty to keep children entertained, including specific children's events which must be booked in advance. (Parents are asked to honour the booking, whatever the weather.)

From the museum, head back down to the river and continue along to the 10 suspension bridge, turning right on the other side to make your way along to the junction. There is a choice here, either to go straight over and into 11 Dock Park, a leafy escape on the banks of the Nith which has been voted 'Best Park in Scotland' by Keep Scotland Beautiful, or to cross diagonally to reach 12 St Michael's Kirk, which stands on the site of a much older 12th-century church. Here in the churchyard is 13 the mausoleum of Robert Burns, with his wife Jean Amour buried next to him. Burns was buried here initially in a different plot but his remains were moved in 1815 to a vault under the mausoleum which was erected to his memory. A plan at the entrance to the graveyard shows the location of his original resting place, as well as the location of the graves of his contemporaries.

From here it's only a couple of minutes' walk to 14 Robert Burns House, Burns Street (☉ all year, seasonal hours in winter; check online ⊘ www.dumgal.gov.uk, then click through 'Tourism and Visitor Attractions'), in which the poet and his wife lived from 1793 until his death in 1796, although Jean continued living there until her death in 1834. The house was bought in 1851 by their son Colonel William Burns and placed in the hands of trustees. The four rooms that make up the house are open to the public and contain a range of period furniture, portraits and personal items.

Coming out of Robert Burns House, turn right and continue down the road to the junction with Shakespeare Street, appropriately named for up to the right is the 15 Theatre Royal, built in 1792 and now the oldest working theatre in Scotland. From here it's a short stroll back down to Whitesands and the river, or alternatively turn up the High Street to take in some more Burns sights (see box, page 111).

⅋ FOOD & DRINK

As you'd expect in a town of this size, there are venues and flavours for every occasion. **Whisky fans**, however, may wish to make their way to **TB Watson Ltd** (11 English St, DG1 2BU ✆ 01387 256601 ⊘ www.drambusters.com). Established in 1909, the company has been through several incarnations but now specialises in wines and spirits, with a vast range of whiskies. The shop's website is very good and has a selection of over 500 whiskies.

Hullabaloo Restaurant Robert Burns Centre, Mill Rd, DG2 7BE ✆ 01387 259679 ⏰ www.hullabaloorestaurant.co.uk. One of the few riverside eateries in Dumfries, with an outdoor terrace beneath a weeping willow that works well on a sunny afternoon, and indoor dining for evenings. Food ranges from soups and salads at lunchtime to mezze and a seafood platter in the evening.

Mrs Green's Tea Lounge 16 Queensberry St, DG1 1EX ✆ 01387 116582. Their description of themselves on their Facebook page says it all: 'Emporium of Delicious Food & All Manner of Cakey Loveliness'.

Nona Lou's Old St Andrew's Primary School, Brook St, DG1 2JL ✆ 07989 031491. A quirky café on the top floor of an old school where the menu is written up each day in chalk on the old roller blackboard. Friendly staff, a convivial atmosphere, and a good range of sandwiches, soups, salads and cakes are on offer. It's a few minutes' walk from the centre but worth the trip. There's also a sizeable free car park if you're driving.

Pizzeria il Fiume Dock Park, DG1 2RY ✆ 01387 265154 ⏰ www.pizza-pasta.co.uk. A family-run Italian restaurant that's been going for over 40 years, specialising in pizza, pasta, chargrilled steaks and seafood and complete with wood-fired oven.

BEYOND THE TOWN CENTRE

Lying just north of Dumfries centre, in a peaceful setting on the banks of Cluden Water where it joins the Nith, are the remains of **Lincluden Collegiate Church** (♀ NY966779; Historic Scotland). On this naturally defensive site was originally an earthenwork castle, or motte, which was gifted to a house of Benedictine nuns, who founded a convent here in 1164. What remains are the ruins of the original chapel and adjoining domestic quarters, worth a visit for their history, the architecture (the choir is one of the finest examples of Gothic architecture in Scotland), and simply for the delight at discovering this place, tucked away as it is at the end of a road on the edge of a suburban housing estate. In the 14th century the nuns were turfed out by Archibald the Grim, Lord of Galloway, who had his sights set on what he saw as a nobler cause: himself, his family and his descendants, prayers for whom were to be said by the priests who replaced the nuns. To achieve his aim, Archibald persuaded the pope to effect the change on the basis that the nuns were running a house of questionable morals, diverting the resources afforded to them to dress their daughters 'born in incest' in the best clothes.

From (or to) Lincluden there is access to the riverside path on the west bank of Cluden Water and the Nith. **Robert Burns** used to walk here on the east side, on a path which now runs from central Dumfries to Dalscone a little further on, and the route is still known as Burns Walk. It was here in 1794 that he wrote the revised version of 'Ca the Yowes tae the Knowes' ('Call the Ewes to the Knolls') one of his most haunting songs, with its reference to Cluden Water.

"Gracefield Arts Centre is home to an impressive collection of between 600 and 700 Scottish paintings from 1700 onwards."

If driving to Lincluden, access is off the A76 Kilmarnock road to your right as you head away from Dumfries. One oddity to keep an eye open for is the **Lincluden Rhinoceros**, a model of a rhinoceros and baby which sits atop what looks like a storage container. In days past this was an art installation on top of a bus stop. When the bus stop was removed, there was such an outcry over the loss of the rhinoceros that it was re-installed in its present location.

To the northeast of the centre, only ten to 15 minutes' walk away, is **Gracefield Arts Centre** (28 Edinburgh Rd, DG1 1JQ), home to an impressive collection of between 600 and 700 Scottish paintings from 1700 onwards, including pieces by the Glasgow Boys and Elizabeth Blackadder, a selection of which are on display at any one time. There are also two temporary exhibition spaces, a shop and café (☉ closed Sun and Mon), all set in pleasant grounds in which further works are on display, including a sculpture by local man Andy Goldsworthy (see box, page 95).

Further out of town to the northeast, flying and plane enthusiasts should head for the **Dumfries and Galloway Aviation Museum** (Heathhall Industrial Estate, Heathhall DG1 3PH ♀ NY000785 ✆ 01387 251623 ⌂ www.dumfriesaviationmuseum.com ☉ seasonal on selected days) 👍, accessible by bike from Dumfries using the Caledonian Cycle Route or the regular No 2 bus service from the town centre. Even if planes aren't your thing, there's a wealth of historical detail here about Dumfries and Galloway during the war which makes for fascinating reading and combines well with a visit to the Devil's Porridge (pages 53–5) to build up a picture of wartime life in the region.

East of town on the road which runs down the eastern side of the Nith Estuary (pages 119–20) is **Castledykes Park**, once the site of Dumfries Castle and now a landscaped hillside retreat with pleasant gardens that links up with the path along the Nith from Dock Park (pages 119–20). It's a good spot to let the kids run around.

¶¶ FOOD & DRINK

Casa Mia 53 Nunholm Rd, DG1 1JW ✆ 01387 269619 ⬦ www.casamiadumfries.co.uk
⊙ for lunch & evening meals. In a peaceful setting, the white linen tablecloths and napkins
set the tone for a smart but relaxed dining experience and a Mediterranean- and Scottish-
inspired menu at reasonable prices. Evenings can be busy so booking is recommended.
Hubbub Gracefield Arts Centre, 28 Edinburgh Rd, DG1 1JQ ✆ 01387 262084 ⬦ www.
hullabaloorestaurant.co.uk. A good option if you want to combine a meal with a gallery visit,
run by the owners of Hullabaloo (page 117).
Kilnford Barns Farm Shop and Restaurant Kilnford Barns, The Glen, DG2 8PT ✆ 01387
253087 ⬦ www.kilnford.co.uk ⊙ daily all year, & evenings on Thu. Located on the western
edge of Dumfries. The Rome family have farmed around Kilnford for over 300 years and, in
transforming their derelict barns into a shop and restaurant, have continued a tradition
of supplying local food that started generations ago. It's a good place for kids, too, with a
nature trail, bird hide and wildlife pond, and an outdoor play area.
Wheelers of St James's Bankend Rd, DG1 4ZZ ✆ 01387 272410 ⬦ www.wheelersdumfries.
com. Marco Pierre White's Dumfries restaurant, where booking is recommended.

NITH ESTUARY: EAST SIDE

From Dumfries centre it doesn't take long to reach a different world down
the east side of the Nith, an agricultural area that feels rural virtually
from the instant you cross the town boundary. This short stretch of
countryside, no more than ten or so miles, links to the southern end of
Annandale and with its quiet outlook across the Nith Estuary stands in
notable contrast to the life of the town on its doorstep. Views to Criffel
and the merse (saltmarsh) on the west side of the Nith abound, with
plenty of opportunities for birdwatching and retreating into the quiet,
gentle landscape.

Immediately south of Dumfries, **Kingholm Quay** was originally part
of the town's port. It's a quiet spot now with a popular local pub (page
121). Downstream another three or four miles lies **Glencaple**, where a
row of cottages strung out along the waterside makes for an attractive
setting. There's a super walk to here along the river from Dumfries town
centre (page 120) and if motivation is needed, an enticing tea room
(page 121) awaits on the quayside. The views of and across the Nith
Estuary to Criffel and the RSPB's Kirkconnell Merse are superb and
many an hour can be whiled away on the riverbanks watching birds
(cormorants and lapwings on our last visit), enjoying the ever-changing

A linear walk along the Nith
from Dumfries town centre to Glencaple

❀ OS Landranger map 84, OS Explorer map 313; start: Devorgilla's Bridge, Whitesands
♀ NX969761; 5 miles/2½ hours one way; easy.

Whitsands is accessible by bus or train and you can return on foot or catch the 6A bus. Note that refreshments are available from numerous cafés in Dumfries, the Swan pub in Kingholm Quay, and the Nith Hotel and Caerlaverock Tea Room in Glencaple.

Starting from **1 Whitesands** cross the 17th-century Devorgilla's bridge spanning the River Nith, turn left, following the riverbank, before re-crossing at the 1875 Suspension Bridge. This stretch offers some lovely views of the bridges and river reflections, plus chance to visit the Old Bridge House and Robert Burns Centre museums. Turn right, cross over the busy road junction in to the newly regenerated area of **2 Dock Park** (♀ NX975755), complete with café, children's play area, bowls green, bandstand and pitch and putt. Also look out for the Titanic memorial and some interesting cast iron furniture.

Follow the tarmac riverside path out of town all the way to the small harbour at **3 Kingholm Quay** (♀ NX975735). Turning right at the road, pass the low harbour-side buildings before picking up a grass track that continues along the riverside. This stretch, while easy to follow, is a little less even underfoot, with the bank and path having been eroded in places. Here you can enjoy a few miles of birds and their song, fine views of the River Nith, saltmarsh complete with lilac sea aster and a skyline dominated by Criffel. The path bends away from the river passing over a series of wooden bridges before following a clear grassy path all the way to Glencaple. Note that after particularly high tides or rainfall in the Nith Valley this area can flood.

Continue around the final meander and the pretty riverside village of **4 Glencaple** (♀ NX995686) can be seen ahead with, on a clear day, the mountains of the Lake District behind. Glencaple makes for a perfect lunch spot, a place to watch the sun set or to see the bore wave from the changing Solway Firth tide.

light and keeping an eye open for otters. Come at the right time and you'll also catch the **tidal bore** as it sweeps up the Nith. Glencaple's history as a port is commemorated in the novel and attractive oak boat benches which line the road south of the tea room, on which words and pictures have been created out of flattened nail heads. One bench notes the fact that 'Enough tea leaves were landed here to make 14 million cups of tea'!

¶¶ FOOD & DRINK

Caerlaverock Tea Room The Quay End, Glencaple DG1 4RE ✆ 01387 770673 ⊘ www.
caerlaverockestate.co.uk. Has a splendid setting on the quay, with great views up and down
the Nith and across the water to Criffel. Popular with walkers, cyclists and birdwatchers, it
serves the usual range of tea room fare plus hot meals at lunchtime.
The Swan Kingholm Quay DG1 4SU ✆ 01387 253756 ⊘ www.theswanatkingholmquay.
co.uk. Stands on the site of an old waterside inn and offers a broad-ranging menu for both
lunch and dinner.

CAERLAVEROCK

❧ Wildfowl and Wetlands Trust Caerlaverock (page 246)

The Caerlaverock Estate, owned by the Duke of Norfolk, covers 5,200
acres on the east side of the Nith, encompasses the villages of Glencaple
(page 119) and Bankend, and includes several farms which incorporate
arable land, permanent pasture, wetlands and woodlands. The estate
also includes part of the Caerlaverock National Nature Reserve
managed by Scottish Natural Heritage, part of which is in turn managed
by the Wildfowl and Wetlands Trust (WWT). For visitors, the main
attractions are walking and wildlife watching, and visiting the splendid
Caerlaverock Castle, dating from the 13th century and now in the
care of Historic Scotland. Full details of the area can be found on the
Caerlaverock Estate website ⊘ www.caerlaverockestate.co.uk, as well as
the websites of the WWT and Historic Scotland, and from Scotland's
National Nature Reserves.

Caerlaverock Church (♀ NY025692) stands on its own at the end of a
lane, through a farm, off the Bankend Road, 1½ miles east of Glencaple.
It is notable as the burial place of Robert Paterson, immortalised by
Sir Walter Scott as **Old Mortality** (page 139), who spent his later years
wandering southern Scotland carving gravestones to mark the burial
sites of Covenanters.

Caerlaverock National Nature Reserve

⊘ www.nnr-scotland.org.uk

Covering almost 20,000 acres, Caerlaverock National Nature Reserve is
a vast flat expanse of sand, sea, mud and merse (saltmarsh) stretching
almost 10 miles along the Solway Coast south of Dumfries. Around 85%
of the area is made up of tidal flats and mudbanks which disappear at
high tide. This is a haven for wildlife of all sorts, from birds to the rare

natterjack toad and the even more obscure tadpole shrimp, a freshwater crustacean that has existed for over 200 million years and which, until its discovery at Caerlaverock in 1994, was thought to exist in only one location in the UK. The name Caerlaverock is derived from the old Scots for a skylark – a laverock – thus Caerlaverock is either 'castle of the lark' or 'lark's nest'. No surprise then that every year there are over 300 pairs of skylarks here.

"Solway Firth remains in a largely natural state and, for the birds that return year after year, a vast natural larder on the saltmarshes and mudflats."

This is a truly special place. Unlike many other firths, the **Solway Firth** remains in a largely natural state, undisturbed for the main and, for the birds that return year after year, a vast natural larder on the saltmarshes and mudflats. Local farmers subscribe to the ethos of the area, too, providing safe grazing for geese in their fields, with any costs incurred being met by the Solway Goose Management Scheme managed by Scottish Natural Heritage.

Visitors can access both the nature reserve generally, which is free of charge, and the WWT reserve, for which either membership is required or an admission fee is charged for non-members. Travelling south down the estuary from Dumfries, once past Glencaple there are one or two waterside benches where it's possible to stop off, but the main parking area for the nature reserve lies roughly halfway between Glencaple and the turning for Caerlaverock Castle. From here there are walks into the reserve, where a good hide is located with views across the flatlands to the Solway. It's a peaceful spot and a great area simply to wander the paths.

2 WWT Caerlaverock Wetland Centre

East Park Farm, DG1 4RS ♥ NY051656 ✐ 01387 770200 ♂ www.wwt.org.uk

Caerlaverock Wetland Centre lies at the end of a lane a short distance on from the turning to Caerlaverock Castle and was the second WWT centre to be opened by Sir Peter Scott after Slimbridge in Gloucestershire. The centre occupies what were the outbuildings of Eastpark Farm and WWT manages the saltmarsh part of the larger nature reserve: 1,500 acres of mainly saltmarsh and goose grazing fields. It's an international place, with connections around the world. In summer the Senegalese flag flies as Senegal is where the Caerlaverock ospreys spend the winter. In winter it's the Norwegian flag (amongst others), for it is to Caerlaverock each year that the entire population – all 35,000 of them – of barnacle geese returns from Svalbard, around 10,000 of which are usually to be found in the WWT reserve. Several bird hides offer good vantage points, and the new Sir Peter Scott Observatory is an impressive state-of-the-art facility at the whooper swan pond, complete with touchscreen swan database, very funky swan wallpaper which reproduces in exact detail the markings and identification tags of a number of swans, and an audio system which facilitates commentated feedings each day during the season (late autumn and winter).

WWT Caerlaverock is, in our view, one of the absolute highlights of Dumfries and Galloway. If you have an ounce of interest in wildlife, or simply in being outdoors in a beautiful place, you could easily lose yourself for a day – or longer – here. And kids will love it, too. There's a Nature's Explorer Passport to be filled with stickers, plus an accompanying rucksack for hire, and a tower to be climbed that offers terrific views over the wetlands and that houses what are believed to be the largest binoculars in Scotland (not yet restored, but they're working on raising the funds for it). There are trails to be followed and nests to be spotted, badger viewing evenings, occasional walks accompanied by rangers, and there's a tank containing the oldest living animal on earth, the tadpole shrimp. And when it all gets too much, there is, of course, a tea room to retreat to.

3 Caerlaverock Castle 👋

Glencaple DG1 4RU ♀ NY025656 ⌀ www.historic-scotland.gov.uk; Historic Scotland; free to members

Next door to WWT Caerlaverock stands the distinctive, red-pink sandstone Caerlaverock Castle, which can be reached by a one-mile waterside path from the wetlands centre or by car. Another great place for kids, this is a castle as you imagine castles should be, with moat, bridge, rooms to run through, towers to climb, and intriguing corners to explore. What's more, it boasts an unusual design as it is triangular, believed to be built on a triangular piece of rock.

Of all the additions and alterations to the castle, perhaps the most impressive is the **Nithsdale Lodging**, an ornately embellished range within the castle walls which was completed by Robert, first Earl of Nithsdale, in 1634. It's an extraordinary sight, a Renaissance frontage with an extravagance of stone carving within the confines of this fortress.

NITH ESTUARY: WEST SIDE

To keep chapters to a manageable size, we have stretched the 'Nith Estuary' to reach as far as Crocketford to the west on the main A75 and then south as far as the RSPB reserve at Mersehead. Strictly speaking this area comes under the old county of Kirkcudbrightshire, much of which equates with the Stewartry (see *Chapter 4*). However, access is easy from Dumfries and it also brings a more rounded view of the Nith estuary as a whole. It's an area of much scenic variety and interest, with a history that incorporates a couple of crannogs at Lochrutton and Milton Loch (although there is little to be seen), the Old Military Road that was previously the main route west, the birthplace of the 'Father of the American Navy', and arguably the most romantic abbey ruin in the country. Cycling is popular, notably at Mabie Forest, part of the 7stanes scheme, and so too is walking, not least to the top of Criffel, only just under 1,900 feet high but one of the most prominent hills in Scotland.

WEST OF DUMFRIES

Between the A75 to Crocketford and A711 to Dalbeattie runs the **Old Military Road**, marked as such on OS maps and featured in many cycle routes in this area. **Crannogs** have been identified at **Lochrutton Loch** just south of Lochfield and **Milton Loch** between Crocketford and Milton. The former was excavated in 1901 and the latter in 1953 after being revealed while the level of the loch was lowered. Finds from both are now held at Dumfries Museum (pages 114–15). At nearby **Crocketford** 🖐, also known as Nine Mile Bar as it is exactly halfway between Dumfries and Castle Douglas, are local amenities, including a shop and post office, and the convenient watering hole and restaurant of the Galloway Arms Hotel. Curiously, Crocketford owes its existence to the arrival in the late 18th century of the strange sect known as the Buchanites, at the centre of which was one Mrs Elspeth Buchan, who claimed to be immortal.

"Crocketford owes its existence to the arrival in the late 18th century of the strange sect known as the Buchanites."

South of Milton off a quiet back road is **Drumcoltran Tower** (📍 NX869684; Historic Scotland), a fine example of a 16th-century tower house, the traditional home of the Scottish landowner. Once owned by the Maxwell family who held the lairdship of Caerlaverock (page 123) and Threave (pages 150–1) castles and many other estates in the region, today it stands on private farm land, but there is access from the road up a fenced pathway. Generally quiet and relatively undiscovered, much can still be seen of how life here would have been lived. Kids will particularly enjoy climbing up the stairs all the way to the top where you can get out on to the roof for views of the surrounding area.

Southeast of Drumcoltran lies **Beeswing**, a small village notable for its name. Originally called Lochend (in reference to nearby Loch Arthur), in the 19th century the local inn was purchased by a racehorse owner who renamed the village in honour of the eponymous British thoroughbred racehorse who won 51 out of 63 races between 1835 and 1842. Next to the village is the very popular **Loch Arthur Camphill Community Creamery and Farmshop** (♀ NX899688; see below).

¶¶ FOOD & DRINK

Loch Arthur Camphill Community Creamery and Farmshop Beeswing DG2 8JQ ✆ 01387 259669 ⬧ www.locharthur.org.uk ◷ closed Sun. Sells all manner of organic goodies and serves delicious teas, coffees and fuller meals from a purpose-built, light and airy shop and restaurant. The outdoor tables are particularly sheltered on a sunny day.

4 MABIE FOREST

A few miles south of Dumfries on the road to New Abbey lies Mabie Forest (♀ NX949712), a Forestry Commission Scotland site and one of the 7stanes biking centres (page 16). Mabie is also one of only three reserves that come under the care of Butterfly Conservation Scotland, and 20 of Scotland's 32 butterfly species can be found here including the scarce pearl-bordered fritillary (*Boloria euphrosyne*). There's plenty to see and do, with **walking** and **biking trails** to suit all abilities, picnic tables, a children's adventure playground with zip-wire, and lots of wildlife to keep an eye open for. There's also a hide at Lochaber Loch. During one visit in May we spotted several pearl-bordered fritillary as well as

"Mabie Forest is one of only three reserves that come under the care of Butterfly Conservation Scotland."

various day-flying moths, plus the big hairy black and ginger caterpillar (commonly known as 'woolly bears') of the night-flying garden tiger moth (*Arctia caja*). We also came across a surprisingly tame roe deer.

There are some fine trees, too. Although this is Forestry Commission land, it's not just a plantation of Sitka spruce but is mixed woodland, including a wide range of trees which provide a more variable habitat. We found one particularly fine example of a sequoia, only a few hundred years old but impressive nonetheless.

The main car park (pay parking) at Mabie is accessed from the A710 between Dumfries and New Abbey. Note that there is a sign into Mabie Farm Park just before the turning into Mabie Forest (which shares an entrance with the Mabie House Hotel), but there is no vehicle access to the forest from the farm park.

AN ALMOST-SECRET WALLED GARDEN

NX961665 www.shambelliewalledgarden.co.uk All year but weather-dependent

In 2005 Sheila Cameron took on a 25-year lease for the walled garden on the Shambellie Estate, on land which had been acquired by the Stewart family in 1625 when it was handed over to them by Sweetheart Abbey, rather than allowing it to be taken by the Crown. Shambellie House, built in 1855 by David Bryce, the principal Scottish architect of that time, used to be open, too, with a costume exhibition but has sadly been closed in recent years. However, Sheila's garden is something of a hidden treat, tucked away on a side road from New Abbey to Loch Arthur (in fact, it makes a good day out to combine the two). When Sheila took it on you couldn't tell what was here was a garden here, let alone see what must have at one time been a productive kitchen garden. 'There were hundreds of trees and every perennial weed you could think of' says Sheila. Ask to see the photographs of how it was, and you'll see what she means. It had been completely abandoned.

Taking it on was a mammoth project and included the controlled demolition and rebuilding of the glasshouse using the original materials. It's now a well-established mixed ornamental garden with benches strategically placed for peaceful contemplation. Bring a book and settle down for a few hours in one of the many sheltered sunny spots, or bring a picnic and a rug and lounge on the lawns. There's lots of wildlife to spot, including honey bees, dragonflies, damsel flies, butterflies, mice and occasional red squirrels.

'All the plants have to work hard' says Sheila, whose planting is based on whatever will thrive here and species that are low maintenance. There are no vegetables or fruits except for blackcurrants simply because Sheila likes them. This is a very personal place which Sheila hopes will give inspiration to other gardeners, either by way of showing what is possible or by allowing people to see aspects that they don't like.

Plants are on sale and occasionally events are held here, too. Keep an eye on the Facebook page for details.

5 NEW ABBEY

⊙ abbey & mill both open all year, reduced hours in winter; Historic Scotland; free to members

Romantic souls will be in their element at New Abbey, a small village which nuzzles up to the northern shoulder of Criffel where it drops to the flat plain of the western side of the Nith. Quaint and historic, its neat rows of houses line the road and sit within what would have been the grounds of the Cistercian New Abbey itself, founded in 1273 and so-called to distinguish it from the then 120-year-old Dundrennan Abbey (pages 181–2). The abbey is now known by the much lovelier name of **Sweetheart Abbey** thanks to the good Lady Devorgilla (page 110). When her beloved husband died, she not only founded the abbey but also had his heart embalmed in a casket and carried it with her wherever she went. On her death in 1290 she was buried here with her husband's heart and the monks subsequently rechristened the abbey *dulce cor*, meaning 'sweet heart'. A good portion of the abbey can still be seen today, both from the surrounding land and also from within the grounds. At 112 feet long, the nave is particularly impressive with its parade of pillars and arches.

The water-powered **New Abbey Corn Mill** at the opposite end of the main street is also cared for by Historic Scotland and, following careful restoration, is now in full working order. The neat whitewashed buildings are picturesquely positioned next to a duck pond and contain all the fixtures and fittings as they were left over half a century ago. The mill is only operated for demonstrations during the summer.

Gardeners – and, for that matter, anyone in search of a peaceful retreat – should head for **Shambellie Garden** (see box, opposite), just west of New Abbey.

¶¶ FOOD & DRINK

Abbey Cottage Tearoom 26 Main St, DG2 8BY ✆ 01387 850377 ⌘ www. abbeycottagetearoom.com. A convenient stop right next to Sweetheart Abbey, with a gift shop attached.

NEW ABBEY TO MERSEHEAD

The coastal road south from New Abbey hugs the skirt of Criffel and offers heavenly views of the Nith Estuary, with a good stopping place at **Drumburn viewpoint** (♀ NX980618) looking out to where the Nith meets the Solway. From here you can see to Wardlaw Wood, site of the Roman fort above Caerlaverock on the other side of the Nith, and south across Carse Sands to Carsethorn. Immediately south is **Drummains Reed Bed**, part of the Solway Site of Special Scientific Interest (SSSI) and Special Area of Conservation, managed by the Scottish Wildlife Trust. The coastal reedbed, saltmarsh and mudflats support wildfowl and waders and are good places to spot sedge warbler and reed bunting. The access path is roughly one mile north of Kirkbean on the A710; park on the grassy verge.

At **Kirkbean** a couple of miles further on, the village church is noted primarily as the burial place of the father of John Paul Jones (see below). Kirkbean developed as an estate village for nearby Arbigland House and if you're visiting the area you may want to dip into the excellent website of the Kirkbean Parish Heritage Society ⊘ www.kirkbeanheritagesociety. org.uk, which offers a wealth of information.

Head out to the coast from Kirkbean, a mile or so northeast, to **Carsethorn**, a picture-postcard village with a row of cottages strung along the waterfront and a popular pub, the Steamboat Inn (see opposite). Once a historic port, during the late 18th and early 19th centuries there were frequent sailings from here to the American and Australian colonies. Carsethorn's importance as a port began to wane following the development of Glencaple (page 119) on the other side of the Nith. Note the wooden bench on which have been carved the names of those who left for Prince Edward Island on the *Lovely Nelly* in 1775.

6 John Paul Jones Cottage Museum 🖐

♀ NX987572 ⊘ www.jpj.demon.co.uk ⊙ seasonal

A mile or so southeast from Kirkbean in the grounds of Arbigland Estate is the John Paul Jones Cottage Museum, the birthplace on 6 July 1747 of the man who was to become a naval hero of the American Revolution and who is regarded as the 'Father of the American Navy'. Born the son of an Arbigland worker, his birth name was simply John Paul, but he changed it to John Jones, and subsequently to John Paul Jones, after killing the ringleader of a mutiny in the West Indies in 1773 and fleeing to Virginia. Although he died at the age of just 45, his career was both distinguished and controversial, ranging from his seaman's apprenticeship at the age of 13 to championing and fighting for the colonists in the American Revolution. In Britain he became regarded as something of a pirate, a reputation which was only enhanced after his victory in 1779 at Flamborough Head.

Jones died in Paris in 1792 and his body then lay in an alcohol-filled coffin in an unmarked grave for over a century until, under the orders of President Roosevelt, a search was undertaken and it was rediscovered. He was finally laid to rest in 1913 in the chapel at Annapolis Naval Academy on Chesapeake Bay, east of Washington DC.

A few minutes' walk from the museum takes you to **Thirl Stane Beach** (parking available), a lovely spot looking straight across the Solway and with views to **Southerness lighthouse**, the oldest in Galloway but sadly long since decommissioned. The rocky beach offers lots of space when the tide is out. Although the name Southerness may seem appropriate for the location, it is actually a corruption of Satterness, derived from Salterness, the saltworks of which were given by Roland, Lord of Galloway, in the 12th century to the monks of Holmcultram, now the village of Abbeytown, in Cumbria.

7 RSPB Mersehead

Mersehead Farm, Southwick DG2 8AH NX925560 01387 780298 www.rspb.org.uk

A couple of miles from Southerness is an extensive wetland and saltmarsh area supporting a range of bird species, including lapwing, reed warbler and, in autumn and winter, pintails and large numbers of barnacle geese. Harbour porpoises, otters and natterjack toads are also found. A small visitor centre by the car park offers information, self-service teas and a cosy viewing area looking out over the merse, while coastal and wetland nature trails, the latter including a couple of hides, are an ideal way to get out into the reserve.

FOOD & DRINK

Steamboat Inn Carsethorn DG2 8DS 01387 880631 www.steamboatinncarsethorn.co.uk. A great waterfront location combined with thoroughly good and filling meals from local produce, especially – and appropriately – fish. Can be busy.

DUMFRIES & GALLOWAY ONLINE

For additional online content, articles, photos and more on Dumfries and Galloway, why not visit www.bradtguides.com/d&g and www.slowbritain.co.uk.

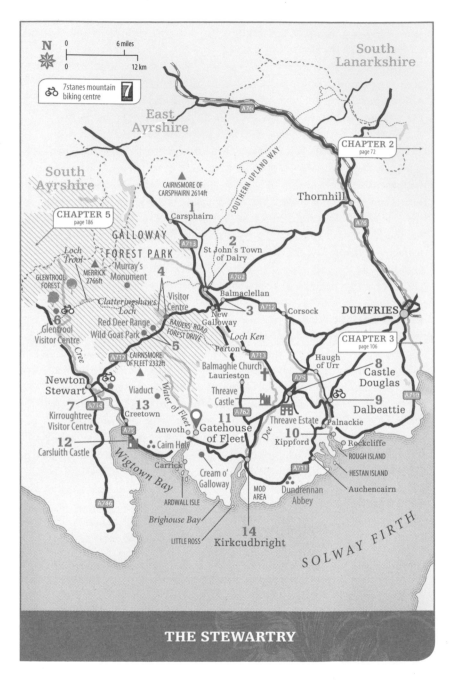

N

0 — 6 miles
0 — 12 km

7stanes mountain biking centre **7**

South Lanarkshire

East Ayrshire

CHAPTER 2
page 72

A76

CAIRNSMORE OF CARSPHAIRN 2614ft ▲

South Ayrshire

CHAPTER 5
page 186

1 Carsphairn

SOUTHERN UPLAND WAY

Thornhill

A76

GALLOWAY

2 St John's Town of Dalry

A713

FOREST PARK

Loch Trool

Murray's Monument

MERRICK 2766ft ▲

4

A762

Balmaclellan

GLENTROOL FOREST

Clatteringshaws Loch

Visitor Centre

New Galloway

3 A712 Corsock

DUMFRIES

6 Glentrool Visitor Centre

Red Deer Range Wild Goat Park

RAIDERS' ROAD FOREST DRIVE

Loch Ken

5

Parton

A713

CHAPTER 3
page 106

Cree

A712 CAIRNSMORE OF FLEET 2332ft ▲

Balmaghie Church

Laurieston

Haugh of Urr

A75

8 Castle Douglas

Newton Stewart

Viaduct

Water of Fleet

Threave Castle

A762

Threave Estate

A710

9 Dalbeattie

7 Kirroughtree Visitor Centre

A714

13 Creetown

A75

Anwoth

11 Gatehouse of Fleet

Dee

Palnackie

10 Kippford

Reckcliffe

12 Carsluith Castle

Cairn Holy

Carrick

Cream o' Galloway

Dundrennan Abbey

A711

ROUGH ISLAND

HESTAN ISLAND

Auchencairn

A746

Wigtown Bay

ARDWALL ISLE

MOD AREA

Brighouse Bay

LITTLE ROSS

14 Kirkcudbright

SOLWAY FIRTH

THE STEWARTRY

4

THE STEWARTRY

Blessed with fine hill and coastal landscapes, replete with history, overflowing with anecdotes and tales of characters past and present, and the location of some of Dumfries and Galloway's most attractive towns, the Stewartry has it all. No wonder that those in the know return to it time and again. It is varied and big, stretching from the north of the wild Glenkens down to the rocky bays of the Kirkcudbright coast, and it would be easy to spend a week in any one of the five different locales into which we have split this chapter, let alone take the time to discover the others.

The name – 'Stewartry' – is a corruption of 'Steward', dating from the 14th century when a steward was appointed by Archibald the Grim, Lord of Galloway, to collect revenues.

The area is the location of the **Galloway Hydroelectric Scheme**, built in the 1930s and consisting of a network of dams and power stations. Much of it falls within the Glenkens, but you will spot the striking Modernist power stations all the way down to the valley of the Dee at Tongland. This is an area with a rich literary heritage, too, the glorious scenery inspiring John Buchan and Dorothy L Sayers to set books here, not to mention local author S R Crockett. And this is the place to come for the **Galloway Kite Trail**, with opportunities to see these impressive birds at close quarters.

A history rich in smuggling characterises the coastal strip. Between Southerness in the east and Fleet Bay in the west there are some 30 bays and coves. This is one of the most stunning stretches of coast in Scotland, yet many parts of it remain relatively undiscovered and it is not unknown to have a beach to yourself. Alternatively, if you prefer wilder places, the Stewartry is also the location of the enormous **Galloway Forest Park**, the country's first Dark Sky Park and a remote and invigorating landscape of moorland and mountains.

With so much history having played out here, there is an ongoing programme of archaeogical digs organised by **The Stewartry Archaeological Trust** (⊘ www.sat.org.uk). The trust is often on the lookout for volunteers, so if you fancy getting your hands dirty while in the area, do drop them a line.

GETTING AROUND

The Stewartry feels a bit like an area of two halves. The Glenkens to the north is a place of fewer main roads, crossed by the A713 and A712, dominated by hills and remote moors dotted with small towns and communities. Closer to the coast the main A75 cuts east to west, passing the more populated areas of Castle Douglas, Kirkcudbright and Gatehouse of Fleet.

PUBLIC TRANSPORT

The Stewartry has no train service; the nearest stations are at Dumfries to the east and Stranraer to the west. With the area's central location in Dumfries and Galloway, **bus services** offer a better option for criss-crossing the area, with numerous services connecting with the railway stations. The fastest service is the 500/X75 Stranraer to Carlisle, stopping at key points along the main A75. From the east, the 501/502 from Dumfries can drop you at Castle Douglas and further down at Kirkcudbright. From the west, the 431/517 also terminates at Kirkcudbright coming from Gatehouse of Fleet. The 520 runs to key points northwards from Castle Douglas through New Galloway, St Johns Town of Dalry and on into Ayrshire. Local public transport information is provided by South West of Scotland Transport Partnership (⊘ www. swestrans.org.uk), or alternatively the traveline (⊘ 0871 200 22 33 ⊘ www.traveline.org.uk).

CYCLING

Quiet coastal lanes, upland tracks and mountain biking trails are typical in this area of green farmland, secluded moors and forestry plantation, the latter dotted with native woods. Much of the area is pleasantly rolling, but there are also many dramatic spots for those looking to work the legs a bit harder. There are two world-class **mountain biking centres** at Kirroughtree (page 146) and

---

i TOURIST INFORMATION

VisitScotland Information Centre Kirkcudbright Harbour Sq, DG6 4HY ✆ 01557 330494 ⊙ Apr–Oct
Castle Douglas Information Centre Market Hill Car Park, DG7 1AE ✆ 01556 502611 ⊙ Apr–Oct
Gatehouse of Fleet Information Point Mill on the Fleet, High St, DG7 2HS ✆ 01557 814212 ⊙ Easter–Oct
Further north, plenty of information is available from the helpful staff and good stock of leaflets at The CatStrand Arts Centre in **New Galloway** (page 139). There are three visitor centres in Galloway Forest Park, details of which can be found on pages 144, 145 and 146.

Dalbeattie (⧉ www.7stanesmountainbiking.com). Forestry Commission Scotland's Kirroughtree Visitor Centre has **cycle hire** (see below), along with some of the best technical single track in the country. Dalbeattie, with its coastal setting and smaller hills, has a relaxed feel but is not without rocky outcrops and fine views. See the Dumfries and Galloway Council's free *Cycling in and around Stewartry* booklet for a good selection. The **Southern Upland Cycleway** is under development and will eventually make use of quiet roads and lanes from Portpatrick on the west coast through to Cockburnspath on the east. So far the section from Glenluce to Sanquhar, through the Stewartry, is signposted.

CYCLE HIRE

Break Pad Kirroughtree Visitor Centre, DG8 7BE ✆ 01671 401303 ⧉ www.thebreakpad. com ⊙ closed Mon. Claims to have the largest bike fleet in Dumfries and Galloway, and hires out road and mountain bikes.
Cycle4Life 54 St John St, Creetown DG8 7JF ✆ 01671 820654. Located opposite the museum and offering free bike hire.
Gorsebank Cycle Hire, Greenhill Farm, A710 Coast Road, Dalbeattie DG5 4QT ✆ 01556 610174 ⧉ www.gorsebank.com. Located 1.5 miles south of Dalbeattie, next to 7stanes cycle trails.
Loch Ken Cycle Hire, Galloway Activity Centre. Loch Ken, Parton DG7 3NQ ✆ 01644 420626 ⧉ www.lochken.co.uk. Located 10 miles north of Castle Douglas on the A713.

WALKING

The Stewartry is an area of contrasting landscapes offering opportunities to enjoy the outdoors for all abilities. The **Southern Upland Way**

($\mathscr{d}$ www.southernuplandway.gov.uk) passes through the heart of the Glenkens. This is the longest stretch at 25 strenuous miles and should only be attempted in a day by the very fittest. Pick-up points at Stroanfreggan Bridge and from the valley of the Scaur Water can be used to break this section into more manageable parts. Down at the coast the short walk from Rockcliffe to Kippford (and back; see page 156) is one of the region's most popular. The district also offers walks to interest art lovers or film location buffs, and there are those encompassing an architectural folly or two, and many fine views.

Dumfries and Galloway Council has produced free 'Walking in and around' booklets to Kirkcudbright and Auchencairn, and Dalbeattie and Colvend, which have a good selection of walking options for this chapter.

THE GLENKENS & LOCH KEN

Remote and wild are adjectives often used to describe the Glenkens and local people here and in the neighbouring Nithsdale villages across the moors might be heard referring to themselves wryly as the 'hill tribes'. Occupying the most northerly reaches of the Stewartry, the Glenkens may lie at a short distance from most of the region's main centres but the area is easy enough to reach while also offering a sense of getting off the beaten track. Outdoor activities are definitely on the cards here: walking and cycling, but also, thanks to lovely Loch Ken, all manner of watersports. There is also wildlife and iconic birdlife (most of the Galloway Kite Trail falls within this area) to be spotted, historic castles, quaint villages with local artisans, and tea rooms stuffed with home baking.

"The Glenkens lie on the eastern fringe of Galloway Forest Park with boundaries defined by the valley of the River Ken."

The Glenkens lie on the eastern fringe of **Galloway Forest Park** with boundaries more or less defined by the valley of the **River Ken**. It therefore incorporates the string of villages which run down the length of the valley from Carsphairn in the north to Parton in the south. **Corsock**, a little further to the east, is also involved in Glenkens community activities, as is **Laurieston** to the west, so both are included in this section, along with the western shore of **Loch Ken**. If you're planning a visit to the area, further information can be found on the community website $\mathscr{d}$ www.visitglenkens.com.

NORTH GLENKENS

The far north of the Glenkens, where Dumfries and Galloway meets East Ayrshire, is an area of wide open space, moorland and hills surrounding the ominously named **Loch Doon**, which can be glimpsed to the west from the main road.

1 Carsphairn 🖐

The Galloway Tourist Route to/from Ayr runs down the A713 offering splendid views, leading to Carsphairn (the name means 'alder meadow'), where the **heritage centre** (DG7 3TQ 📍 NX559934 ✎ 01644 460653 ✍ www.carsphairnheritage.org ☺ seasonal) at the northern end of the village offers information on the surrounding area and local community. (If you plan to stop off at Polmaddy or Dundeugh leaflets are usually available here.)

In the 19th century this was a lead mining area: **Woodhead lead mine and village** were located in the hills a couple of miles to the west and the remains of the village can still be visited.

Carsphairn was also a Covenanter village and claims its own martyr, **Roger Dunn**, whose tombstone is found near the churchyard gate. It is recorded that he was killed on the night of Carsphairn Fair in June 1869, though some records claim that it was a case of mistaken identity. The village was also for a few years the home of **John Loudon McAdam**, the great engineer and road builder, whose family lived just outside Carsphairn at Lagwyne Mansion. The house

> "Carsphairn was a Covenanter village and claims its own martyr, Roger Dunn."

burned down when McAdam was six, just about taking him with it, after which the family returned to Ayrshire, where he had been born. Despite his Ayrshire connections, McAdam remains associated with Dumfries and Galloway. Not only is there a memorial to him here in the church, but he also died in the region, in Moffat, where he is buried (page 34).

If you're stopping off in Carsphairn, there is a good tea room on the main street, **Carrick's of Carsphairn** (DG7 3TQ ✎ 01644 60211 ☺ daily).

2 St John's Town of Dalry 🖐

There is a choice of roads to reach St John's Town of Dalry from Carsphairn, the main A713 or the smaller B729/B7000 both offering a glimpse of the dams of the hydroelectric scheme (page 131).

The intriguingly named St John's Town of Dalry (often shortened to Dalry, but not to be confused with the Ayrshire town or Edinburgh suburb of the same name) is an attractive Galloway village of painted cottages tumbling down the hill. The village as it appears today has its roots in a late 18th-century medieval hamlet which was developed by the Earl of Galloway. At the top end of the village is a natural stone in the shape of a chair. Legend has it that John the Baptist rested upon it, thus giving the village its name, but the more commonly accepted truth is that the land was owned by the Knights Templar (or, later, the Knights Hospitaller, also known as the Knights of St John) who administered to pilgrims travelling south to the shrine of St Ninian at Whithorn (pages 200–4).

"The intriguingly named St John's Town of Dalry has its roots in a late 18th-century medieval hamlet which was developed by the Earl of Galloway."

At the foot of the village on a high bank of the Water of Ken and with good views of the Rhinns of Kells is **Dalry Parish Church**, completed in 1831, with its distinctive tower and red-tiled roof. Believed to be the third on this site, details of the first church are sketchy but a ruin stood here in 1427. In the churchyard is the **Gordon Aisle** of 1546, the resting place of the Gordons of Lochinvar, whose seat, Lochinvar Castle, stood on an island in Loch Lochinvar, three miles across the moors to the northeast. (For a trip into the wilds of the surrounding countryside, take the Moniaive road out to lonely Lochinvar.) The castle was lost when the Lochinvar Dam was built and the waters rose. Sir Walter Scott's poem 'Marmion' tells the tale of 'Young Lochinvar', a character associated with the 15th-century Sir William Gordon.

St John's Town and the surrounding area have a strong Covenanting history, which is commemorated in the **Covenanter Memorial** (see box, opposite) and the grave of Robert Stewart and John Grierson in the parish church. Stewart and Grierson had been active in freeing Covenanters held in Kirkcudbright tollbooth (page 177) and had also been involved in the murder of the curate of Carsphairn. They were marked men, pursued by John Graham of Claverhouse, 1st Viscount Dundee (page 24), who caught and killed them. Their bodies were brought to Dalry for burial.

Dalry is a good spot to linger and explore, with plenty of walks in the surrounding area, notably the **Southern Upland Way** which passes

THE PENTLAND RISING

The striking **Covenanter Memorial** of 2004 stands in the park at the southern end of the village and is based on the 'Burning Bush' from Exodus chapter 3. Donated by one Bill Dunigan, a member of the Scottish Memorials Association, it was decided to erect it here to mark the start of the Pentland Rising, one of the most significant events of the period, which was precipitated by a skirmish in St John's Town in 1666. What started with four Covenanters coming out of the hills in search of a meal turned into an attempt to rescue an old farmer from soldiers, which then escalated with the involvement of Covenanters holding a Conventicle at nearby Balmaclellan (page 139). Rebellion had begun and culminated in 900 Covenanters marching to Edinburgh where, on 28 November at Rullion Green on the edge of the Pentland Hills, they were met by around 3,000 soldiers. Carnage followed with around 100 Covenanters reported killed on the field and a further 300 as they tried to escape. Around 120 were taken prisoner and sentenced to death.

through the centre of the village. Slightly to the east is a path to **Holy Linn Waterfall**, a Covenanter's meeting and baptism place, accessed from either the A702 or through mixed deciduous woodland and along the Garple Burn from the B7075 to Balmaclellan.

The **Donald Watson Bird Walk** is a circular loop taking about 1½ hours that is detailed on a leaflet available from The CatStrand in New Galloway (page 139) and online (⊘ www.watsonbirds.org). It was one of the favourite walks of Donald Watson, an internationally renowned wildlife artist and author who made Dalry his home from 1951 until his death in 2005. There is also a leaflet detailing the **Donald Watson Art Trail**, a 47-mile route around the Glenkens which includes many of the locations that provided inspiration for his paintings.

If you happen to be in the Dalry area at the weekend, the **Glenkens Farmers' Market** is held on the second Saturday of every month throughout the year in Dalry's Town Hall.

¶¶ FOOD & DRINK

Clachan Inn 8–10 Main St, DG7 3UW ⊘ 01644 430241 ⊘ www.theclachaninn.co.uk. Perfectly located at the heart of Dalry, the Clachann has a strong reputation and is described by the Campaign for Real Ale as 'one of the most attractive pubs in southwest Scotland'. A fine range of Scottish real ales, craft beers and malt whiskies is offered, not to mention quality food using local ingredients. Open fires in winter make for a cosy retreat.

3 NEW GALLOWAY & BALMACLELLAN ✋

🏠 **Glenlee Holiday Houses** (page 247)

New Galloway

John Rennie's graceful bridge of finely dressed granite over the Ken sets the tone for New Galloway, a village of undeniable charm, which exudes an air of calm country life but is far from inert. In fact, New Galloway is positively brimming with cultural life thanks to the development of The CatStrand, a community arts initiative developed by the Glenkens Community and Arts Trust. New Galloway lies just two miles outside the eastern edge of **Galloway Forest Park** and is on the **Red Kite Trail**, both factors which help to bring in the visitors.

New Galloway is **Scotland's smallest royal burgh**, a status conferred upon it after Sir John Gordon of Lochinvar (page 136) obtained a charter from Charles I in 1629. The village was popularly referred to as the 'New Town of Galloway', which in time has been shortened to today's name. It lies in the parish of Kells and the **parish church** of 1822 with its battlemented tower stands on a hill above the northern end of the village with delightful views over the surrounding hills and a number of interesting headstones in the graveyard.

"John Rennie's graceful bridge of finely dressed granite over the Ken sets the tone for New Galloway, a village of undeniable charm."

In more recent days New Galloway's profile has been raised, partly thanks to actor Sam Heughan – who plays Jamie Fraser in the *Outlander* series based on Diana Gabaldon's novels – who hails from here, and partly because of the **Alternative Games** which are held on the first Sunday in August. The games were first held in 1977 for the Queen's Jubilee after a local farmer, Mungo Bryson, found an old rusty gird n' cleek when he was tidying the barn. (A gird n' cleek is a metal hoop which is attached to a metal rod via a smaller hoop. The aim is to hold the rod and roll the hoop along the ground; it's much trickier than it sounds.) Recalling childhood games, he began to dream up other pursuits and thus the annual contest was born. An alternative to the traditional Highland Games, sports include Tossin' the Sheaf (throwing a sheaf of corn over a high bar with a pitchfork), Hurlin' the Curlin' Stone (like a shot putt), Tug o' War, the official Gird n' Cleek World Championship, Tractor Pull and Snail Racing.

The **CatStrand Arts Centre** (High St, DG7 3RN ✆ 01644 420374 ⚲ www.catstrand.com) is the village's modern jewel in the crown. 'Strand' is an old name for a small stream, while 'Cat' was the name of the stream which ran beneath the old school, the building which was converted to house the new facility. Everything about The CatStrand is buzzing with creativity, from the small channel of stream water which runs beneath glass panels in the floor, to the sculpture of a tup (ram) in the garden made out of recycled corrugated iron from the old lean-to which stood (leaned) at the back of the building. A regular programme of music, drama and films is offered; full details are available on the website.

Balmaclellan 🖐

Neighbouring Balmaclellan (meaning 'House of McLellan' [sic]), two miles to the northeast, is smaller than New Galloway, has a village shop and enjoys eye-catching views westwards over the Rhinns of Kells from the war memorial. Balmaclellan once had links with the monks at Dundrennan (pages 181–2) through sheep farming, but is noted more often these days for the memorial in the churchyard to **Robert Paterson** (1715–1801), immortalised as Old Mortality by Sir Walter Scott in his novel of the same name. A stonemason by trade, Paterson spent the last 40 years of his life searching out unmarked graves of the Covenanters and carving their tombstones. He and his wife lived at Balmaclellan (his wife started the school here), but Robert spent much of his time away. He died in Bankend, just south of Dumfries, aged 86 and was buried in the cemetery of the church at Caerlaverock (page 121).

"In the churchyard is a memorial to Robert Paterson, immortalised as Old Mortality by Sir Walter Scott in his novel of the same name."

🍴 FOOD & DRINK

The CatStrand High St, New Galloway DG7 3RN ✆ 01644 420374 ⚲ www.catstrand.com. A light and airy café at the back of the arts centre building, offering sandwiches, salads and home baking. Internet access also available.

The Smithy Tea Room and Craft Shop High St, New Galloway DG7 3RN ✆ 01644 420269 ⚲ www.thesmithy-newgalloway.co.uk ⊙ closed Nov–Feb. Marion and David Briggs run a popular tea room right next to the Mill Burn in the heart of New Galloway. Homemade soups and beef burgers, home-cooked ham, sandwiches and baked potatoes, and a tempting array of home baking. Indoor seating and outdoor tables by the burn.

LOCH KEN

Loch Ken stretches southwards for nine miles, fed by the Water of Ken from the north and the River Dee (also known as Black Water of Dee) from the west. Part of the Galloway Hydroelectric Scheme, the loch is a Ramsar area, included in the list of sites on the Ramsar Convention designed to protect wetlands (named after the city of Ramsar in Iran, where the convention was signed in 1971). A section of the loch has also been designated an Environmentally Sensitive Area and the habitats here support internationally important roosting numbers of Greenland white-fronted geese and Icelandic grey geese. The loch is also popular for its watersports and on its shores and in the surrounding area are a number of attractive villages worth exploring.

Kenmure Castle

♀ NX635764

If we ever win the Lottery, Kenmure Castle could make for an exciting renovation project. We wouldn't be the first to try, for in the 1950s it was a hotel. What's left of this imposing mansion house is a very curious mix of ancient and modern, consisting of a roofless shell of 17th-century stonework ornamented by the trappings of a more modern age such as TV aerial and external connection point for telephone wires.

Situated around one mile south of New Galloway, Kenmure can only be approached on foot. Head down the A762 and just after a row of white cottages, park by a five-bar gate on the left-hand side, from where the way in is through the gate and down the avenue of trees. Kenmure sits raised up on what looks like a motte or manmade mound, though it is in fact partly natural, and seen from below at first sight has the appearance of a fortress. It doesn't help that the original stonework has been covered on the outside by grey harle, lending it a somewhat sinister mien. It is, perhaps, not unfitting as the site is said to have been occupied by a defensive structure of the Lords of Galloway.

John Balliol, husband of Galloway's good Lady Devorgilla (page 110) was born here in 1249, while in later years Kenmure became the seat of the Gordon family of Lochinvar (page 136). In the 19th century it was one of the Kenmure Gordons who moved to America where he acquired in the state of Virginia a plantation house which had been built by the sister of George Washington and her husband. In tribute to his home he renamed it Kenmore.

Today's ruinous building is the sort of place you want to dive into and explore. Do be warned, though, that much of the building has collapsed and by all accounts more of it may follow. Entrance is at your own risk.

Surrounding the castle is what would have once been parkland with some fine trees and a walled garden, now completely overgrown. It is an atmospheric and moody place, both enchanting and austere.

The east side of Loch Ken

🏠 **Galloway Activity Centre** (page 247), ⚓ **Loch Ken Holiday Park** (page 248)

Courses in all manner of watersports are offered at the **Galloway Activity Centre** (Near Parton DG7 3NQ ♀ NX657735 ☏ 01644 420626 ⊘ www.lochken.co.uk) on the east shore. Alternatively, if you're an experienced hand you can hire equipment for your own use. There's also a **café** and an interesting range of accommodation (page 247).

Waterskiing and wakeboarding are run from Loch Ken Marina a mile or so further south, out of which the **Loch Ken Waterski and Wakeboard School** (Parton DG7 3NF ☏ 01644 4670333 ⊘ www.skilochken.co.uk) operates. Immediately south of the marina is the Glenlaggan Loch Ken information point, with a noticeboard giving information about the **Red Kite Trail**, parking and access to the pebbly shore of the loch, a pleasant spot for a picnic.

"Parton is home to one of the region's quirkiest listed buildings, the Parton Privy."

The hamlet of **Parton** was built in 1901 as an estate village for Parton House (now demolished) and consists of a cute row of black-and-white, Arts and Crafts style cottages with a church at one end. It still wears its motto proudly and *Floreat Partona* ('Let Parton Flourish') is proclaimed above the door to the village hall. Parton is home to one of the region's quirkiest listed buildings, the **Parton Privy**, an octagonal building housing the communal toilets for the cottages. Not so long ago one of the loos was still open for viewing, complete with visitors' book! Today the privy stands in a private garden behind the cottages and is not open to the public but can be seen from the road.

In the **churchyard** at Parton is a monument to the physicist **James Clerk Maxwell** who is buried here. His family home, Glenlair, lies a short distance to the northeast, near Corsock. Maxwell is credited with one of the most significant discoveries of the modern age, the theory of electromagnetism, and his work received plaudits from many notable scientists, including Albert Einstein. **Glenlair House** (Knockvennie DG7 3DF ✆ 01556 650209 🖰 www.glenair.org.uk) 🖐 has a small visitor centre dedicated to Maxwell which is open by appointment.

The village of **Corsock** sits in rolling countryside and is home to what sounds to modern ears like a contradiction in terms, an 18th-century **Temperance Inn** (now private) near the bridge. Immediately south of the village is **Corsock House** (DG7 3DJ ✆ 01644 440250 🖰 www. scotlandgardens.org), part of the Scotland's Gardens scheme.

The west side of Loch Ken

At **Glenlochar** the waters of Loch Ken flow southwards as the River Dee. A barrage here controls the flow of water and a bridge crosses the river. **Balmaghie Church** (♀ NX723664) is found about 1½ miles up the west side of the loch. Built on a slight rise, the church of 1794 has a lovely position with delightful views up the loch and to Crossmichael on the other side. In the churchyard is an early 18th-century table stone commemorating two Covenanting martyrs and the grave of **S R Crockett** (1859–1914), novelist, who was born in the parish at Duchrae. Another mile or so beyond the church lies the **RSPB Ken Dee Marshes** (♀ NX699685), where the River Dee meets Loch Ken. Come and enjoy the wetland here which supports a range of birds, wildlife and plants, including nuthatches, elusive willow tits and red squirrels.

"RSPB Ken Dee Marshes supports a range of birds, wildlife and plants, including nuthatches, elusive willow tits and red squirrels.

The endearing village of **Laurieston** to the southwest is known for its **Red Kite Feeding Station** (Bellymack Hill Farm, DG7 2PJ ♀ NX688652 ✆ 01556 670464 🖰 www.gallowaykitetrail.com), a good place to see these impressive birds. There is daily feeding at 14.00.

Laurieston is also home to photographer Phil McMenemy, who is always happy to welcome visitors to **The Gallery at Laurieston** (Woodbank House, DG7 2PW ✆ 01644 450235) to view his work, have a cup of tea and a natter. It can be found on the Gatehouse Road, immediately west of the crossroads. Phil was awarded Visual Artist of the Year 2013 by local magazine *Dumfries & Galloway Life* and has also worked and published a book with popular artist Julie Dumbarton from Langholm in the east of the region (page 60). His images, printed on a range of materials, including aluminium and wood, are increasingly sought after, can be spotted in various places around the region, and have been exhibited internationally.

Tom van Rooyen's **Earth's Crust Bakery** (The Croft DG7 2PW ✐ 01644 450624) is in Laurieston, too. Tom grew up on a Dumfries and Galloway smallholding and, after travelling and working abroad, returned to the area. In 2011 he set up his bakery, from where he now offers several bread-baking courses. As he only bakes on certain days, if you wish to visit please telephone in advance and make an appointment rather than just stopping in.

At the northern end of the village, on a rise above the road, stands a **memorial to S R Crockett**. From Laurieston the B795 runs back to Glenlochar, offering a good view of Threave Castle (pages 150–1) to the south along the way. Alternatively, the minor road heading west through Laurieston Forest is a memorable way to approach Gatehouse of Fleet (pages 158–61), with superb views down to Fleet Bay and, on a clear day, beyond to the Isle of Man and the Machars.

GALLOWAY FOREST PARK

The most comprehensive source of information is the Forestry Commission Scotland website ✐ www.scotland.forestry.gov.uk, which details access points, activities, viewpoints, memorials & visitor centres; parking is charged at the visitor centres, but not at the smaller parking areas elsewhere in the forest.

Established in 1947, at 300 square miles Galloway Forest Park is Britain's largest. Sometimes referred to as 'the Highlands of the Lowlands' it encompasses some of the region's most dramatic scenery and the highest peak of the Southern Uplands, Merrick (2,766 feet), part of the range of 'The Awful Hand', so-called because of its resemblance to the fingers of a hand. No matter what sort of outdoor pursuits you're looking for, there's every chance you will find it here. Notable are the **7stanes mountain biking centres** at Glentrool and Kirroughtree.

The park has a particular reputation as the first **Dark Sky Park** in the UK. Galloway has some of the darkest skies in Europe with a resident population so small that light pollution is minimal. Over 7,000 stars and planets are visible with the naked eye from here and the nightly show changes constantly as the seasons pass. On the Sky Quality Meter scale, the night sky of the park scores between 21 and 23.6. The scale runs from 0 to 25 and in the middle of a major city the reading would be around 8, while in a photographer's dark room it would be 24. This really is the place to come for some uninterrupted star-gazing.

It has to be said that plantation forests *per se* don't usually excite us, but the effort and creative thinking that has gone into Galloway Forest Park is striking. Not only are there three worthwhile **visitor centres** (at Clatteringshaws, Glentrool and Kirroughtree, further details of all of which are given below and on pages 145 and 146), but Forestry Commission Scotland is actively involved in developing its assets for local enjoyment, often working in partnership with local community and arts initiatives to enhance the natural environment. **Sculptures** are positioned around the forest, for example, and parts of the forest have also been used for experimental **music and light installations**. Keep an eye on the website to see what is going on when you are here.

For a full daytime experience of the park, head out along the **Raiders' Road Forest Drive**, which for most of its way follows an old drove road featured in the book *The Raiders* by local author S R Crockett. This ten-mile track runs through the forest from the west side of Loch Ken to Clatteringshaws, passing Stroan Loch and viaduct along the way. Further along, about halfway, is the **Otter Pool**, a lovely riverside picnic spot (with toilets).

For grand views and an eclectic range of attractions, the A712 from New Galloway to Newton Stewart, known as the **Queen's Road**, makes for a fine leisurely amble. All points of interest are detailed on OS maps of the area, and they are mentioned below running east to west.

4 CLATTERINGSHAWS LOCH & VISITOR CENTRE

 NX552764 01644 420285 Mar–Nov

Overlooking Clatteringshaws Loch, with views on a clear day of Merrick, the visitor centre is good for birdwatching in the summer and it's also a short stroll from here to the site of one of two **Bruce's Stones** (the other is at Glentrool, page 145). The loch was created in 1934 by the construction of a dam across the River Dee to flood adjacent marshland as part of the Galloway Hydroelectric Scheme. The visitor centre offers information and a café, complete with wood-burning stove for cooler days. Look out on the path to Bruce's Stone for the surfboard-like plinths set to one side of the trees. Try them out: lie down on them and gaze upwards. Even a bit of daytime sky-watching has its rewards.

5 RED DEER RANGE & WILD GOAT PARK

The Red Deer Range (♀ NX521731) is a purpose-built hide from which to view red deer. The best time to see them is between April and October. In autumn listen out for the roar of the stags at the start of the rut.

Up a dirt track on the right hand side of the road between the deer range and Wild Goat Park is the **Black Loch** and **the Eye sculpture**. You can't miss the Eye, a 25-foot conical terracotta obelisk, so-called because of a hole that runs through the middle of it at eye height.

Beyond the track to Black Loch, a couple of miles on from the Red Deer Range is **Wild Goat Park**, where wild goats roam on a hillside of craggy rock. Park up and the chances are they will make their way down pretty quickly to see you in the hope of a snack. Please note the request not to feed them bread, vegetables are preferred!

MURRAY'S MONUMENT & THE GREY MARE'S TAIL

Clearly visible from the road below, the monument (♀ NX487718) commemorates **Alexander Murray** (1775–1813), son of a local shepherd who despite his humble beginnings became a professor of Oriental Languages at Edinburgh University. His simple cottage can be visited, and you can also walk to a viewpoint for the **Grey Mare's Tail waterfall** (not to be confused with one of the same name just outside Moffat; see page 39).

6 GLENTROOL VISITOR CENTRE ✋

♀ NX372786 ✎ 01671 840302 ◷ Mar–Nov

North of the A712 and towards the west side of the park, **Glentrool** has been described as the centre of the Galloway Highlands. Access is via the A714 from Newton Stewart, then turn off at Bargrennan to reach the **Glentrool Visitor Centre**, a welcoming cabin in a lovely spot in the heart of the forest at the Black Linn (falls or pool) on the banks of the Water of Minnoch. In the car park is a nifty sign showing different views of the night sky and from here you can either walk or drive the three-mile forest track to **Bruce's Stone**, set high above Loch Trool with superlative views all round, from where a track up Merrick can be followed. It was from the Glentrool area that Bruce launched the campaign which culminated in Bannockburn, and it was also in this area that John Buchan set much of *The Thirty Nine Steps*.

7 KIRROUGHTREE VISITOR CENTRE

♀ NX452646 ☎ 01671 402165 ⊙ Apr–Oct

At the southern end of the park, Kirroughtree Visitor Centre offers a different experience again. Accessed off the A75 east of Newton Stewart (page 192), the sign on the main road says it's half a mile, but in fact it's exactly one mile up the lane to reach the turn-off to the left up to the visitor centre. The centre is big, bright and airy, with information at one end and a café and bike hire at the other. It was built using local stone and larch, has been designed so that no light escapes into the night sky, and is heated using geothermal energy from deep underground. There's a good kids section with nature snippets such as blue tits are known as blue bunnets (bunnet means cap or bonnet) and the Scots pine tree is known as the Bunnet Tree because of its distinctive shape. This is a **7stanes** centre, too, and **bike hire** (page 133) is available.

> *"Kirroughtree Visitor Centre has been designed so that no light escapes into the night sky, and is heated using geothermal energy from deep underground."*

▯▮ FOOD & DRINK

All three visitor centres offer hearty fare but in very different settings. **Glentrool** is the smallest, more like a log cabin on the banks of the river, while **Clatteringshaws** has a lovely lochside setting. Further south, the café at **Kirroughtree Visitor Centre** is larger and is in a new purpose-built chalet-style cabin with glass windows along one wall beyond which there is seating on the decking for warm days. Sitting here in the sun the whole place feels almost alpine, with views through the trees towards Cairnsmore of Fleet.

House O' Hill Hotel Bargrennan (on the west side of the park) DG8 6RN ☎ 01671 840243. The reasonably priced seasonal menu consistently finds favour with both locals and visitors, and is generally regarded as the best in the area. The owners, Helen, Karen and Daniel, took over the hotel in 2010 and have put their all into making it the place it is today.

CASTLE DOUGLAS & THE EAST STEWARTRY

Local food specialities, beaches, a plethora of history and a wonderful rolling landscape characterise this part of the region, much of which lies within the **East Stewartry Coast National Scenic Area**. If you're arriving from the east you may prefer to avoid the A75 and take advantage of the quieter **Old Military Road** of the 18th century, built by General Wade's successor, Major Caulfeild, to assist in the passage of troops to Ireland. Alternatively, a little further south the A711 runs through some pretty country and skirts **Kirkgunzeon**, with its mighty obelisk in the churchyard, almost taller than the church itself.

If coming from the west, you can detour off the A75 up to **Barstobrick** just north of Ringford, where you can walk up to Neilson's Monument and enjoy the views of the surrounding countryside from the top. This striking pyramid was erected in 1883 to commemorate James Beaumont Neilson, who invented the 'hot blast' process of smelting iron.

8 CASTLE DOUGLAS

🏠 **Douglas House** (page 247), **Gelston Castle Holidays** (page 247), **Orroland Holiday Cottages** (page 248) ⛺ **Lochside Caravan and Camping** (page 248)

Galloway has long been known for its independent spirit and one of the places where that spirit continues to be championed is Castle Douglas. This small market town has bucked the trend of recent years and retained its position as a bustling centre at the heart of local, commercial and agricultural life. A seasonal **tourist information centre** (page 133) operates from its office in the main public car park at the top of end of town, where there are also local and regional information boards.

Castle Douglas's history is long, as is testified by the **Carlingwark hoard**, a cauldron filled with ancient artefacts that was brought up in 1868 by two men fishing in Carlingwark Loch at the southwest end of town (now a good spot for birdwatching). Dating from the 1st or 2nd century AD, many of the items are now exhibited in the National Museum of Scotland in Edinburgh.

"In the Middle Ages Castle Douglas was the domain of the so-called Black Douglases, noble earls and Lords of Galloway."

In the Middle Ages Castle Douglas was the domain of the so-called Black Douglases, noble earls and Lords of Galloway, whose mighty Threave Castle (pages 150–1) nearby was the main administrative centre until their demise. Despite the association with the Black Douglases, the town was named for and by a Douglas of a different ilk altogether. William Douglas was a pedlar from Penninghame in the Machars, whose fortune was made in what were most likely dubious trades in Virginia before he returned to Scotland to indulge his ego. First he tried,

THE DIFFERENCE BETWEEN A KEG & A CASK 👆

Sulwath Brewers Ltd 209 King St, DG7 1DT ☏ 01556 504525 ⬧ www.sulwathbrewers. co.uk ⊙ closed Sun; entrance is down the alleyway between Carlo's restaurant & 215 King St.

Having handed over the day-to-day running of the business to his son Allan, Jim Henderson is usually on hand to welcome visitors to Sulwath Brewers Ltd. Convivial, canny and courteous, 'I blame my mother-in-law for the fact I turned to drink' he says with a smile. It was while visiting his wife's family in the Malvern Hills that he was smitten by the pubs serving ale made from local hops.

In 1995 he set up Sulwath Brewers, operating from 'cousin Bob's dairy farm' near Southerness. The business soon outgrew the space, so Jim relocated to Castle Douglas, to what had previously been a baker's premises, and since then it has gone from strength to strength (3.5% to 5.5%, but no pun intended) and now turns out around 8,000 bottles a year.

You can pop in at any time to sample the beer, or to have a pint and a pie (the latter supplied by another Henderson, one of the local butchers).

Tours of the brewery run on weekdays at 13.00 and include the main working area, all gleaming steel and malty aromas. Draft and bottled beers are on sale, including gift packs of mixed bottles. Jim is an expert guide, full of facts, figures, terminology and snippets of brewing trivia. If, like me, you don't know the difference between a keg and a cask before you go in, you will by the time you come out.

and failed, at Newton Stewart (page 190) before turning his attention eastwards, where he re-christened Carlingwark as Castle Douglas, laid out the town in its current grid pattern, and built himself a somewhat fanciful turreted castle at nearby Gelston. His **mausoleum** (⚲ NX758603) is just outside Castle Douglas to the south, a short distance beyond the gates to Threave Gardens. It was built by his nephew who inherited the estate, and is a fitting tribute for a man who has become known for his trademark grandiloquence. A strange, squat bunker with pagoda-like roof, it looks like something out of an episode of *Dr Who*, sitting in a woodland clearing and providing eternal shelter for not just Sir William but 24 other family members, too.

There has been a **cattle market** in Castle Douglas since 1819 and it still operates today, run by Wallets Marts, the main local employer, at the top end of Queen Street. Come on a Tuesday to see the weekly livestock sale or on one of the other dates publicised online (⬧ www.walletsmarts. co.uk) for cattle sales.

In more recent years Castle Douglas has worked hard to establish itself as the **Food Town** of Dumfries and Galloway, an initiative which got fully underway in 2002 and which since then has successfully built a reputation that is known not just locally but well beyond the region for its range and quality of local produce. Despite the opening of Tesco, **King Street** is one of the best high streets in the region for independent shops. Down the length of it can be found delicatessens, a wholefood shop with enough loose-leaf teas to satisfy the most discerning connoisseurs, a traditional sweet shop, bakers, a greengrocer, not one but two chocolatiers and not one but three, yes *three*, butchers. There are also cafés, sandwich bars, new and secondhand book shops, antiques and bric-a-brac shops, gift shops, galleries and art shops, traditional tweedy outfitters, jewellers and craft shops. There's even a traditional clockmaker with a striking model clock on the wall outside at No 71. For a town with a population of around 4,000 people, it's an impressive list. To top it off, Castle Douglas also boasts its own **independent brewery** on the High Street (see box, opposite). Full details of all the local shops can be found on the comprehensive website, ⊘ www.cd-foodtown.org.

¶¶ FOOD & DRINK

For something a little different and superb cooking, reserve a space at **Craigadam** near Kirkpatrick Durham, a 15-minute drive east of Castle Douglas (page 152).

Carlo's 211 King St, DG7 1DT ✆ 01556 503977 ⊘ www.carlosrestaurant.co.uk. Described as a 'real' Italian and 'the best Italian in the southwest' by one restaurant reviewer. The restaurant itself is relatively small, the menu not extensive (this is no typical trattoria: pizzas don't feature!) but the quality and atmosphere are good.

Designs Gallery & Café 179 King St, DG7 1DZ ✆ 01556 504552 ⊘ www.designsgallery. co.uk. Offers an appealing mix of gallery, gifts, garden and café serving coffees, speciality teas, home-baked organic bread, cakes and sandwiches. Specials and homemade soup are on the menu every day.

Street Lights Coffee House and Bistro 187 King St, DG7 1DZ ✆ 01556 504222. Has a wide-ranging menu, from haggis panini to bacon rolls, from falafel and chargrilled veg to hummus and halloumi.

Moore's Fish and Chips 254 King St, DG7 1HA ✆ 01556 502347 ⊘ www.mooresfishandchips. co.uk. Since June 1977, the Moore family have been serving up haddock, scampi, prawns and a whole lot more besides, including build-your-own pizza. Most of their fish comes from the North Sea and every day their fish buyer visits the fish market at Peterhead up beyond Aberdeen on the east coast. Moore's regularly wins awards for the best 'chippy' in Scotland.

THREAVE CASTLE & ESTATE

Threave Castle and Threave Estate are two separate but connected sites. The former, northwest of Castle Douglas, lies on land owned by the National Trust for Scotland but is run by Historic Scotland. The latter, southwest of Castle Douglas, is purely National Trust for Scotland; in fact it's one of their top ten attractions. Both were acquired in 1867 by Liverpool businessman William Gordon and were subsequently passed to the National Trust for Scotland by his grandson in 1948.

"Threave Castle and Threave Estate are two separate but connected sites acquired in 1867 by Liverpool businessman William Gordon."

On an island in the River Dee stands the forbidding **Threave Castle** (DG7 1TJ ♀ NX739623 ☉ seasonal; Historic Scotland; free entry for members). 'High, sombre and – despite its ruinous state – magnificent in its attitude of aggressive medieval power' as one guidebook writer of old describes it, it was built in 1369 for Sir Archibald Douglas, Lord of Galloway, commonly known as Archibald the Grim. He died at Threave on Christmas Eve in 1400.

Threave Castle was the seat of the 'Black Douglases', who by the mid 15th century had established a stranglehold on power. James II spent much of his reign trying to break the Douglases and in 1455 laid siege to Threave, gaining entry after two months but only after bribing the garrison. Threave was – and is – a formidable structure, with walls almost 100 feet high and ten feet thick. Depending on which story you wish to believe, it is said that James II had the enormous cannon, Mons Meg (now at Edinburgh Castle), forged in Castle Douglas for the attack on Threave.

One of the modern-day delights of a visit to Threave Castle is its accessibility, or rather its inaccessibility. The only way to reach it is by rowing boat from the jetty on the banks of the Dee. If the boat isn't there, ring the bell and wait for the boatman to return from the other side.

Threave Estate (DG7 1RX ♀ NX755605 ✆ 0844 493 2245; National Trust for Scotland; free entry for members) consists of four areas: the house, gardens, sculpture garden and nature reserve. William Gordon built Threave House towards the top of the gardens with good views. Access to the house is by guided tour only; parts of it are now used as flats for students, while the rest has been restored and furnished in 1930s style.

The **gardens** at Threave are a delight. Even if you're not particularly green-fingered, there's a blackboard in the visitor centre on which helpful notes are written with suggestions of what to look for depending on the time of the year. There are glasshouses, a sculpture garden, nature reserve, a walled garden and various themed garden rooms, including a secret garden, rhododendron garden and a rose terrace. Threave is particularly popular in spring for its specialist and extensive range of daffodils.

Wildlife plays a significant role on the estate. **Ospreys** have been a feature for several years, either passing through or nesting, notably down near Threave Castle on the banks of the Dee. There are five bird hides along the river and marshes. Since 2010, Threave has also been the location of Scotland's first reserve especially for **bats**, with more species found here than anywhere else in Scotland, including the rare whiskered bat.

THE LOWER URR VALLEY

🏠 **Craigadam Country House Hotel and B&B** (page 247)

The River Urr rises at Loch Urr near Moniaive in Nithsdale and flows for 35 miles down to the Solway at Kippford in the Stewartry. A meander down its lower reaches through the Stewartry makes for a leisurely sojourn.

THE KING'S MOUNT

📍 NX815647

Motte of Urr is also known as The King's Mount, a name which has its roots in a far-fetched story which is nonetheless good for the telling. The story goes that at this site Robert the Bruce fought an English knight and was aided in his battle by the wife of Mark Sprotte, who lived on the motte. Madame Sprotte, seeing that Bruce was in danger, plunged into the affray and brought the knight to his knees. Not wishing to take advantage, Bruce sheathed his sword and the gentlemen retired. Mrs Sprotte then served up a bowl of porridge to Bruce but offered none to the knight, refusing to serve an Englishman in her house. To defuse the situation, Bruce told her that he would grant to her all the land she could cover while he ate his porridge. The lady duly went out and Bruce shared his porridge, with one spoon, with the knight.

As unlikely as the story may seem, it has been noted that the Sprottes held the lands of the motte for 500 years, on condition that a bowl of porridge should be served to any Scots monarch that happened to be in the area. (One observer has commented wryly that perhaps this accounts for the fact that there have been relatively few royal visitors to Galloway.)

Kirkpatrick Durham lies slightly to the east of the river and, like many local parishes, has a 19th-century church built by Dumfries architect Walter Newall, who also designed nearby Glenlair (page 142). In the **graveyard** there is a stone to the wife of Covenanter John Neilson of Corsock Castle, who gave refuge to Gabriel Simple, the minister of Kirkpatrick Durham, when he was driven from his church. Semple's preaching at nearby Corsock (page 142) is said to have been the start of field preachings or Conventicles. Neilson himself was hanged at the Mercat Cross in Edinburgh.

"Kirkpatrick Durham has a 19th-century church built by Dumfries architect Walter Newall."

A couple of miles south, the River Urr tumbles down the rocks at **Old Bridge of Urr**, where the village nestles in the hollow of the valley. From here it flows southeast to **Haugh of Urr** and on past the eastern edge of the remains of the **Mote of Urr**. One of the most impressive in Scotland, the motte was built in the mid 12th century, destroyed in 1174 and then rebuilt six feet higher. The spacious bailey is ringed by a mighty ditch, about eight feet deep and almost 50 feet wide and the summit is 85 feet above the river. This is a real hum-dinger of a motte, a magnificent earthwork.

¶¶ FOOD & DRINK

Craigadam near Kirkpatrick Durham DG7 3HU ☎ 01556 650233 ⊘ www.craigadam.com. A 15-minute drive east of Castle Douglas, Craigadam is quite special and offers something a little bit different. Celia and Richard Pickup run a country-house-style B&B from their traditional Galloway farmhouse and non-resident guests are welcome to book for dinner, which is taken family-style around the large table in the wood-panelled dining room. Much of the food comes from their own farm or within a few miles of it and the cooking is superb.

9 Dalbeattie

Dalbeattie has had a tough time over the years but keeps bouncing back. Originally planned in the 1790s, the town came alive when local man Andrew Newall started quarrying on a small scale. It wasn't until the early 19th century though that the serious business got underway when the **Craignure quarry** came into operation, yielding up its granite which was shipped so far and wide that it became renowned the world over. Stone from here was used in the base of the Eddystone lighthouse and in the construction of Sydney harbour. Ironically, the one project it wasn't used in was the construction of its own bridge across the Urr, which was built from stone brought in from Kirkgunzeon (page 147).

Despite being six miles from the sea, the Urr is tidal as far as Dalbeattie and at that time there was a thriving port just to the west. Ships were walked up the Urr pulled by horses to deposit their goods and pick up cargo from the busy industrial town. It was a canny operation, an early example of recycling with rags, bones and scrap metal brought in by ship to be transformed by local mills into brown paper, shovels, ploughs and fertiliser. Dalbeattie folk didn't miss a trick and groceries, too, came in by boat, used as ballast. The port today is no longer used and had fallen into disrepair, but thanks to the work of the Dalbeattie Community Initiative various improvements have been made, interpretation boards installed and access opened up.

"Despite being six miles from the sea, the Urr is tidal as far as Dalbeattie."

Dalbeattie Museum (81 High St, DG5 4BS ✆ 01556 611657 ⌂ www. dalbeattiemuseum.co.uk ⊙ seasonal) tells the town's story in fuller detail and is one of those irresistible local museums that is packed with all manner of intriguing artefacts. Tommy Henderson started the museum in 1993 having been inspired by the determined Miss Drew (see box, page 191) from Newton Stewart. Dalbeattie born and bred, there's not much that Tommy doesn't know about the town, and he and his trusty team of volunteers make terrific hosts for anyone visiting the museum. Exhibits include a collection of artificial glass eyes, a piece of the Enigma machine donated by a Dumfriesshire lady who worked at Bletchley, paintings by local artist Jim Sturgeon, who was known as the 'Galloway Colourist', and a couple of model churches made from icing sugar (not for eating, you understand). There are also a number of items relating to Dalbeattie's most famous son, William McMaster Murdoch, First Officer of the *Titanic*.

While in Dalbeattie, pop in to **The Nail Factory** (56 Southwick Rd, DG5 4EW ✆ 01556 611686 ⌂ www.nailfactory.org.uk ⊙ daily during exhibitions), which was once (200–300 years ago, it is believed) exactly that, but which today provides a sympathetic space for an ongoing programme of exhibitions for up-and-coming artists.

South of town lies **Dalbeattie Forest**, one of the **7stanes mountain biking centres**, from where the six-mile **Colvend Trail** offers a route for both walkers and cyclists to the coastal community of Kippford (pages 155–6).

FOOD & DRINK

The Granite Kitchen 62a High St, DG5 4AA 🕿 01556 610361. Offers the Dalbeattie take on traditional dishes such as ploughman's ('quarryman's') and a classic hamburger ('the slab'). In addition to good Scottish fare, French and Spanish/Basque dishes also make an appearance.

From Dalbeattie to the coast

Much of the area around Dalbeattie falls within the parish of **Buittle** (pronounced 'Bittle') 🖐, notable for its historic connection with John Balliol under whose control it came through his wife, Lady Devorgilla (page 110), who is said to have financed the building of the now ruined **Buittle Old Church** (♀ NX808598).

A couple of miles south of Buittle is the village of **Palnackie**, home to the very curious annual **World Flounder Tramping Championship**, in which competitors, who number in the hundreds, tramp through the mud looking for flounders. At the bottom of the village is the still working old **harbour basin**, while from the minor road south to Glen Isle there are good views high above the Urr estuary. Within the village are a popular pub and restaurant (see opposite).

"South of Buittle is the village of Palnackie, home to the annual World Flounder Tramping Championship."

At **Glen Isle**, there are walking trails in Forestry Commission Scotland's **Tornat Wood**, where a plan is afoot to restore large areas of the forest to native broadleaved species. Keep heading down the track from here and you reach the shoreline at Glen Isle, an enchanting spot, little frequented, with superb views across to Kippford, out to Rough Island and beyond to the Lake District.

South of Palnackie is the imposing and unique mid 15th-century **Orchardton Tower** (♀ NX817552; Historic Scotland; free entry), the only circular laird's tower house built in late-medieval Scotland. Much of it is intact and you can climb all the way to the top to enjoy the views (mind your head on the low doorway at the top).

Beyond Orchardton to the south at the end of the peninsula is **Almorness Point**. This private land can be accessed on foot if you leave your car at the parking area at the gate to Almorness House. It's a 4½-mile **walk** around the point, with superb coastal views and a bay of fine white sand.

¶¶ FOOD & DRINK

Glenisle Inn Port Rd, Palnackie DG7 1PG ✎ 01556 600429 🖧 www.glenisleinn.co.uk ⊙ seasonal. Appropriately for Palnackie, flounder is often on the menu. The Glenisle has also teamed up with local butcher Griersons to offer a fine selection of locally sourced dishes.

The Willow Tree Glen Rd, Palnackie DG7 1PH ✎ 01556 600092 🖧 www. thewillowtreepalnackie.co.uk ⊙ closed Mon. Cheryl Radwell took over The Willow Tree in 2014 having spent three years working at the Balcary Hotel nearby. This is a wee place with a big reputation for food, from traditional breakfasts to evening meals that might include parmesan panna cotta, scallops and sea bass on lemon risotto. Good value in a fun bistro-style setting with some impressive wickerwork.

THE COLVEND COAST

If Scotland were on the Mediterranean, the Colvend Coast is what it would look like. This stretch of shoreline from south of Dalbeattie eastwards to Mersehead (page 129) is the most developed part of all of Dumfries and Galloway's 200 miles of coastline, but unlike the worst excesses of the Med, here there is very little of the uncontrolled sprawl of modern holiday resorts. For more than 75 years part of this coast has been in the care of the National Trust for Scotland and, despite the high number of visitors, there is still a timeless quality to much of it. I have memories of building sandcastles here over 40 years ago and – notwithstanding rose-tinted glasses and a few more people – not that much has changed.

South of Palnackie the Urr Water broadens out where river meets Solway, with a long thin peninsula to the west, flat and sandy, and a rocky coastline to the east. North of Palnackie, cross the Urr at Dalbeattie and head south again to reach first Kippford and then Rockcliffe, both enchanting coastal villages in their own right, but quite different in feel.

10 Kippford

Kippford harbour was used in the early 18th century to accommodate large ships at the most northerly navigable point of the Urr. A boat-building industry subsequently developed but in time the village became more of a tourist retreat than a centre of industry. Today, it is a busy and popular holiday spot, good as a base (especially in the quieter low season) or for a day visit. The beach at the southern end can look positively tropical when covered in gleaming white shells, and a couple of pubs, a café and a village store can be found on the waterfront.

From Kippford the **Jubilee Path** runs over the hill to Rockcliffe, offering splendid views over the Urr estuary and the Solway, known here where they meet as **Rough Firth**. There are two paths, a lower one and an upper one. Take one in one direction and the other coming back. There's also a detour off the path to the **Mote of Mark** on the summit of a hill above Rockcliffe, from where the views are even better. This early Dark Age fort or citadel is believed to have been the seat of a powerful chieftain in the 5th and 6th centuries before being destroyed by fire in the 7th century. Keep an eye open for adders as they are known to be here, and are sometimes seen lying in the sun on a warm day. The route is covered in daffodils and gorse in spring, with wild garlic and bluebells also making an appearance. There's plenty of birdlife (we've spotted the migratory chiff-chaff here), gardens are full of rhododendrons and moss-covered walls mark the edge of mixed deciduous woodland.

"The route is covered in daffodils and gorse in spring, with wild garlic and bluebells also making an appearance. There's plenty of birdlife too (we've spotted the migratory chiff-chaff here)."

Rockcliffe

No matter how busy the beach, the small village of Rockcliffe is one of the prettiest in Dumfries and Galloway, and even in the height of season somehow retains its air of gentility. With its rocky bay, Victorian villas and cottages, and lush gardens and lawns, it has an almost exotic atmosphere. Offshore lies **Rough Island** (National Trust for Scotland), a 20-acre bird sanctuary, home to oystercatchers and ringed plovers. It can be reached on foot at low tide but do check the tide times (the website of the Solway Firth Partnership includes links to tide times for specific locations; ⊘ www.solwayfirthpartnership.co.uk) before setting out and it is requested that you avoid the island in May and June to prevent disturbance during the breeding season.

In addition to the Jubilee Path walk, there is also a four-mile **coastal walk** northeastwards from Rockcliffe to Sandyhills over more challenging terrain, details of which are given on the noticeboard in the parking area at the top of the village. Incidentally, if you drive to Rockcliffe, parking in the official area is advised as space along the waterfront is very limited.

The A710 runs parallel to the coast, passing through the village of **Colvend** with its shop and café, and on to the RSPB reserve at Mersehead (page 129). Various minor roads drop down to the shoreline, which is celebrated here for the many coves, inlets and rock formations with evocative names: Gutcher's Isle, Cow's Snout, Gillis Craig… and further on towards Balcary (page 182) the natural arch of the Needle's Eye.

¶¶ FOOD & DRINK

The Anchor Hotel Kippford DG5 4LN ✆ 01556 620205 ◈ www.anchorhotelkippford.co.uk. On the banks of the Urr estuary, this inn with a public bar and a smarter lounge bar for food, plus outdoor tables, is popular with both locals and visitors. There are a mix of staples on offer such as steak and Criffell Ale pie and fish and chips, as well as specialities such as the chef's seafood chowder with prawns, clams, smoked haddock and mussels. Dogs are allowed in the bar and snug, where there's an open fire in winter.

The Garden Room The Brae, Rockcliffe DG5 4QG ✆ 01556 630402. Rose Vernon moved to Rockcliffe 25 years ago from Norfolk to her traditional house on the road down into the village, the lower floor of which she opens as a café, plus a shop selling a small but very perfectly formed range of antiques. Teas, coffees and homemade baking are offered at outdoor tables only in her suntrap of a back garden. It's a pretty spot, and a convenient one too as it's located right next to the public car park. Generally open five days a week, but it can depend on what else is going on. From the front of the house there is often a selection of cans of drink and home-baked treats on offer, complete with honesty box for payment.

GATEHOUSE OF FLEET & THE WEST STEWARTRY

The western end of the Stewartry is dominated by Cairnsmore of Fleet, at 2,333 feet the most southerly Graham in Scotland. (A Graham is a peak between 2,000 and 2,499 feet, named after Fiona Torbet, née Graham, who published her own list of them in the 1990s.) Cairnsmore lies at the heart of its eponymous national nature reserve (see ◈ www.nnr-scotland.org.uk for more information). Travellers are spoiled for choice in this area when it comes to choosing routes, since the two minor roads that cut across the lower slopes of Cairnsmore to Creetown also traverse the Fleet Valley National Scenic Area, designated as such over 20 years ago for its outstanding beauty and to protect it as part of Scotland's heritage. The coast road offers panoramic views to Wigtown Bay.

11 GATEHOUSE OF FLEET & AROUND 🖐

🏠 **Cally Palace Hotel** (page 247), **The Ship Inn** (page 247) ⛺ **Sandgreen Caravan Park** (page 248)

There is a pleasing neatness and quietude about Gatehouse that always leaves us feeling content. It may be its wide main street lined with painted cottages, or the fact that even when busy it's still imbued with an air of calm gentility. Or it could just be its setting, cosily enveloped within the hills on the banks of the Fleet. Suffice to say, it is a delightful place to while away a few hours or as a base for exploring the surrounding area. You may wish to make use of the good local website, ⊘ www.gatehouse-of-fleet.co.uk.

The **Murray Arms Hotel** at the top end of town was at one time the original 'gate' house ('gate' comes from 'gait' or road) and also the only house, a staging post on the route west to Portpatrick and Ireland. Gatehouse might

A LASTING LEGACY

No coverage of Gatehouse would be complete without mention of the Murray Usher family, in particular Mrs Elizabeth (Betty) Murray Usher, who died in 1990. I didn't know her personally, but since those early childhood holidays in the area I have always known about her. Such was her standing within the community that anyone who spent any time here could not fail to be aware of her enormous contribution to the development and well-being of not just the town, but of the wider area and its traditions as a whole. Along with The Stewartry Drystane Dyking Committee, she was, for instance, the founder in 1968 of the Drystone Walling Association of Great Britain.

'We do miss her' said one Gatehouse resident when asked about her and she is remembered with great fondness. Many a story could be (and still is) told by those who knew her, usually accompanied by a wry smile as they recall her tactics to make things happen and get her voice heard. At one time, unsuspecting visitors who were coming for a meeting with her, for example, would be offered on their arrival one of the gobstoppers which she kept on her desk.

Antony Wolffe, a retired architect and long-time resident of Gatehouse has kindly written a few words about her for this guide. He first met her in the 1950s and worked with her on a range of projects over 40 years.

Elizabeth Murray Usher of Broughton and Cally OBE (1904–90) succeeded her father Colonel Frederick Murray-Baillie in 1924 and at the age of 20 she took charge of the Cally Estate in the parishes of Girthon, Anwoth, Borgue and Twynholm, about 40,000 acres in total.

have remained like this, had it not been for James Murray of Broughton, entrepreneur and grandson of the fifth Earl of Galloway. It was a time of expansion, the Act of Union of 1707 had created opportunities for growth and James's father, Alexander of Broughton, approached William Adam, the leading architect of the day, about building a fine mansion on lands at Gatehouse. Unfortunately, he died before his project came to fruition, but his son James took up the baton, developing not just the estate but also creating an industrial settlement on the banks of the Fleet. First came a tannery and then breweries followed by a cotton mill in 1785, the year the village was made a Burgh of Barony. So successful were these endeavours that Gatehouse became known as the 'Glasgow of the south'. However, development faltered in the early 19th century, after which the population declined to around 1,000 people, which is where it has remained ever since.

Cally mansion was let and Cushat Wood was the Dower House for her mother, and Betty lived with her until she married Neil Usher in 1929, when they moved to Carstramon. From 1924 until 1990 – for 66 years – Mrs Murray Usher ran the Cally Estate and took a leading part in the local affairs of Gatehouse of Fleet. As Feudal Superior she took special interest in all new developments and long before the post-war planning legislation she exercised control over local building by insisting on slate roofs, white walls, sash and case windows and black chimney pots. She maintained that in the Stewartry, which is granite country with black soil, red tiles and ridges or natural brick walls are foreign and were not to be used in new building. The original layout of the planned burgh has been protected and by putting surrounding land under a restrictive agreement with the National Trust for Scotland, the original core of the town became an Outstanding Conservation Area.

The powers of the Superior have now been taken over by the Planning Authority, but we can thank Mrs Murray Usher for having made use of these powers for the benefit of the local community. She latterly served on the Fine Arts Commission but had been on the Scottish Economic Development Council and supported the National Trust for Scotland, as well as many local societies and clubs.

She did not waste words but would send a memo with the name of the property or person(s), with a – ? – which was enough to get a response. And for attention she would ring a bell or sing a cock-a-doodle!

In 1923, Cally House with its policies was sold to the Forestry Commission on the condition that part of it would become a forest nursery to provide local employment. This worked well, but the nursery is now part of the Cally golf course.

Despite such fluctuations, James Murray's grand Georgian mansion has survived and today is run by local business McMillan Hotels as the **Cally Palace Hotel** (page 247), sitting in extensive grounds south of the town (the grounds and hotel are now in separate ownership).

"Within the grounds are a number of points of interest, including Cally Gardens specialising in unusual perennials, and Forestry Commission Scotland's Cally Woods."

Within the grounds are a number of points of interest, including **Cally Gardens** (✆ 01557 815029 ♂ www.callygardens.co.uk ☉ seasonal; closed Mon & weekday mornings), specialising in unusual perennials, and Forestry Commission Scotland's **Cally Woods** with a selection of easy waymarked trails. There are also a number of curious buildings tucked away: the 'Temple' of 1779, a battlemented two-storey folly designed to impress passing traffic, and **Cross Cottage**, originally the chapel to the main house and now a holiday cottage available for rent. Just beyond the southern boundary of the grounds lies **Girthon Old Parish Church**, where in the churchyard is the grave of Robert Glover, one of the earliest gardeners at Cally. He died in 1775 and on his tombstone are carved a hoe, rake and spade.

One local Gatehouse resident tells me that when she moved here 52 years ago the town had 16 shops. Today it's a smaller but eclectic selection: delicatessen, charity shop, a lovely small secondhand bookshop/gallery, post office-cum-gift shop, kilt-making shop and, down at the bottom end of the High Street, the **Mill on the Fleet**. This converted mill building has a visitor information centre and riverside café on the ground floor and on the second floor the splendid **Garvellan Books**, with around 20,000 new and secondhand books in stock. Pop in to the information desk downstairs and say hello to manager Pat Jacques who is a mine of information about the local area and who runs the café under the memorable name of **Tart n' Tea**.

Cultural life in Gatehouse is thriving with a range of artists and writers choosing to make this their home. Writer, poet and artistic director Chrys Salt organises literary events at **The Bakehouse** (44 High St, DG7 2HP ✆ 01557 814175 ♂ www.thebakehouse.info), which are advertised on posters around the region. Chrys is building on the town's literary heritage which famously includes John Buchan, who set much of *The Thirty-Nine Steps* in the area, and Dorothy L Sayers, who visited on several occasions and is known to have stayed at the Anwoth Hotel (now The Ship) while writing *Five Red Herrings* in 1930.

Just to the north of Gatehouse on the east side of the Water of Fleet lies **Carstramon Wood**. Some of my earliest childhood memories are from here, the sight and pungent scent of a mass of bluebells flowering in the woods. We used to come on holiday to Culreoch farmhouse at the end of the track through the wood (now private but Culreoch Cottage is available for holiday lets). These 200-year-old woods are known for their bluebells (in May) and pollarded oaks. Come and walk here. The wood is managed by Scottish Wildlife Trust and is one of the largest semi-natural broadleaved woodlands in the area.

⏹ FOOD & DRINK

Galloway Lodge Preserves Fleetvale DG7 2HP ✎ 01557 814001. Popular with both locals and visitors, and has convenient parking in the public car park next door. Nigel Hesketh's family firm has been producing fine quality marmalade, jams, chutneys, jellies and mustards for over 40 years. Fiona Hesketh is at the helm these days and the company now supplies coffee shops, restaurants and hotels around the UK, as well as running coffee shops of its own. Breakfast and brunch, soup and sandwiches, toasties and jacket potatoes, afternoon teas and even packed lunches (to order) are on offer, with as many locally sourced ingredients as possible: meat from a Castle Douglas butcher, rolls from Kirkcudbright, eggs from the Glenkens.

The Masonic Arms 10 Ann St, Gatehouse of Fleet DG7 2HU ✎ 01557 814335 ⏹ www. masonicarms.co.uk. Always popular, this historic Gatehouse hostelry run by Jimmy and Sofia offers a wide-ranging menu using local ingredients wherever possible. Booking advised for evenings and Sunday lunch.

Mill on the Fleet High St, Gatehouse of Fleet DG7 2HS ✎ 01557 814099 ⏹ www. millonthefleet.co.uk. Good food is served throughout the day, but for tea and scones it's hard to beat the Mill's sunny riverside terrace. Take-away fish, chips and burgers are also offered on Friday and Saturday evenings.

Cardoness Castle 👋

DG7 2EH ♀ NX591553 ⏹ seasonal; Historic Scotland; free to members; no link with Cardoness Estate

Cardoness Castle stands prominently just beyond the southwestern end of Gatehouse. Built for the McCullochs in the late 15th century it was lost to the Gordons of Lochinvar (page 136) in the 17th century before being abandoned. The six-storey tower house is roofless but otherwise remarkably intact, complete with murder hole from the guardroom above the entry to help repel unwanted visitors. There are terrific views from the battlements looking south to Fleet Bay and the Solway beyond.

Immediately to the north of Cardoness is **Trusty's Hill**, an archaeological site which in recent years has gained much significance. Pictish symbols discovered here were first described in 1794, but it has only been since work undertaken in 2012 that the full importance of the site has been recognised. Archaeologists were puzzled for many years why such symbols were located here, so far away from the northern territories of the Picts. After much research and analysis, the evidence suggests that Trusty's Hill could have been a royal site of the Britons who were familiar with Pictish symbols at some time between AD500 and AD900, very possibly the location of Rheged, one of the most mysterious kingdoms of Dark Age Britain.

Gatehouse of Fleet to Anwoth

✻ OS Landranger map 83, Explorer map 312; start: Gatehouse of Fleet, ♀ NX600564; 3 miles (without detours)/1½ hours; easy to moderate (some inclines).

Note that refreshments are available in Gatehouse, which is accessible by bus 431/500.

Starting from the main car park in **1 Gatehouse of Fleet**, turn left and follow the road over the River Fleet until it bends left and the sign is pointing right to Anwoth. Here is the first of a number of mini-detours that are worth exploring along the way, **Venniehill** is a wildflower meadow offering drifts of common spotted orchids in early summer followed by a stunning display of knapweed and devil's-bit scabious in August. Return to the road and follow the lane, signposted 'Anwoth'. After a short distance the **old brickworks** is on your right, now a small nature reserve complete with boardwalk.

Continue along the lane as it bends left and go straight ahead at the bench and green, remembering to look back for some fine views. Pass through the **2 metal gate** and along the drystane dyke-edged path, climbing over the steps in the wall at the end and follow the waymarkers as they meander up and over the hilltops. **3 The wooden sign** 'Trusty's Hill/ Anwoth' offers another short detour contouring up on to **Trusty's Hill**, site of an ancient hillfort and **Pictish rock carvings** (♀ NX589560). Retrace your steps and follow the path in the direction of Anwoth, through a drystane dyke and over gorse- and bracken-covered moorland. The path appears to go away from the hilltop monuments you are heading for, but eventually reaches a wooden sign, 'Rutherford's Monument/Anwoth'. Head left on a gradual climb

Anwoth

It was the minister of Anwoth who first described the symbols at Trusty's Hill (see opposite). Here, in a picturesque setting are the remains of the very **Old Parish Church**, in the centre of which a sarcophagus monument from around 1635 commemorates the mother and two wives of John Gordon, who by that time had taken ownership of Cardoness Castle (pages 161–2). It's an atmospheric spot which was used as a location in the cult film *The Wicker Man* (page 204). Opposite the ruin the **Old Schoolhouse Gardens** are open one day a year as part of Scotland's Gardens scheme. A short way down the road stands Walter Newall's 'new' **Parish Church** of 1826–27.

Above Anwoth to the east is the prominent **granite obelisk** (♀NX587557) commemorating **Samuel Rutherford**, minister at Anwoth

up to **Rutherford's Monument obelisk** (♀ NX587588), dedicated to Anwoth's first parish minister, and enjoy sweeping views of the bay and, on a clear day, to the Isle of Man.

Having rested awhile soaking up the scenery, head to the next hilltop monument, dedicated to the work of the ministers of Anwoth and Girthon, and then on to the trig point (♀ NX586559). Go straight ahead and in the bottom of the dip turn right following a rough

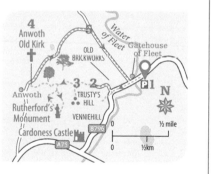

path until it re-joins your earlier route. Turn left and then on to the path for Anwoth. Head down the hill and over a soggy field to the track running alongside the **4 Anwoth Old Kirk** (♀ NX582562) turning right at the road. Take time to explore this atmospheric old kirkyard with its fine gravestone carvings and the impressive Maxwell family tomb. For fans of *The Wicker Man*, this will be a familiar location. Follow the quiet road out of the village turning right at the **5 T-junction** (♀ NX592570) and following it back to Gatehouse of Fleet. Go left at the T-junction (♀ NX598562) to return to the start point. This last section is perhaps less interesting but take time to enjoy the smaller pleasures, such as the beauty of the fine oaks and the joy of the hedgerow flowers.

1627–38. The monument was raised in 1842, struck down by lightning in 1847 and raised again in 1851. Rutherford was a diligent soul who was eventually banished from Anwoth due to his non-conformity. By then, though, he was regarded so fondly by his parishioners that when it was decided to knock down his manse, which had stood opposite the old church, and use the stones to build the new church, the masons refused to work and went on strike, not for higher wages but out of respect for his memory. A **millennium cairn** opposite the monument lists the names of all of the ministers of Anwoth and nearby Girthon (page 160) up until the year 2000.

South of Gatehouse, the Water of Fleet flows out to Fleet Bay, with its half-mile tides and warm shallow waters. Down the east side of the Fleet is **Sandgreen**, site of a holiday park (page 248) with its own beach, while nearby is one of the region's most visited attractions, the ever-popular **Cream o' Galloway** (see below). To the west of the Water of Fleet is **Cardoness Shore**, with six sandy bays which can be accessed either from the Skyreburn Teapot Café in the layby on the A75 (park here and walk back along the shore, generally only possible when the tide is on the way out), or through **Cardoness Estate Holiday Park** (DG7 2EP) south of the A75 and just beyond the Skyreburn Teapot, where you will need to buy a day ticket from the estate office. From the estate car park, dinghies can by launched from trailers.

Cream o' Galloway
Rainton DG7 2DR ✆ 01557 814040 ⊘ www.creamogalloway.co.uk

The Finlay family have been farming at Rainton since the 1920s and over the years have developed, diversified and reinvented themselves several times in order to survive. The result is impressive and Cream o' Galloway is now not only known for its fully organic ice cream and cheese, but caters for a broad range of interests and offers a number of entertainment options for kids and adults alike (3-D maze, adventure playground, bike tracks and bikes for hire, nature trail, to name a few). But this is also part of a working farm, which means there's a whole lot more besides, from a farm tractor tour to tasting sessions of the homemade ice cream and cheese, and visits to the milking parlour to meet the cows. Underpinning it all is the Finlay family's commitment to ethical farming and 'cow contentment'. Their story is an interesting one, especially the new methods which they have been trialling to reach new standards of animal husbandry.

THE COAST ROAD
FROM GATEHOUSE TO CREETOWN

There is a story that Thomas Carlyle (page 47), when asked by Queen Victoria which was the finest road in the kingdom, replied 'the coast road from Creetown to Gatehouse'. And when he was asked whether there was not another one as good, he replied 'Yes, the coast road from Gatehouse to Creetown'. (Penpont poet Hugh McMillan references this in his piece in the Nithsdale chapter, see pages 78–9.) Carlyle's attachment to the scenic delights of this route was not unjustified. Pinched between the hills on one side and the dramatic sweep of Wigtown Bay on the other, there are some fine views, especially on a sunny day when the sea is sparkling blue. This is the fastest route west along the A75 and offers some entertaining and interesting diversions, including the **Laggan Outdoors Centre** (DG7 2ES ✆ 01557 840217 ⌂ www.lagganoutdoor. co.uk) with one of the longest zip wires in Europe, and **Mossyard Bay**, where the perfectly formed small sandy bay affords good views of the islands at the mouth of Fleet Bay.

Cairn Holy (♀ NX518538; Historic Scotland) is an easy jaunt, around half a mile up a single-track road. Here lie two chambered cairns, Cairn Holy I and Cairn Holy II, the former the more elaborate of the two but the latter of which has been named as the tomb of the legendary Galdus, the great warrior king of the Scots. Up this same road is **Kirkdale Sawmill and Nature Trail** (⌂ www.kirkdale-sawmill.org.uk). The Kirkdale Estate has been in the Hannay family since 1532 and the present Kirkdale House (private) was designed by Robert Adam. The sawmill dates from the early 19th century and was restored by Neil Hannay. Today it is open to visitors (seasonally, limited hours) who can come and watch what is probably the only working water-powered sawmill in Scotland. A nature trail runs by the mill pond behind the sawmill; look out for red squirrels, otters, deer and a good selection of birdlife in Kirkdale Glen.

12 CARSLUITH CASTLE
♀ NX494541; Historic Scotland

Carsluith Castle sits just off of the A75 towards Creetown on the edge of the sea overlooking Wigtown Bay. Built in the 1560s, it was a typical tower house, the home of one Richard Brown, whose family remained here until emigrating to India in 1748, after which it lay empty.

Gilbert Brown, the last abbot of Sweetheart Abbey (page 127) was born here. Visitors can climb right to the top where a balcony offers superb views out over the bay.

Next to the castle is the **Marrbury Smokehouse** (see below), a convenient stopping place, and one of two smokehouses along this route. The second is the **Galloway Smokehouse** (DG8 7DN), just a little further west.

FOOD & DRINK

Marrbury Smokehouse Just off the A75 at Carsluith Castle, DG8 7DY ✆ 01671 820476. The smokehouse itself is at the home of owners Ruby and Vincent Marr up at Bargrennan near Glen Trool (page 145), but the *fruits de mer* of their labours can be enjoyed here and/or bought to take home. Outdoor tables by the castle make for a pleasant stop on a sunny day, alternatively inside seating in the cosy café is also an option. Ruby and Vincent are very much hands-on and do everything themselves, from the fishing to the smoking. Marrbury is the house smoker for the famous Gleneagles Hotel in Perthshire.

THE HIGH ROADS
FROM GATEHOUSE TO CREETOWN

The high roads to Creetown offer slower, single-track alternatives to the coast road. Our suggestion would be to take the coast road in one direction and one of the high roads in the other. And if you have time, we'd recommend exploring both of the high roads, partly for the jaw-dropping views but also for the chance to visit the **Big Water of Fleet Viaduct** on the old railway line.

Cairnsmore of Fleet
National Nature Reserve (NNR) 👆

Cairnsmore NNR covers 4,650 acres in the hills above Gatehouse of Fleet and Creetown, and makes up around half of the area of the Cairnsmore of Fleet SSSI. One of the wildest and most remote areas of southwest Scotland, it is dominated by the imposing granite hill of Cairnsmore (2,333 feet). The privately owned Cairnsmore Estate was at one time the home of the wildlife photographer F W Champion.

Dromore Visitor Centre (📍 NX555637 ⊙ all year) is reached on the B796 north of Gatehouse, up the western side of the Water of Fleet, and then by taking the turning to the right where indicated. The area is a walker's paradise and there are three suggested routes detailed in a leaflet available at Dromore and from the Mill on the Fleet in Gatehouse (page 160). There is also a path to the summit of Cairnsmore from Palnure, about three miles east of Newton Stewart. Summit heath, heather moorland and blanket bog make up the terrain, supporting a range of iconic birdlife, including both red and black grouse, peregrine falcon and (if you're lucky) golden eagle. Also to be spotted are red deer, mountain hare and adders.

A short walk from the visitor centre stands the **Big Water of Fleet Viaduct**, an impressive 900-foot span of 20 arches. It was built in the late 1850s as part of the Portpatrick and Wigtownshire Joint Railway (the 'Port Road') linking Stranraer to Castle Douglas. Alas the line didn't survive the Beeching cuts and closed in 1965. The viaduct is not as graceful as it would have been originally as its piers have been strengthened by brick encasings; however, it has fared better than its smaller sister, the Little Water of Fleet Viaduct, which was blown up some years ago by the military as part of a training exercise.

"Beyond Pibble the road drops down into Creetown, following the course of the teasingly named Moneypool Burn."

The 18th-century Pibble Mine is found in the hills between here and Creetown. Beyond Pibble the road drops down into Creetown, following the course of the teasingly named Moneypool Burn.

Corse of Slakes Road

NX535587

In 1808, in the First Report from the Committee of the Highways of the Kingdom to the House of Commons, it was recorded that the Marquis of Downshire, despite 'having labourers with tools attending his coach, which was then a necessary part of the retinue' while travelling through Galloway, was forced to spend a night in his coach on the Corse of Slakes (corse is old Scots for 'crossing' while slake is from an old Galloway word meaning 'an opening in the hill'). This unfortunate incident prompted consultation between the Marquis and the Duke of Queensberry (of Drumlanrig) (page 90), which resulted a couple of years later in a workforce of soldiers being sent to construct a road through the hills, a task which kept them busy for almost 30 years. The result is the **Old Military Road** (marked as such on OS maps) which, unlike other such roads, notably General Wade's in the Highlands of Scotland, was not built to repel the Jacobite threat but to allow easier passage of troops to Ireland.

Today the **Corse of Slakes** takes off up into the hills via a track from Anwoth. Alternatively, it can be accessed by car through the lovely countryside north of Skyreburn (take the Skyreburn turning off the A75 west of Gatehouse). It is a route of exquisite hill and moorland vistas which, towards the western end, opens up into a glorious panorama taking in points west and south to the Rhins and right down to the Mull of Galloway, as you come around Stronach Hill. This is countryside to be savoured, take it slowly (it would be difficult not to on this single-track lane) and keep an eye open for birds. We spotted a hen harrier up here. **Walking** it is also an option, starting from Gatehouse, taking in Trusty's Hill and Anwoth, and then taking the gated track at the Old Church.

As you head down into Creetown, for something completely different you may want to stop in at **Garrocher Market Garden** (see box, page 170), where, believe it or not, tea is being grown in the Galloway Hills. I wonder what the Marquis of Downshire would have had to say about that?

13 CREETOWN

Towards the far western fringe of the Stewartry lies Creetown, feeling as if it is more of the Machars than points east, not least in its outlook to Wigtown Bay and its proximity to Newton Stewart. However, Creetown is definitely within the boundaries of the Stewartry as any local will tell you. In early days it was called Ferrytown of Cree, providing a crossing point across the Cree for pilgrims on their way to Whithorn (see pages 200–4). In the 19th century it became one of the wealthiest towns in Scotland thanks to its famous local quarries, granite from which was used to build the town itself, and was shipped far and wide for use in, among other places, the Liverpool Docks, Thames Embankment and London Bridge. Creetown is therefore noticeably different from most other local towns in its physical appearance, the grey granite is cold and austere on a dull day but in the sun it sparkles.

"Crystals, minerals, fossils, meteorites and even a dinosaur egg are on display."

Appropriately for somewhere that has relied so heavily on rock, Creetown is the location of the excellent **Gem Rock Museum** (Chain Rd, DG8 7HJ ✆ 01671 820357 ◊ www.gemrock.net ☉ throughout the year, reduced hours in winter), which was started by the father of Tim Stephenson, who now runs it with his wife, and which houses a

HIDEO FURUTA

Hideo Furuta died in 2007, not long after completing work on Adamson Square in Creetown. The following text is extracted and adapted from the obituary by Professor Duncan Macmillan that appeared in *The Scotsman* newspaper on 18 December 2007.

Born in 1949 in Hiroshima, Furuta studied art and philosophy and aesthetics there and in Tokyo. A crucial experience for him, however, was a year spent as a stonemason and quarryman in the Ishizaki quarry on Kurahashi Island, Japan. It was there that he learned to work granite, which became his chosen medium. He taught briefly in Japan before going to Chile in 1984, then coming to Britain in 1985. He came to Scotland in 1989 to a residency at Edinburgh University, where he made an immediate impact by setting up his studio in the open air in the back garden of what was then the fine art department in George Square. He would light a fire in the morning to temper his tools afresh each day and, incidentally it seemed, to cook his breakfast. After that he settled in Scotland, where the geology of the country, like that of Japan, is rich in granite.

He persuaded Tarmac to give him the use of Kirkmabreck quarry, near Creetown in Galloway. He made his home there for many years, living in a dilapidated house that went with the quarry and working a seam of beautiful white granite. When Tarmac eventually asked him to move, with the support of the people of Creetown he found another disused quarry near Carsluith, which in turn became his base.

He most frequently worked with simple Euclidian shapes, spheres especially, but also cylinders, cones, pyramids and cubes (latterly he added low relief or inlaid figuration to the hewn surface of the stone) but his geometry was always intuitive.

Furuta came to be regarded with great affection in Galloway and he repaid this regard with one of the last of more than 40 public works he had carried out, the remodelling of Adamson Square in Creetown. It is a major project that he initiated and largely completed himself. It will now be his monument.

very impressive and wide-ranging collection. This is a lovingly curated showpiece with an impressive and fascinating range of items, presented in a smart exhibition space complete with mini-film theatre, café and shop. Tim is often on hand himself to talk about how the museum got going and what it offers today, and how he was inspired by his father to become not just a gemmologist but also a lapidary (stone polishing takes place here, too). Crystals, minerals, fossils, meteorites and even a dinosaur egg are on display, as well as the complete skeleton of a 50,000-year-old fossilised Russian female cave bear. The range of stones and rocks is extraordinary and displays the most fantastic spectrum of colours.

For a closer look at the area's local and natural history, **Creetown Heritage Museum** (91 St John St, DG8 7JE ℰ 01671 820267 ℰ www.creetown-heritage-museum.com ☉ seasonal, otherwise by appointment; small entry fee) offers a mix of insights, including images from *The Wicker Man*, some of which was filmed in this area (notably in the Ellangowan Hotel, which is now closed). Bike hire is available opposite the museum (page 133).

The main street is dominated by two notable features. The granite **clock tower** with its drinking troughs and bowl was built in 1897 from public subscription to commemorate Queen Victoria's Diamond Jubilee and

TEA IN THE GALLOWAY HILLS

Angela Hurrell, Garrocher Market Garden

Saying we are one of a small number of tea growers in Scotland invariably gets a wide-eyed reaction and a 'you're joking' comment. Wine growers in Wales must have had the same reaction.

As I write this, Garrocher Market Garden hasn't had tea bushes growing on its terraces for very long. The early signs are good and I intend to extend the planting in the next couple of seasons, weaving a tapestry of tea, flowers, fruit and vegetables through the extent of the garden. I've wanted to grow tea for years and knew of tea growing in Cornwall but it was just happenstance that led me to The Wee Tea Plantation, a Scottish tea-growing co-operative in the wilds of Kinross in Fife, and the discovery that I would be able to grow tea in Dumfries and Galloway.

If you visited the garden, what would you see? Well, a work in progress is the main answer, areas of raised beds among wild nature. I use the word planting, but much of it wasn't 'planted' as such. There are times when a little more order seems an attractive idea, but

the thought passes and the garden goes back to its dream state. Nothing is out of hand, I just edge out as the need arises. Slowly the bits join together, and the swaying wild grasses are inter-planted with swathes of tall border plants, fruit bushes, wild flowers, vegetable beds, trees and now tea. I have no plan; well, not on a piece of paper, but I do have a feeling or idea, the sort of feeling that says 'over there would be just the place for a seat', or 'that place ought to have roses'. And then there's the thinking rests, little places – well they would have to be named tea houses – just for sitting and thinking in, or for drinking tea.

At some point in the not too distant future I will be opening the garden for just such times: an invitation to pass a day in quiet reflection, to sit and think, stroll around the garden or through the woods, paint, read, write, or just 'be', while the work of the garden carries on or carries you along. We aren't ready yet the garden and I, but it won't be long, and in the meantime, if you would like to visit, just drop me a line.

is reminiscent of the clock tower in Gatehouse. Next to it is **Adamson Square**, which was remodelled in 2007 and is itself dominated by a stark granite sphere. The square was designed and created by renowned Japanese sculptor Hideo Furuta, a remarkable man who lived in the area for many years before his death (see box, page 169). A film of his work can be seen in the Creetown Museum, outside which one of his sculptures, depicting quarry workers, is built into the wall.

Garrocher Market Garden

By appointment only; please make contact via Garrocher Market Garden on Facebook or by emailing ✉ garrochermarketgarden@gmail.com

For a real taste of the Slow life, head for Garrocher Market Garden, a horticultural oasis tucked into an old sand quarry in the hills above Creetown. The owner, Angela Hurrell, moved here in 2005 and lives a low-impact lifestyle dedicated to nurturing the garden she and her partner have created from scratch. Angela can often be found selling her fruit and veg from her stall at the farmers' markets in Dumfries and Moffat, but she is also happy to receive visitors by appointment at Garrocher. If you come at the right time, you may even be able to enjoy a pot of home-grown tea, for Angela is one of a very small number of people who are experimenting with growing tea in Scotland, and the only tea grower in Dumfries and Galloway (see box, opposite). Hers is the first Scottish Lowland Tea Plantation and she is producing a Single Estate Tea Blend.

KIRKCUDBRIGHT & THE SOUTHERN COAST

The southernmost part of the Stewartry is considered by many to be the jewel in Dumfries and Galloway's highly ornamented crown, and there are many who return here year after year for their annual holiday. What makes it so special is its mix of attractions: the historic harbourside town of Kirkcudbright and the strikingly beautiful and unspoiled coastline abutting the pastureland of gently undulating lush green hills, with the higher ranges of the Galloway Hills in the background. Combined with a pleasant climate for much of the year, we have heard this area and the neighbouring Colvend Coast (page 155) being referenced as the 'Scottish Riviera' and, much as the description smacks of a brashness which is far from the reality, we can understand why the soubriquet might stick (though we hope it doesn't). Genteel, cosy, couthy even, are adjectives which more accurately fit the bill.

Coverage in this section extends eastwards up to and including Auchencairn, west to Carrick, and north to the A75, though most of the attractions lie in the south along the coast.

NORTH OF KIRKCUDBRIGHT

The village of **Twynholm**, just off the A75, is the birthplace of Formula 1 racing driver David Coulthard and the location of the **David Coulthard Museum** (2 Burn Brae, DG6 4NU). For access, you need to go to the **Star Hotel** (18 Main St, DG6 4NT ✆ 01557 860279) in the village and ask for entry. Do note that there are no set opening hours, so it is best to telephone in advance. Also in Twynholm is **The Cocoabean Factory** (Ashland DG6 4NP ✆ 01557 860608 ⬠ www.thecocoabeancompany.com ☉ daily), a family-run business started by Claire Beck in 2005 on her kitchen AGA, which has since grown and moved to these purpose-built premises. Children's chocolate-making workshops, kid's play area, a factory-viewing area and a café combine here to make a family day out. Adult workshops (make your own truffles) are run from time to time, too. Combine it with Cream o' Galloway (page 164) for a truly calorie-tastic day.

The other place of note north of Kirkcudbright is **Tongland**, where the main thing you will notice is the striking power station, the most southerly in the Galloway Hydroelectric Scheme, in a Modernist building of 1935 on the banks of the Dee. Tongland was also the location in the 1920s for the **Galloway automobile plant**, a subsidiary of Arrol-Johnston in Dumfries (page 112). The plant was housed in an old World War I factory and was started up by the engineer T C Pullinger, who was a manager at Arrol-Johnston. Pullinger's daughter, Dorothée (see box, opposite), was instrumental in persuading her father to keep the factory going to provide employment.

In medieval times, Tongland was the site of a **Premonstratensian monastery** founded by Fergus, Lord of Galloway. Its remains can still be seen. The monastery's most famous resident was John Damian, an Italian (real name Giovanni Damiano de Falcucci) who attended the court of James IV of Scotland and who was abbot at Tongland in the early 16th century. He was, by all accounts, quite a character. Much involved in organising entertainments, he was also an alchemist and directed the

'A CAR BUILT BY LADIES, FOR THOSE OF THEIR OWN SEX'

The Galloway car plant at Tongland owed its existence to Dorothée Pullinger, who persuaded her father, a manager at Arrol-Johnston, to make use of the disused World War I factory to provide employment. At the age of just 20, Dorothée had been in charge of 7,000 women in an aircraft and ammunition factory during the war. Once her father opened the Tongland plant, she managed production in a workplace that famously included a tennis court on the roof, a swimming pool, a hockey team and a piano room for relaxation. Many of the employees were women and Dorothée ran a ladies engineering college, which offered apprenticeships in three years rather than the five undertaken by men, since women were believed to be faster learners.

The car which they produced was the Galloway 10/20HP, a light-weight vehicle designed specifically for women and described as 'a car built by ladies for those of their own sex' (*The Light Car and Cyclecar* magazine, 1921). It was the first car with a standard mounted retro-visor and it was designed without protruding handles or pedals that could snag a woman's skirt. As women were on average shorter than men, measurements and fittings were adjusted so that the driver could look over rather than through the steering wheel.

Dorothée was not only a founding member of the Women's Engineering Society but was also accepted as the first female member of the Institution of Automobile Engineers (albeit having to apply twice, since the first application was turned down on the grounds that 'the word person means a man and not a woman'). In 1920 she was awarded an MBE for her work during World War I and in 1924 she won the Scottish Six Day Car Trial driving the Galloway. After the war she came in for flack, like so many women did, for taking jobs which were perceived to be men's. She subsequently moved south with her husband, to Croydon, where she opened a large, technically innovative steam laundry, commenting that 'washing should not be doing men out of a job'. During World War II she set up the women's industrial war work programme and later she was the only woman on a post-war government committee formed to recruit women into factories.

Dorothée Aurélie Marianne Pullinger: born France 13 January 1894, died Guernsey 28 January 1986.

building of chemical furnaces at Stirling Castle and Holyrood. His most infamous venture was his attempt to fly when he launched himself from the battlements of Stirling Castle. The birds' feathers he was wearing failed to do the trick and he was lucky only to break his thigh.

From Tongland it's a short hop down into Kirkcudbright, crossing **Thomas Telford's bridge** of 1808 over the River Dee.

14 KIRKCUDBRIGHT 🖐

🏠 The Grange (page 248), **Orroland Holiday Cottages** (page 248), **The Selkirk Arms Hotel** (page 247)

Kirkcudbright ranks highly for having one of the most confounding names in Scotland. Pronounced 'kir-coo-bree', the popular belief is that it is derived from the church/kirk of St Cuthbert, but it is also possible that this in itself was a derivation of an earlier name, Caer Cuabrit, meaning 'fort on the bend in the river'. Whatever the truth, there is no doubting that the first Christian church here was dedicated to Cuthbert, the 7th-century saint whose uncorrupted body was carried around the country in the late 9th century by monks from Northumbria fleeing attacks from the Danes. The church was most probably situated on the hill to the east of town, where St Cuthbert's graveyard can now be found.

Kirkcudbright's – and Galloway's – history is both long and abundant, with more twists, turns and anecdotes than can be told in full here. From Celtic tribes to the Roman general Agricola, Galloway Picts and St Cuthbert and one of the earliest Christian churches in Scotland, so the town developed. By 1140, on land at Lochfergus east of today's town, Fergus, Lord of Galloway lived in his castle, the first of five hereditary lords who ruled Galloway for a century. Edward Bruce, younger brother of Robert, was granted the Lordship of Galloway in 1308 following his efforts to rid the area of the English in the Wars of Independence. Douglas rule and disharmony followed until on 26 October 1455 Kirkcudbright became a royal burgh. The 16th century was a time of prosperity but despite the Union of the Crowns in 1603 more trouble was to follow, for nowhere was religious persecution felt more harshly by the Covenanters than in Galloway. During the 17th and 18th centuries the town fell into decline, so much so that Daniel Defoe commented:

> Here is a pleasant situation yet nothing pleasant to be seen. Here is a harbour without ships, a port without trade, a fishery without nets, a people without business; and that, which is worse than all, they do not seem to desire business, much less do they understand it.

The 19th century saw the beginning of the revival of Kirkcudbright's fortunes, not least thanks to the influx of artists who made this their base (see box, pages 176–7), drawn by the quality of the light and the availability of affordable housing. The cachet that had always been attached to the town was enhanced further and its profile as the county town and capital of Kirkcudbrightshire was raised, although economically it was given a run for its money and ultimately overtaken by Castle Douglas.

Kirkcudbright today is still known as 'The Artists' Town' and is as enticing a place as you can imagine. Compact but with wide airy streets, the old town with its brightly painted houses clusters around the remains of the 16th-century **MacLellan's Castle**, which stands prominently overlooking the fishing boats moored at the harbour. Such a mix of attractions has a timeless appeal

"The old town with its brightly painted houses clusters around the remains of the 16th-century MacLellan's Castle overlooking the harbour."

which gives this small town a perpetual charm. It is a place to explore, to linger, and to get to know. Standing at the harbour, reflect on the fact that Kirkcudbright can claim over 800 years as a commercial port, from warfare to piracy and smuggling, from passenger services to international trade. And what's more, it's still in use today.

Start off with a visit to **The Stewartry Museum** (St Mary St, DG6 4AG ✐ 01557 331643 ☉ all year but with seasonal variations in hours). The museum was purpose-built in 1892–93 and stepping inside is a like stepping back in time. Glass-fronted wooden cabinets are positioned around the ground floor while the upstairs balcony is fitted with glass topped display cases of the type that are only found in museums of this vintage. The collection is crammed with items of historical interest, from artworks and book covers designed by the celebrated illustrator Jessie King (see box, page 176), to newspaper clippings telling the gruesome story of the 'Lighthouse Murder' in 1960 on Little Ross Island at the mouth of Kirkcudbright Bay. There's a fine collection of old rifles and pistols, a model railway, an 1898 Bechstein piano, and even a jigsaw which is there for anyone to sit down and have a go at. Upstairs is dedicated to natural history, with stuffed animals, birds and fish, as well as pinned butterflies and birds' eggs. This really is a museum of its time, but one which has also been kept relevant and alive, and where children as much as adults will find plenty of interest. There's usually also some sort of activity on offer for kids; last time we were there it was an 'elephant hunt'.

Just around the corner from the museum is the old High Street, lined with period cottages and houses. The **Selkirk Arms** (High St, DG6 4JG;

page 247) dates from 1777 and is somewhat confusingly named, for it has no connection at all with the town of Selkirk in the Scottish Borders but is instead derived from the Earl of Selkirk, whose family had acquired lands in Wigtownshire and the Stewartry through marriage and who were the original owners of the inn. Thomas Douglas, fifth Earl of Selkirk was born in 1771 at St Mary's Isle to the south of Kirkcudbright and became one of the town's most famous sons. A **plaque** commemorating him is affixed to a plinth on the green near the corner of St Mary's Street and St Cuthbert's Street. The Selkirk Arms's most famous guest was Robert Burns, who came to stay here in 1793, during which visit it is believed he may have written his famous Selkirk Grace.

Further down the High Street stands the 17th-century **Tolbooth**. Fans of the film *The Wicker Man* (page 204) will recognise both it and some of the narrow closes (passageways) that run off the High Street. On top of the outside stone staircase is the **Market Cross** of 1610, below which

KIRKCUDBRIGHT – ARTISTS' TOWN

Anne Ramsbottom is Museums Curator of Dumfries and Galloway West and looks after a range of museums and galleries from Castle Douglas to Stranraer, including The Stewartry Museum and Tolbooth Museum in Kirkcudbright. She has kindly written this piece on Kirkcudbright's rich artistic heritage.

Kirkcudbright has a unique place in the history of Scottish Art as the only town where an artists' community or 'colony' flourished for a long period.

By the early 1880s, inspired by the success of the Faed family of artists from nearby Gatehouse of Fleet, a group of local artists were regularly exhibiting in the town alongside several of the 'Glasgow Boy' artists who found inspiration for their painting in the Kirkcudbright area. The town's reputation was established by 1900 with the Kirkcudbright-born 'Glasgow Boy' E A Hornel, the pre-eminent resident artist.

A younger generation of artists was drawn to visit the town, some of whom eventually settled here. Of these residents perhaps the most famous, both within the town and throughout Scotland, were Jessie M King and E A Taylor. This husband and wife team were multi-talented with Jessie M King designing jewellery and fabrics for Liberty of London, illustrating books and decorating ceramics while E A Taylor, a prolific artist, also designed musical instruments. In the 1920s and 1930s they set up artists' studios behind their home in Kirkcudbright's historic High Street, and through their teaching they encouraged and nurtured a further generation of younger Scottish artists up to 1940.

Post-war, the town was noted for its summer art school involving artists and is **St Cuthbert's Well**. Look for the town **jougs** or iron collar on the wall of the Tolbooth, in which ne'er-do-wells of days past were chained. In 1698, Elspeth McKewan was held here before being burned alive, the last witch to be executed in Scotland. She was accused of making 'a compact and correspondence with the Devil', of drawing off milk from her neighbour's cows with a magical wooden pin and of interfering with the hens' egg laying.

The following century the Tolbooth was prison to a number of Covenanters, and it was from here that on 16 December 1684 there was a **mass break-out**, assisted by Robert Stewart and John Grierson (page 136), both of whom ultimately paid for their sympathies with their lives. In the 18th century **John Paul Jones** (pages 128–9) was held in the Tolbooth. During a voyage in 1770 Jones flogged Mungo Maxwell, one of his sailors, for being negligent in his duty. Later that year Maxwell died on a different ship and rumours circulated that it was

resident craft workers such as Tim Jeffs and the potter Tommy Lochhead. The Stewartry area still has a high number of practising artists and craft workers. With a thriving Wasps facility in the town (Wasps is an arts-based charity that provides studio spaces across Scotland), a nationally acclaimed summer exhibition programme, a range of art galleries and a well-established branding, the Artists' Town has come into its own.

Kirkcudbright's artists have been a part of the town's social history for the last 150 years, and they have engaged with the local community in many different ways – from serving on the town council to arranging pageants, and operating local craft businesses. Kirkcudbright's artist community inspired Dorothy L Sayers to write her Lord Peter Wimsey crime novel *Five Red Herrings*, and the daughters of the artists Bill Johnston and Dorothy Nesbitt were the models for Ronald Searle's 'St Trinian's Girls'. The town itself is a character in this story where the homes and studios of artists can still be identified.

The material evidence of this unique story survives in Broughton House, the home of E A Hornel, now a National Trust for Scotland site, The Stewartry Museum and the Tolbooth Art Centre. Each displays a fine collection of these artists' paintings and crafts, including jewellery, ceramics, woodwork and sculpture. The Stewartry Museum collection also boasts a significant archival, documentary and photographic record of the artists' lives and careers. The Tolbooth Art Centre displays a ten-minute film on Kirkcudbright Artists' Town telling a short history of the primary artists such as Jessie M King, E A Taylor and E A Hornel and their influence on the town today.

as a result of the wounds he had suffered while under Jones's command. Jones was subsequently imprisoned in the Tolbooth but released shortly afterwards on bail when he produced papers intimating that Maxwell had in fact died of yellow fever. Despite this apparent exoneration, the story of Maxwell's death stuck with Jones for the rest of his life.

The **Tolbooth Arts Centre** houses a shop on the ground floor and, upstairs, exhibition space for some of the town's permanent collection of artworks.

Continuing down the High Street from the Tolbooth, on the left-hand side at number 46 is **Greengate** (now a B&B), the home of the artist, illustrator and designer Jessie M King and her artist husband E A Taylor for much of the first half of the 20th century. Students would come and stay with them here and Jessie gathered around her a group of Glasgow-trained female artists who became known as the Greengate Close Coterie, which was still in existence when she died in 1949.

The town also has a range of shops and is particularly noted for its **galleries**. Full details of the town's galleries (and more besides) can be found on the local website ⊘ www.kirkcudbright.co.uk.

Broughton House & Garden
12 High St, DG6 4JX; National Trust for Scotland; free entry for members

Broughton House is one of Kirkcudbright's star attractions. The building was originally two separate town houses which were acquired by Alexander Murray of Broughton (page 159) in 1740 who remodelled them into one. Thomas, fifth Earl of Selkirk later lived here and the house was occupied over the centuries by a succession of Kirkcudbright dignitaries. Eventually in 1901 it was bought by E A Hornel, whose ancestors had lived in Kirkcudbright since the late 1500s and who had by then achieved fame as one of the Glasgow Boys. To the back of his home Hornel added a large studio, which along with the rest of this fine Georgian building is now open to the public. In addition to around 40 Hornel paintings on display at Broughton, visitors can also see Hornel's **library**, which by the time of his death contained a staggering 15,000 items. His Burns collection is one of the largest in private hands and contains many early and valuable editions, including the first 'Kilmarnock' edition of Burns's *Poems, Chiefly in the Scottish Dialect* from 1786. Behind the house is Hornel's garden, a serene and beautiful retreat looking out over Kirkcudbright harbour.

MacLellan's Castle

DG6 4JD ⊙ closed Oct–Mar; Historic Scotland

The northern end of the High Street bends round to the right on to Castle Bank, site of the remains of MacLellan's Castle, a fine example of late 16th-century domestic architecture as it evolved from more heavily defended tower houses.

A much earlier castle, first mentioned in 1288, had stood on a site to the west on the banks of the Dee near what is now Castledykes Road. The town also had a Franciscan convent, founded in the mid 15th century, the site of which was granted to Thomas MacLellan of Bombie, provost of Kirkcudbright, in 1569, and it was here that he built his own mansion partly from stones from the convent and early castle.

Today, the castle is remarkably complete inside apart from the roof. Of particular note is the **Great Hall**, over 42 feet long and almost half that in width, where the enormous fireplace boasts a lintel over ten feet long made out of a single stone. Hidden at the back of the fireplace is a **peephole**, a 'lairds lug' (literally 'lord's ear'), from where the castle owner could keep an eye on, and listen to, his guests.

Thomas MacLellan himself is commemorated in the **Episcopalian church**, which stands across from the castle on Moat Brae. The current building dates from 1919 but incorporates various parts of older churches. One of the 19th-century buildings was used as a school and it is said that the children used to sharpen their slate-pencil on Thomas's nose!

BILLY MARSHALL, THE TINKER KING (1672–1792)

On the hill to the east of the town lies **St Cuthbert's Graveyard**, the site of the early church. Here lies Billy Marshall, of Romany stock, who was regarded as the king of the gypsies in southwest Scotland in the 18th century. His was a colourful life which included serving as a private soldier first in King William's army at the Battle of the Boyne and, later, under the Duke of Marlborough in Germany. He is said to have been instrumental in organising the 'Levellers', a band of people who in 1723–24 destroyed the dykes which had been raised by farmers enclosing their land. Prior to this time there had been a common right of grazing, but with the price of cattle increasing landlords chose to close off sections of their land, which in turn led to revolt.

Billy Marshall lived to the age of 120, claimed to have been married 17 times and is said to have fathered many children, including four after the age of 100.

On the outskirts of Kirkcudbright

Galloway Wildlife Conservation Park (Lochfergus Plantation, DG6 4XX ✆ 01557 331645 ⬧ https://gallowaywildlife.org.uk) above the town to the east is set in 27 acres of mixed woodland and is home to a varied collection of nearly 150 animals from all over the world.

On the road in from Tongland is the **Elizabeth MacGregor Nursery** (Ellenbank, Tongland Rd, DG6 4UU ✆ 01557 330620 ⬧ www.elizabethmacgregornursery.co.uk ☉ end Apr–mid-Oct, closed Sun & Thu) where for over 20 years owners Elizabeth and Alasdair MacGregor have been cultivating their half-acre walled garden to take advantage of Galloway's mild climate and specialise in choice perennials.

One of the best **views of Kirkcudbright** is from the The Stell on the west side of the Dee, from where the town presents itself, pretty as a picture, clustered around the harbour with the mixed deciduous woodland of Barrhill behind. From here there's a glimpse of Broughton House and, next door to it, the imposing white Blair House, of the fishing boats and yachts in the marina, and of the castle. It is a scene so inviting that it makes quite clear, if it weren't already, just why so many artists have been attracted to the town.

🍴 FOOD & DRINK

Polarbites Fish and Chips Harbour Sq, DG6 4HY ✆ 01557 339050 ⬧ www.polarbites.co.uk ☉ closed Mon. This place is legendary! Sit in or out, or take away, this is not your average chippy. Scallops, lobster and crab might be found on the menu or, if not, can be sourced from the sister shop, Polarpak, next door. Cod and haddock are on the menu too, along with lemon sole, monkfish, mussels, and so the list goes on. This is one serious fish and chip shop.

The Selkirk Arms High St, DG6 4JG ✆ 01557 33040 ⬧ www.selkirkarmshotel.co.uk. Chef Paul Somerville has built a strong reputation for his locally sourced dishes, with starters such as a smokehouse board with duck, salmon, chicken, beef and egg with olives, capers, aioli and garlic bread. Mains might include Galloway beef or venison and the menu is replete with indulgent desserts.

THE KIRKCUDBRIGHT COAST

The coastline in the area around Kirkcudbright is one of the finest in the UK. There are enough rocky bays, sandy beaches and tales of smugglers to make you feel as if you've stepped into a Famous Five story. To top off the spirit of adventure, there's even a **Ministry of Defence (MOD)**

Exercise Area to the southeast of Kirkcudbright which was used during World War II for training for the D-Day invasion. Take note though: it's still in use today (see below).

East to Auchencairn

The A711 south of Kirkcudbright hugs the shoreline for a short distance with views out to **St Mary's Isle** (a peninsula, not an island), once the seat of the Earl of Selkirk. It was to the earl's house in 1778 that John Paul Jones came, landing his ship the *Ranger* on St Mary's Isle and intending to capture the fourth earl. On reaching his house, however, Jones's men discovered that the earl was away from home. Jones did nothing more than authorise his men to loot the house of its silver, which he later purchased back from them and returned to Lady Selkirk along with a lengthy note of apology.

Heading east you very quickly hit **MOD land** (see ⊘ www.gov.uk/public-access-to-military-areas#scotland) which reaches as far as Dundrennan. No restrictions apply to the main A711 road itself, nor to the land north of the road but if you want to explore the area to the south of the road you will need to be clued up on where you can go and at what times it is safe to do so. Access to the area is possible at four different points, at each of which you must leave your car and walk. The MOD publishes a leaflet which is available from Kirkcudbright tourist information centre (page 133), which shows the extent of the area and walking routes within the range. It also emails out

"*Of the 13 Cistercian monasteries in Scotland, the most impressive that still remains is Dundrennan Abbey.*"

times of live firing exercises two weeks ahead of time to the tourist information centre and library, so if you want to walk in the relevant area make sure to check in advance if it is safe to do so. If in doubt, the MOD flies a flag during the day and has red lights at night to indicate that no access is allowed. You can also telephone the Guard Room at the Kirkcudbright Training Centre which is manned 24 hours a day (✆ 0141 224 8502). The number has a Glasgow code but goes through the exchange automatically to reach Kirkcudbright.

Of the 13 Cistercian monasteries in Scotland, the most impressive that still remains is **Dundrennan Abbey**. It was founded by Fergus, Lord of Galloway in 1142 and the monks who came here went on to found the abbeys at Glenluce (page 220) and New Abbey (page 127). The graceful ruins that can be seen today are known for their bucolic setting, for the well preserved transepts from the late 12th century, and for the fact that it was here that Mary, Queen of Scots spent her last night on Scottish soil.

"It was here at Dundrennan Abbey that Mary, Queen of Scots spent her last night on Scottish soil."

From Dundrennan it's a short hop over the hills to Auchencairn, passing on the way East Kirkcarswell Farm where the large **straw effigy** in the field at the side of the road marks the location of the annual **Wicker Man Festival**. Wickerwork is also on display in **Auchencairn** itself, for this pleasant, unpretentious village is the home of Trevor Leat (⊘ www.trevorleat.co.uk), one of the UK's foremost creators of willow sculptures, whose work can usually be spotted on the main street and who each year creates the Wicker Man which is burned at the end of its eponymous festival at nearby Kirkcarswell. Auchencairn, and more specifically Auchencairn Bay, was smugglers' country, with the most ostentatious sign of those times being **Balcary House** (now a hotel) at Balcary Point. Depending on which account you read, the house, which dates from 1625, was built either by a shipping firm or on the proceeds of smuggling. The road out to Balcary Point is a dead end but worth the trip. It runs for two miles up the side of Auchencairn Bay with fine views out over the sands and, from the end, to the diminutive **Hestan Island**, which in the 12th century was used by the monks from Dundrennan for fishing and which in slightly more recent times became the Isle of Rathan in *The Raiders* by S R Crockett (page 142). A short **circular walk** can be done around Balcary Point taking in the pillar of stone called **Lot's Wife** and, further on, a natural rock seat known as **Adam's Chair**. It's possible to walk over to **Hestan Island**, too, but only at certain low tides. Misjudge it and you risk getting into trouble, so caution is advised and any attempt is at your own risk. Ask locally for the best advice before setting out.

🍴 FOOD & DRINK

The Old Smugglers Inn 11–13 Main St, Auchencairn DG7 1QU ⊘ 01556 640331 ⊘ www. solwaysmugglers.co.uk. Serves traditional pub fare in either the restaurant or bar. At the time of going to press, the pub was closed but it is hoped a community buy-out will ensure its future. Check ahead if visiting.

West to Carrick

To get the most out of the west side of the Dee head out of Kirkcudbright across the stark concrete-arched bridge of 1926 and take the B727 south, signposted for Brighouse Bay. The road hugs the shoreline of the Dee offering ever-changing views of the estuary and passing a convenient stopping point at **Dhoon Bay**, a pleasant spot for a picnic. From the small housing estate above the bay it's possible to walk eight miles straight down the estuary through the woodland to Ross Bay and then around the headland to Brighouse Bay. Alternatively, keep heading south on the road as it turns inland and take the first turning on the left for both Brighouse and Ross bays.

This stretch of coast is a succession of slow-shelving bays and inlets, ideal spots for bathing. The sandy horseshoe of **Brighouse Bay** is a

THE GALLOVIDIAN ENCYCLOPAEDIA

A short walk across the fields from the road to Ross Bay lie the remains of **Senwick Church** (♀ NX655460) on the west side of Kirkcudbright Bay. Here in the kirkyard is buried **John Mactaggart**, author of *The Gallovidian Encyclopaedia* ('Gallovidian' being 'of Galloway'), published in 1824. The full title of his work, as it appeared on the title page, was more than just a mouthful: 'The Scottish Gallovidia, or the original, antiquated, and natural curiosities of the South of Scotland, containing sketches of eccentric characters and curious places, with explanations of singular words, terms, and phrases, interspersed with poems, tales, anecdotes, &c., and various other strange matters; the whole illustrative of the ways of the peasantry and manners of Caledonia, drawn out and alphabetically arranged, by John Mactaggart'.

Mactaggart was in his lifetime poet, teacher, author, and engineer, forging his various careers in Scotland, London and Canada. It is his notorious *Encyclopaedia*, though, for which he is remembered, though not necessarily for the right reasons. Into this book he poured his heart and soul. No character and no custom of his native land did he leave unexplained, all told in his own inimitable, perplexing style. In a display of uncharacteristic *sangfroid* he then declared: 'It will be a book that will never create much noise, yet still it will not be in a hurry forgotten'. He was almost right, for not long after publication his book was withdrawn due to the threat of libel from the father of a local Kirkcudbright girl and the story of both the man and his work has endured ever since. In fact, so persistent has the story been that in recent years the Wigtown Book Festival (pages 195–6) commissioned Penpont poet Hugh McMillan (see box, pages 78–9) to write a sequel or modern-day version, *McMillan's Gallovidian Encyclopaedia*.

particular favourite and rarely gets too busy. The surrounding parish of **Borgue** 🍴 has long enjoyed a reputation as 'the land of milk and honey', with fine pastureland for grazing and farms famed for producing honey. The area was the home in the 18th century of one Hugh Blair whose condition it is believed may have been the first recorded case of autism.

The coast from **Borgue to Knockbrex** and then on to Carrick is gorgeous. It takes in a few curiosities, all of them dating from the late 19th and early 20th centuries and attributable to James Brown, part owner of Affleck and Brown, Manchester's 'Harrods of the north' in what is now the city's iconic Smithfield Buildings. **Kirkandrews Kirk, Corseyard Farm and Model Dairy** and the estate house at **Knockbrex** all display a unique style, combining influences from the Arts and Crafts movement, Celtic motifs and Brown's fondness for outlandish castellated finishings. So extravagant is the model dairy (visible from the road at Corseyard) that it has for years been known the 'coo [cow] palace'! Look out for the castellated **bathing hut** on the beach at Knockbrex.

Beyond Knockbrex the sandy bays give way to a wonderful rocky shore. Keep going to **Carrick**, though, down a rough track, and you'll reach another small sandy bay among the little chalets dotting the shoreline.

Lying just offshore between Knockbrex and Carrick is **Ardwall Isle** (♀ NX572493), the largest of the Islands of Fleet. This is a magical place for kayaking and makes for a popular walk, too. Walkers beware, though, for the island can only be reached at low water and the tides can be treacherous. Check tide times before setting out (the website of the Solway Firth Partnership includes links to tide times for specific locations; ⤢ www.solwayfirthpartnership.co.uk) and keep an eye on them on the way. The island itself is believed to have been an early Christian site possibly dating from the 5th century. In the 13th century a hall house stood here, and towards the end of the 18th century a tavern, catering – one likes to think – to the many smugglers who made this their haunt.

🍴 FOOD & DRINK

Borgue Hotel Main St, Borgue DG6 4SH ✆ 01557 870636 ⤢ www.borguehotel.co.uk. Serves bar meals and snacks and rates consistently highly with both locals and visitors for a warm welcome and good quality food.

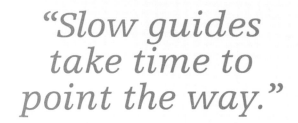

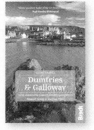
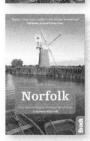

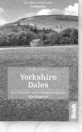

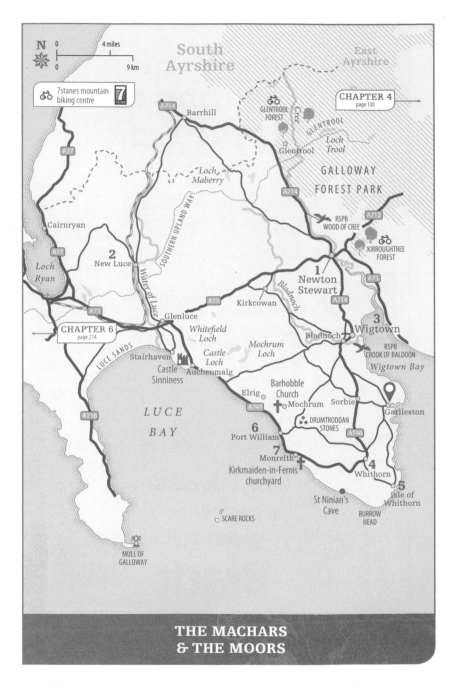

0		4 miles
0		9 km

7stanes mountain biking centre

South Ayrshire

East Ayrshire

CHAPTER 4
page 130

GLENTROOL FOREST

Cree

GLENTROOL

Glentrool

Loch Trool

Barrhill

A714

A77

A714

Loch Maberry

GALLOWAY

FOREST PARK

RSPB WOOD OF CREE

A712

Cairnryan

SOUTHERN UPLAND WAY

A77

KIRROUGHTREE FOREST

A75

2
New Luce

Loch Ryan

Water of Luce

1
Newton Stewart

Bladnoch

A714

A75

A75

Kirkcowan

Glenluce

3
Wigtown

Bladnoch

CHAPTER 6
page 214

Whitefield Loch

Mochrum Loch

RSPB CROOK OF BALDOON

Castle Loch

Wigtown Bay

LUCE SANDS

Stairhaven

Castle Sinniness

Auchenmalg

Barhobble Church

Garlieston

A716

Elrig

Mochrum

Sorbie

LUCE BAY

A747

DRUMTRODDAN STONES

A746

6
Port William

7
Monreith

4
Whithorn

Kirkmaiden-in-Fernis churchyard

St Ninian's Cave

5
Isle of Whithorn

SCARE ROCKS

BURROW HEAD

MULL OF GALLOWAY

THE MACHARS & THE MOORS

5

THE MACHARS
& THE MOORS

Occupying the tract of land between the high hills and ragged coastline of the Stewartry to the east and the gentler landscapes of the Rhins to the west, the Machars and Moors offer a compelling mix of upland wilderness, undulating interior and idyllic coast for discerning travellers in search of somewhere just a wee bit off the beaten track. North of Newton Stewart stretches empty moorland, while to the south, the peninsula of the Machars – from the old Scots word meaning low-lying coastal plain – is perfect for pootling around quiet lanes by car or bike or venturing into the countryside on foot. Exploring is a real treat with a wealth of attractions and features that are as notable for their diversity as they are for their compact geography: it takes less than an hour to drive the 28 miles from Newton Stewart down to the Isle of Whithorn (though the going is slower if you head north to the moors).

"Culture and history abound, notably in Wigtown and at Whithorn, the cradle of Christianity in Scotland."

Culture and history abound, notably in **Wigtown**, Scotland's National Book Town, and at **Whithorn**, the cradle of Christianity in Scotland. There is also a plethora of prehistoric sites: stone circles, cup and ring marks, Iron Age settlements, crannogs, chambered cairns … historical evidence of life down through the centuries in such abundance that separate books have been written on them alone. We have selected some of the best to include here, but there are lots of leaflets and information points around the region, so if you have a specific interest, keep an eye open for relevant literature. As ever, OS maps provide an indispensable reference source, too.

Strictly speaking, the Machars start at Newton Stewart on the west side of the River Cree, which means that Minnigaff, on the east side, falls into the Stewartry. However, it makes no sense to separate the two and so both are dealt with in this chapter.

GETTING AROUND

The Machars and Moors are bisected east–west by the A75/European route E13 and north–south by the A714 from Whithorn up into Ayrshire and beyond. The sometimes busy A75, particularly shortly after a ferry docks at Cairnryan, masks the tranquil areas and quiet roads that lie just a short distance either side.

Ferries operate between Northern Ireland and Cairnryan, on the eastern side of Loch Ryan, which is 26 miles from Newton Stewart. P&O Ferries operates services to Larne, and Stena Line sails to Belfast.

PUBLIC TRANSPORT

The Scotrail **train service** has two railway stations within 25 miles of Newton Stewart at Barrhill (18 miles) to the north, and Stranraer (25 miles) to the west, which connect to Glasgow. Dumfries station is 48 miles, with services also operated by Scotrail, which has more frequent services along its Newcastle, Carlisle to Glasgow route.

There are regular **bus services** between Dumfries and Stranraer, which stop at Newton Stewart, Kirkcowan and Glenluce. Stagecoach Western services 500 and X75 between them offer seven departures daily Monday to Saturday from Dumfries railway station and Whitesands to Stranraer. The journey can take up to 2½ hours depending on the time of day. McCulloch Coaches also offers one service a day. On Sundays there are three departures of service 500. Return journeys run as frequently.

Once at the Machars, daily buses run from Newton Stewart through many of the key villages and towns to Port William (Service 415 – James King Coaches/Stagecoach Western). Stagecoach Western also runs the infrequent 416 service from Stranraer down to Whithorn and back up to Newton Stewart.

Local public transport information is provided by South West of Scotland Transport Partnership (⊘ www.swestrans.org.uk), or alternatively the traveline (✆ 0871 200 22 33 ⊘ www.traveline.org.uk).

CYCLING

The quiet, triangular-shaped peninsula of the Machars is fertile low-lying ground, making for flatter cycling when compared to the rest of the county. The rolling pastures and the varied coastal scenery, from rugged cliffs at Burrow Head to merse (saltmarsh) in the Cree

ℹ TOURIST INFORMATION

VisitScotland Information Centre Newton Stewart Dashwood Sq, Newton Stewart
DG10 9JU ☏ 01671 402431 ⊙ www.visitdumfriesandgalloway.co.uk ⊙ seasonal

estuary, offer an interesting mix of views for the cyclist. Further north the countryside opens up to mile upon mile of moorland, ever more imposing hills, and remote lochs and glens, and is a treat for wildlife watchers. **National Cycle Network Route 7** passes Newton Stewart on its way north to Inverness.

The Machars has four **colour-coded signposted routes**. The yellow route (25 miles) passes through the northern Machars, visiting Kirkcowan, Bladnoch and Wigtown. The orange route (22 miles) explores the central eastern Machars, taking in Kirkinner, Garlieston, Sorbie, Whauphill, Bladnoch, and Wigtown. The green route (20 miles) heads along the coast of the southwest Machars, passing through Mochrum, Port William, Monreith and Whithorn. The red route (17 miles) is around the countryside of the southeast Machars overlooking Wigtwon Bay, visiting the Isle of Whithorn, Sorbie and Whithorn.

Dumfries and Galloway Council's free *Cycling in and around Wigtownshire* booklet offers a good selection of routes.

⅋ CYCLE HIRE

Courtyard Cycle Hire 67 Main St, Kirkcowan, DG8 0HQ ☏ 01671 830286 ⊙ www.courtyardcyclehire.co.uk

WALKING

The quiet peninsula of the Machars and the wild and remote moors to the north provide a fine range of scenery for walkers to explore. The rugged moors and hills offer a wonderful sense of isolation. The **Merrick Trail** from Loch Trool takes you to the highest point in Dumfries and Galloway rising to 2,766 feet. Along the way, look out for some of the rarest plants in Scotland such as dwarf willow, mossy saxifrage, thrift and juniper, all montane species and extremely tough, surviving harsh mountaintop conditions.

The long distance **Southern Upland Way** wiggles its way across this northern area. Heading south from the Southern Upland Way the **Pilgrim's Way** is about 25 miles long and passes through the pretty village of New

Luce and on to the early Christian holy sites of Whithorn and St Ninian's Cave. On the coast, green pastures roll to the water's edge and merse (saltmarsh), providing contrast with stretches of dramatic cliffs carpeted in coastal flowers. Inland, pockets of native broadleaved woodlands, particularly along the River Cree, are important sites for birds and wildlife. Dumfries and Galloway Council has produced free 'Walking in and around' booklets to the Machars, and Newton Stewart and Creetown.

1 NEWTON STEWART & AROUND

🏠 **Kirroughtree House** (page 248), **Cairnharrow** (page 249)

Pleasantly positioned on the banks of the 'silv'ry winding Cree', Newton Stewart is a likeable and functional town, servicing all of the outlying areas (the next town of any size is Stranraer (pages 224–6), 25 miles to the west) with its mix of restaurants, shops and supermarkets. 'Gateway to the Galloway Hills' is a description that's used to describe it today, while the novelist S R Crockett, who came from neighbouring Kirkcudbrightshire, said it was the 'natural gateway and distributing point for much enchanted ground'. No surprise then that it's the hub for southern Scotland's largest **walking festival** which is held each year in May.

In times past this was a river crossing point on the cattle droving route from the west along to Dumfries and beyond to the markets in England. Cattle (and sheep) continue to play a role in the life of the modern town thanks to Wigtownshire's last remaining **livestock market**, which can be found in a listed octagonal building on Station Road at the southern end of town. Sales are held weekly, and at the end of the trading year in October there is a world-famous Blackface Ram sale.

Newton Stewart developed when William Stewart, second Earl of Galloway, secured the royal burgh charter from Charles II in 1677. Two hundred years later, however, its name was changed to Newton Douglas when aspiring merchant William Douglas, of Castle Douglas fame (pages 147–8), bought the estate. In this instance Douglas's ego surpassed his business acumen, for the £20,000 cotton mill that he built here failed and he was compelled to retreat from the Shire, leaving locals to revert their town name without fuss to Newton Stewart.

For an introduction to the town, take a short **circular walk** from the riverside car park next to the supermarkets at the southern end of Victoria Street. Cross the bridge and head back along the east bank and

NEWTON STEWART'S ALADDIN'S CAVE ✤

York Rd, DG8 6HH ✧ www.newtonstewart.org ⊙ seasonal, check the Newton Stewart town website for details

Perhaps the greatest unsung attraction of Newton Stewart is its **museum**, housed in the former St John's Church in a residential area above Victoria Street. A carving of Old Mortality (page 139) in the grounds welcomes you, and although the random mix of items that surrounds it hints at the mass and range of the collection to come, nothing really prepares you for the sight that hits you on stepping inside. Thousands of exhibits are crammed into every nook, niche and cranny, a fantastic collection of accumulated paraphernalia, worth exploring for the joy of its interest, local personality, anomaly and the downright bizarre. The collection was started in the 1970s having originated as an idea in 1966 and then been pursued with vigour by a number of local people, not least Miss Helen Drew, a name which according to local newspaper the *Galloway Gazette* is 'synonymous not just with the museum but with Newton Stewart as a whole'. Miss Drew, who passed away in 2010, purchased the church and gifted it to be used as a museum.

She also spent her life collecting for it and donated around 50% of the items which are on display.

The collection here is one of the most eclectic and wide-ranging that we have ever come across in a local museum, rivalled perhaps only by the collection at Dalbeattie's museum (page 153). Exhibits are arranged into themed bays and include everything from old dolls and games to a penny farthing bicycle, a martyrs stone commemorating Covenanters, and a medical and dental section complete with ear trumpet and false teeth. There are royal items and china, 1920s dresses and old hand-held fans along with an explanation of the 'Language of the Fan'. A costume room at the back is full of old mannequins and as you open the door you can't help but feel that creepy sensation that they have all been alive and moving until the moment you turned the handle. Perhaps the most bizarre exhibits, though, are the elephant molar and a necklace of horse teeth.

then return via the handsome granite **Cree Bridge** of 1813. Here on the west bank stands a **monument** to Randolph Stewart, ninth Earl of Galloway, by all accounts a credit to his title having held the position of Lord Lieutenant of both Wigtownshire and Kirkcudbrightshire.

From the monument continue along Victoria Street, noting the **Art Deco cinema**, which celebrated its 80th anniversary in 2014. Still functioning as a cinema, it's a community-run venue staffed by volunteers and operating on a not-for-profit basis. Beyond the cinema, walk up the hill and turn left to drop back down to the riverside car park.

GALLOWAY FOREST PARK

🏠 **House o' Hill Hotel** (page 248)

From Newton Stewart there is easy access to Galloway Forest Park, its many attractions and its various visitor centres. This western side of Galloway Forest Park also offers the only vehicular access to **Glentrool Visitor Centre** (📍 NX371787) north of Newton Stewart, while immediately east of Newton Stewart is **Kirroughtree Visitor Centre**. For more information on Galloway Forest Park see pages 143–6.

RSPB WOOD OF CREE RESERVE 🖐

Running up the east side of the Cree north of Minnigaff is the **RSPB Wood of Cree** reserve, the largest ancient woodland in southern Scotland and a good place to spot some of the UK's declining population of willow tits. There are various stopping points and parking areas along the wood edge, from where different trails head off.

🍴 **FOOD & DRINK**

The Belted Galloway Visitor Centre Riverside View, DG8 6NQ 🖉 01671 403458 👆 www.thebeltedgalloway.co.uk. Café, shop and information in a convenient location by the riverside car park.

House o' Hill Hotel Bargrennan DG8 6RN 🖉 01671 840243 👆 http://houseohill.co.uk. The only hotel within Galloway Forest Park and has also established a strong reputation for its food from local ingredients. It's a 20-minute drive from Newton Stewart but worth the trip. Alternatively, plan your day's touring to include it for lunch or dinner.

Kirroughtree House Newton Stewart DG8 6AN 🖉 01671 402141 👆 www. kirroughtreehousehotel.co.uk. Up the hill to the east of town, this hotel is open to non-residents serving traditional, locally sourced food in its comfortable dining room.

The Riverbank Restaurant Goods Lane, DG8 6EH 🖉 01671 403330. On the riverside next to the supermarket, a popular café serving sandwiches, soups, fish and chips and more.

THE MOORS

Miles upon miles of empty moorland lie north of the A75 where it runs between Newton Stewart and Glenluce. If you feel like getting away from everyone and everything, this is the place to come and, depending on how you like your countryside, you will either love it or loathe it. There is a stark beauty in the endless moorland vista, but there is also a loneliness and isolation that can shake even the most positive spirits.

CASTLES & HISTORIC HOUSES

Fought over long and often, Dumfries and Galloway has, of necessity, had to arm and defend itself through successive centuries. An impressive legacy of fortified buildings now punctuates the landscape.

1 The striking pink sandstone façade of Drumlanrig Castle. 2 MacLellan's Castle in Kirkcudbright. 3 Remote and mighty Threave Castle on an island in the Dee.

1

HOLY PLACES

The region is home to a wide range of religious architecture, reflecting the many and varied influences which have been brought to bear over the centuries. From simple handmade crosses to extravagant marble monuments, the variety is striking.

2

3

4

5

6

1 Romantic Sweetheart Abbey. 2 The Durisdeer Marbles. 3 Dalswinton Mission Church. 4 St Ninian's Cave. 5 Kagyu Samye Ling Tibetan Monastery. 6 Irongray Church. 7 Ghoulish gravestones in the cemetery of St Kentigern Monastery. 8 Anwoth Old Church. 9 The Ukrainian Chapel near Lockerbie.

7

9

8

GLORIOUS GARDENS

All manner of gardens and outdoor spaces can be found across the region. The far west is known for its mild climate and southern hemisphere plants, while in the east there are curiosities such as the new Crawick Multiverse, an intriguing project by landscape architect Charles Jencks.

1 Crawick Multiverse occupies a 55-acre site in northern Nithsdale. **2** Logan Botanic Garden boasts an astonishing array of southern hemisphere plants. **3** Shambellie Garden has been nurtured back to life in recent years.

One way to experience this area is to take the Glasgow train from Stranraer (pages 224–6) up to **Barrhill** in South Ayrshire, get off there and then catch the next train back, but train times don't tie in very neatly and you're likely to find yourself killing time for several hours. Barrhill is a small village with limited amenities and the station is a 15-minute walk outside the village itself. Alternatively, driving – or cycling for the very fit – offers greatest flexibility. Whether you start at Glenluce or Newton Stewart, it's just less than 20 miles by road to Barrhill.

If going from **Glenluce**, once north of New Luce (see below), stick to the road on the east side of the Main Water of Luce and you'll find isolated hilltop farms and views that make you feel as if you're on top of the world. There really is nothing here. It is bleak, desolate, wonderful, superlative moorland where black-faced sheep roam the road and the old disused station at **Glenwhilly** (♀ NX173715) sits forlorn and empty since closing in 1965. The road follows much the same route as the train line and you may be forgiven for wondering if you have reached the emptiest place in Scotland. From Newton Stewart the A714 travels through large stretches of Forestry Commission plantation, as does the smaller B7027, the latter having the added interest of a series of lochs roughly halfway. The **River Bladnoch** rises at pretty **Loch Maberry** (♀ NX285755), which marks the regional boundary and which is gemmed with a number of small islands, on one of which stand the remains of a fortified castle. **Canoe trips** are run here by the Adventure Centre for Education (✆ 07920 406982 ⊘ www.adventurecentreforeducation. com), catering to both adults and (accompanied) children.

2 NEW LUCE

The pretty village of New Luce sits at the junction of five roads and the confluence of the Main Water of Luce and Cross Water of Luce. At one time it was a bustling small community of tradesmen and labourers serving the surrounding farms, but today it's a quieter place of whitewashed cottages, neat gardens and hanging baskets, with a post office, shop and, right by the river, the Kenmuir Arms Hotel. Located just a mile or so north of the **Southern Upland Way**, it's a good spot for walkers in search of retreat.

During the 17th century, from 1659 until his ejection in 1662, New Luce came under the care of the renowned Prophet Peden, one Alexander Peden, Covenanter preacher and minister. He was one of the 300 or so ministers who were forced to leave their churches after the restoration of Charles II. He spent 11 years on the run, during which time he preached in fields all over southern and central Scotland, gaining notoriety and making government troops ever more eager to catch him. Eventually he was arrested in 1673 and spent four years imprisoned on Bass Rock in the Firth of Forth. In 1678 he was put on a slave ship bound for the US but he was set free by the captain and spent most of the rest of his life in Ireland. It is said that when he left New Luce, after preaching his farewell sermon, he closed the door of the pulpit and, knocking on it three times with his Bible, declared 'I arrest thee in my Master's name, that none ever enter thee but such as come in by the door as I have done.' His prophecy was correct for the pulpit at New Luce wasn't used again until after the Revolution.

Various places of archaeological interest are found in the surrounding area, all of them detailed on a sign at the top end of the main street, from Neolithic cairns to remains from the Bronze and Iron ages.

North of New Luce the road follows the line of the railway over rolling hills and farmland for 13 miles up to Barrhill.

3 WIGTOWN

🏠 **Glaisnock Café and Guest House** (page 249), **Hillcrest House** (page 249)

With its plethora of bookshops, quiet streets, views over Wig Bay, abundant birdlife and a colourful history, Scotland's National Book Town is an overgrown village where you can wrap yourself in the comfort of a slower way of life. There is something unreservedly appealing about a town that has a bowling green at its very heart, set out neatly in the town square in front of the disproportionately large and imposing County Building, a sign of past prosperity. Looking at today's peaceable town with its gaily coloured houses and its delightful dedication to matters bookish, it is difficult to believe that this was once a major centre with a trade built upon the fortunes of a port that is now silted up, where cattle were corralled in the railed enclosure in the town centre and the green was the common dunghill, and where the savage murder of innocent victims occurred during Covenanting times.

Settled for at least 1,000 years, Wigtown was once the main town of Galloway west of the Cree. It also lent its name to the old county of Wigtownshire, an administrative region which was lost in the reorganisation of county boundaries in 1975, but which still exists as a lieutenancy area for the Queen's representative, the Lord Lieutenant of Wigtownshire. A castle was built here by the 13th century, but little is known about it other than the fact that, contrary to the siting of most defensive buildings, it was located on the flat plains of the River Bladnoch, where it could command control of the port, while the town and church were above it on the hill.

A Royal Charter was granted in 1457 and during the 15th and 16th centuries the port of Wigtown thrived, competing first with Kirkcudbright (page 174) and then, later, with nearby Whithorn (pages 200–4). It was in the 17th century, during the Killing Times (pages 24–5), that Wigtown gained notoriety for the execution of the **Wigtown**

"Wigtown lent its name to the old county of Wigtownshire, an administrative region which was lost in the reorganisation of county boundaries in 1975."

Martyrs, including a 63-year-old woman and a girl of 18 who stood accused of attending 20 field Conventicles. Margaret McLachlan and Margaret Wilson were sentenced to death by drowning and on 11 May 1685 both were tied to the stake in the channel of the Bladnoch near the entrance to Wig Bay, where they were left to the incoming tide. They were laid to rest in **Wigtown Parish Church** at the bottom of Bank Street, where their graves can still be seen along with those of other martyrs, and they are also commemorated in the **Martyrs Memorial**, an obelisk built on Windy Hill in 1858, from where there is a good view over the town down to the bay (and which is a good place to come bat-spotting of an evening). To reach the memorial head up High Vennel from the main square, turn left at the garage and take the last turning on the left at the top.

Down on the bay stands the most poignant of all the memorials, the **Martyrs Stake**, which can be reached via a path past the Parish Church and leading on to a boardwalk across the merse. Standing here in this lonely spot it is awful to contemplate the horror that befell those who lost their lives for remaining true to themselves.

By the end of the 20th century, Wigtown was beginning to lose its life and lustre. That all changed when it won a competition to become the National Book Town, since when its fortunes have been significantly revived. Now the town boasts more than ten independent bookshops specialising in just about every subject imaginable, and every year in late September/early

LEAF YOUR WAY
THROUGH WIGTOWN'S BOOKSHOPS

All of Wigtown's bookshops and their areas of speciality are detailed in a useful leaflet available from, well, all of the bookshops! Copies are also held at the Book Festival office and can be viewed online at ⌀ www.wigtown-booktown.co.uk (click on 'Books' and then select 'Bookshops').

October it becomes a hive of activity when it hosts the annual **Wigtown Book Festival**. It's a fun affair with a wide range of talks on all manner of topics given by everyone from international celebrities to local authors. Further details can be obtained at ⌀ www.wigtownbookfestival.com or from the festival ticket office in the County Buildings.

Wigtown Bay, a huge expanse of saltmarsh and mudflat, is the largest Local Nature Reserve in the UK, brimming with food that attracts waders throughout the year, notably in winter when some of the Svalbard geese that make it to Caerlaverock further east (pages 120–3) find their way along here. Ospreys have also nested here for the past few years and can sometimes be seen via osprey cams at the **wildlife centre** on the top floor of the County Buildings, from where there's a great view over the bay. Immediately south of Wigtown is the new **RSPB Crook of Baldoon reserve** (♀ NX445531), accessed through nearby Bladnoch and across an old World War II airfield. From the reserve a shore footpath runs to Wigtown harbour, while a noticeboard and audio installation offer further information on what to look for.

On a separate note, if you head down to Crook of Baldoon, keep an eye open for the remains of **Baldoon Castle** (private) 🖐 at Baldoon Mains.

AROUND WIGTOWN

The area around Wigtown encompasses gentle scenery, ancient standing stones, small villages and all the attractions of the coast. To the northwest is **Kirkcowan**, a friendly, sleepy village with a good **bike hire** option (page 189). East from here on the B733 in a field just next to the road is the impressive **Torhouse Stone Circle** (♀ NX383565; Historic Scotland). Known as a recumbent stone circle due to one of the stones being laid flat, it is one of the best examples of its type in Britain and something of a rarity in Scotland.

Bladnoch, just south of Wigtown, was for many years known for its whisky distillery, the buildings of which can still be seen but which is now closed. It's a pleasant spot on the banks of the eponymous river, which grew up as a crossing point for pilgrims on their way to Whithorn. It is also the location of a popular pub (page 198) and home to a community of artisans and musicians. Six miles south of here is **Sorbie**, a small village once known for its damask weaving and with an exceptionally solid-looking church, immediately east of which is the half ruined 16th-century **Sorbie Tower** (♀ NX451471) ⚘, notable as the seat of the Clan Hannay. Occupied until 1748 it was abandoned until coming into the care of the Clan Hannay Society in 1965, who have carried out a number of remedial works. The tower's setting is pleasant, surrounded by trees and with a small colourful garden with picnic tables.

The pristinely maintained waterfront cottages of **Garlieston** on the east coast look out to Wig Bay, making an endearing setting which draws in the visitors to the local caravan park. This was once the richest village in Galloway thanks to industries such as boat building, fishing and cargo, while in more recent times nearby Rigg Bay was a testing site for the Mulberry Harbour used in the Normandy Landings. In the 18th century the sixth Earl of Galloway redesigned the village to incorporate the neat terraces, and it's from his eldest son, Lord Garlies, that it takes its name. The Earl also built neighbouring **Galloway House** (⊘ www. gallowayhousegardens.co.uk), an enormous pile which now sits empty having been sold off by the 11th Earl in 1909 and passed through various hands before being abandoned. (At the time of writing it was on the market once again.) Its grounds are open seasonally to the public and are well worth a visit. From the small parking area (honesty box for payment) there are delightful walks through what were once fine woodland gardens which are today maintained by a stalwart team of volunteers. A short stroll brings you to the sands of the exquisite **Rigg Bay**.

South of Garlieston on the B7063 stands **Cruggleton Church** (♀ NX478428), the former chapel of nearby **Cruggleton Castle** (♀ NX485428), only a fraction of which can still be seen on a rocky peninsula about one mile south of Rigg Bay (see box, pages 198–9). Situated above farmland, the church is surrounded by a walled burial ground and was restored in the 1890s by the Marquis of Bute. Its chief point of interest is the 12th-century chancel arch inside, one of the few surviving examples of early Norman architecture in the area.

Garlieston to Cruggleton Castle

❄ OS Landranger map 83, Explorer map 311; start: Village Hall, Garlieston, ♀ NX478463 (accessible by bus 415/416); 6.5 miles/2½ hours; easy to moderate (some inclines). Note that refreshments are available in Gatehouse.

S tarting from the **1 Village Hall** on Garlieston waterfront, head towards the caravan parks and on to the old harbour. Take the track at the end of the harbour wall as it passes along the water's edge through old gnarled oaks, past fine estuary views and in front of the stately **Galloway House**. Look out for grey seals, the silhouette of open winged cormorants and a motley crew of wading birds. Follow the path around the headland and in to the lovely **Rigg Bay**. The track becomes less distinct **2** but follow your nose along the small paths through the woods, enjoying the estate gardens as you go and keeping the bay to your left.

Once at the **3 picnic area** (♀ NX476447) the path becomes clearer along the back of the bay and on in to the woods. At the cottage ruins veer off to the left and enjoy the gentle climb up through beautiful mixed woodland and over numerous bridged small streams. When the path meets the stone dyke (wall) and turns right, pause a second and head over to an old **wooden bench 4** and enjoy the view.

Exit the wood to find yourself by a solitary cottage standing atop towering cliffs complete with stunning views – if you feel like staying a while longer the cottage can be rented out (⊘ www.gallowayhouseestate.co.uk). Continue along the clifftop following the dry stone dyke; go through the gate, turn left and along the edge of the fields to **5 Cruggleton Castle**

To gain access, make contact via Scotland's Churches Trust (⊘ www. scotlandchurchestrust.org.uk) or, if you are here in late summer, a service is held once a year on the first Sunday in September at 15.00.

⑪ FOOD & DRINK

Wigtown isn't short of cafés, all of which are detailed on the Wigtown Book Town website ⊘ www.wigtown-booktown.co.uk.

Beltie Books & Café 6 Bank St, DG8 9HP ⊘ 01988 402730 ⊘ www.beltiebooks.co.uk ⊙ closed Tue. Proprietor Andrew Wilson offers a warm welcome, lots of information about the area, and bakes a scrumptious range of cakes, scones and bread.

Bladnoch Inn Bladnoch DG8 9AB ⊘ 01988 402200 ⊘ www.bladnochinn.co.uk. Always popular for both lunch and dinner, and especially on a sunny evening when you can sit outside on the banks of the river.

(♀ NX485428). All that remains of this 13th-century castle is a reconstructed arch, but what it lacks in walls it certainly makes up for in atmosphere and views.

Retrace your steps back to the picnic area at Rigg Bay. Once at the benches and information board take the hard surface track to the left, through the gate and on past the cottages and walled garden. Turn right and follow the signs through the gardens to the car park and out along the access road, with its fine views of Galloway House. At the **6 crossroads** go straight ahead over the cattle grid, through the field, over another cattle grid and through a farmyard. At the end of the track turn left at the T-junction and follow track back to Garlieston.

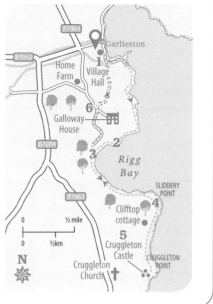

Hillcrest House Maidland Pl, Station Rd, DG8 9EU ✆ 01988 402018 🖉 https://hillcrest-wigtown.co.uk. For over ten years Deborah and Andrew Firth have been welcoming guests to their late 19th-century home/guesthouse. A hearty three-course set menu is offered every evening and non-residents are welcome (booking essential). Deborah knows all the best places to get local ingredients: she buys Wigtown saltmarsh lamb by the lamb from her preferred butcher and sources vegetables from a market garden in the hills above Creetown. It's friendly, intimate, and something just a little bit different.

Glaisnock Café & Bookshop 20 South Main St, DG8 9EH ✆ 01988 402249. Carl and Stephanie Davis's intimate café is welcoming, friendly and serves good wholesome food.

ReadingLasses Bookshop and Café 17 South Main St, DG8 9EH ✆ 01988 403266 🖉 www.reading-lasses.com. Cosy and comfortable, and serves irresistible cakes. This is the sort of place you could happily sit for hours.

4 WHITHORN

🏠 **Whithorn House Hotel** (page 248), **The Pend** (page 249)

With a population of less than 1,000 people, Whithorn at first glance appears to be little more than a quiet country town, isolated from the rest of the world towards the southern tip of the Machars. But Whithorn's

WHITHORN: CRADLE OF CHRISTIANITY IN SCOTLAND

Julia Muir Watt is the Development Manager for the Whithorn Trust. She kindly agreed to provide the text below for this guide.

The international importance of Whithorn as an archaeological site, and its seminal role in Scottish history is not immediately apparent from this small royal burgh's attractive and well-preserved Georgian streetscape. Yet the observant eye will already detect from the narrow ports closing either end of George Street that a medieval town underlies its later frontages; glimpses of the 'burghage plots' – the narrow strip gardens running down from the houses to the back – further confirm Whithorn's early credentials.

Its real claim to national importance, however, lies after you leave behind the secular world at the mouth of The Pend, the arched gateway into the former Priory precincts, adorned with the Stuart Coat of Arms (c1500), and walk up historic Bruce Street to the crown of the small hill. In so doing, you walk in the footsteps of countless pilgrims, who came to seek forgiveness, healing and even absolution from crimes at the shrine of St Ninian, Scotland's earliest saint, whose cult reached a peak in the high medieval period. At the top of the hill, the roofless ruins of the medieval cathedral, once a tall structure dominating the

surrounding countryside, are what remain of the latest of a series of churches built on the site of the earliest Christian shrine and church in the country.

Much scholarly controversy surrounds the exact date and identity of St Ninian, a debate begun by the Venerable Bede in the early 8th century, when he wrote that the saint's evangelising mission had pre-dated the much better-known Columba's by a great many years. A series of archaeological excavations from the late 19th century onwards have sought the grail of the original white-plastered Ninianic church, *Candida Casa*, or the 'white shining house', and in so doing have uncovered, if not the church itself, a remarkable body of evidence which proves that Whithorn, probably by the 5th century ad, was a thriving, sophisticated and literate community with Christian beliefs, importing luxury goods, in touch with the outside world of ideas and trade, with a complex and Latin-speaking church hierarchy and a specialised economy. Much of the evidence for this was excavated during the 1980s and 1990s by archaeologist Peter Hill, and the finds from the dig are on display in the appearance today belies its past, for it was once a major trading centre located conveniently close to major shipping routes. What's more, its place in history is assured thanks to the story of **St Ninian**, Scotland's first saint who, according to many, helped to make this small settlement the **cradle of Christianity** in Scotland. Tomes have been written on this subject, but in brief the story goes that within 50 years of Roman

Whithorn Trust's visitor centre. The inscribed 'Latinus' stone, the iconic stone which testifies to the very early origins of the Whithorn site, dates from its earliest Christian period and can be seen at the adjacent Priory Museum.

The continuing reverence in which the early church and its saint were held is attested by the way in which Whithorn was constantly resettled and reinvented in the following centuries and by successively invading or colonising peoples. In Bede's day, the Anglo-Saxons dominated Whithorn, claimed St Ninian as their own, and an 8th-century poem speaks of the volume of pilgrims seeking miraculous cures at his shrine. Just after, Whithorn (which has kept its Anglo-Saxon name, 'Hwitan-Aerne', the White House) acquired its own school of sculpture and the distinctive disc-headed crosses, seen in the museum, were carved here and have been found at critical points in the countryside, as preaching crosses, at places of judgement or at the sites of other medieval churches within Whithorn's sphere of influence. The later carved stones of the 10th and 11th centuries display perhaps less skill, but show how those of Norse origin, originating from Viking Dublin, came to Whithorn, bringing their own culture and symbols, blending them with Christian imagery

and incidentally giving their name to Galloway (the 'Gall-Ghàidheil', or the foreign Gaels).

Wealth and power accumulated from the pilgrimage trade (the pilgrims' detritus fortunately survived for archaeologists to analyse) and allowed Whithorn to become a broker in the murky world of Scottish medieval power politics. Whithorn's Prior had the power of life and death within his extensive lands, a trading fleet sailing from the Isle of Whithorn, and was in the confidences of princes. At the peak of its influence, James IV of Scotland visited this remote, and not always obedient, part of his kingdom yearly on pilgrimage, dispensing largesse and begging forgiveness for his sins at the shrine of Scotland's most powerful saint. His treasurer's accounts paint a lively picture of his visits, occasionally accompanied by Italian minstrels, dancers and a baggage train, arriving from across Scotland. The wide open space in front of The Pend still has a ceremonial grandeur, and the town's older civic buildings cluster round the entrance to the Priory.

With the banning of pilgrimage after the Reformation, Whithorn settled into a more modest role as a small centre for trade and a service centre for the surrounding, rich countryside, and that is what it remains today.

withdrawal from Britain there was a Christian community here, who were harried by the barbarous Picts from the north. It was to these dangerous tribes that St Ninian brought his message, with the date AD397 being taken to be the start of his mission. Significantly, this would mean that St Ninian arrived more than half a century before Columba, his rival saint, reached the community of Iona in the north of Scotland. And it was in Whithorn that he built his *Candida Casa*, from which Whithorn takes its name (see box, pages 200–1).

"Robert the Bruce came to the shrine of St Ninian in 1329, just three months before his death, to pray for a cure for leprosy."

To get to grips with the ins and outs of this crucial part of Scottish history, head straight for the well-planned **Whithorn Story Visitor Centre** (45–47 George St, DG8 8NS ⌀ www.whithorn.com ☉ seasonal) run by the Whithorn Trust, where an introductory film sets the scene followed by a wander through the chronologically arranged exhibition which lays out clearly the town's development. The importance of this small community to the evolution of a nation can't be overstated and the insights offered here make all the difference in appreciating just how special a place this is. Over the centuries many Scottish kings and queens have visited, including – so tradition has it – Robert the Bruce who came to the shrine of St Ninian in 1329, just three months before his death, to pray for a cure for leprosy. Pick up copies of a couple of leaflets while here: *Whithorn Story* and *Whithorn Town Trail*.

The entry ticket to the Whithorn Story also includes access to Historic Scotland's **Whithorn Priory & Museum** (DG8 8PY ⌀ www.whithornpriorymuseum.gov.uk/ ☉ seasonal) just around the corner, which forms an integral part of the tale. Enter through the arched gateway of **The Pend**, noting James IV's sculpted coat of arms above, who was known for his devotion to the veneration of the relics of the saints and who visited Whithorn frequently. Of the original large compound only the roofless nave and crypts survive, the latter gloomy but impressive in their scale. The neighbouring museum houses an effectively displayed collection of stone crosses from the 10th and 11th centuries. Even if this sounds like a dry subject, we recommend a visit, as there is much to be learned and discovered especially if Debbie, the museum curator, is on hand. Her father looked after the museum before her and there is little that she doesn't know on this subject, helping to bring it alive in ways that are truly enlightening. Crosses such as these would have been spread across the landscape in centuries past and the collection here is particularly fine, including the so-called Whithorn School crosses and carvings from AD800–1100.

There is still an **annual pilgrimage** at Whithorn on the last Sunday in August, when between 500 and 600 people gather and make their way to **St Ninian's Cave** (♀ NX422361), four miles southwest of Whithorn at Physgill on the southwest coast of the Machars. Tradition has it that here on this pebbly shore St Ninian would retreat to the cave at the end of the beach for personal prayer. The cave can be visited at any time by parking in the car park around one mile from the beach and wandering down through the woods. A small enclave with a good view back along the beach and coast, it's an ideal spot for quiet contemplation. Over the centuries many pilgrims have come to give thanks for a safe

"There is still an annual pilgrimage at Whithorn on the last Sunday in August, when between 500 and 600 people gather and make their way to St Ninian's Cave."

journey and, in among the offerings from present-day visitors, are 8th-century crosses carved into the walls. Depending on when you come, look out for the house martins nesting above the entrance to the cave and the dainty purple thrift flower dotted along the edge of the beach. We've also spotted seals just off shore.

Whithorn's main street hasn't changed much since 1760 and still retains much of its medieval shape. Scattered along it is a goodly range of local shops, including the appropriately named **Priory Antiques** at 29 George Street with a small but interesting collection in an outhouse at the back and the **Central Café** just a few doors along offering tasty homemade ice cream. If you're here in July look out for venues opening for the annual **Arts Trail** run by the Creative Whithorn Arts and Crafts Association.

West of Whithorn lies **Rispain Camp** settlement, a source of much debate over the years but which Historic Scotland now asserts, thanks to archaeological excavations between 1978 and 1981, is not a Roman fortlet, nor a medieval manor-place, but was probably the home of a tribal chief, inhabited between 100BC and AD200. The defences are among the most impressive surviving from Iron Age Scotland.

¶¶ FOOD & DRINK

Whithorn House St Johns St, DG8 8PE ✆ 01988 501081 ◷ https://whithornhouse.com. Offers one of the finest afternoon teas you'll find on the Machars, in the light and airy front room of this traditional 19th-century stone built house. Period wallpaper and original cornicing set the tone, along with lace finishings on the table cloths and beaded crocheted sugar covers. Choose from 30 teas (split between black, white, green, oolong, herbal and fruit infusions and wellness teas), and nine different types of scones, not to mention all manner of homemade cakes and traybakes. Savouries are on offer, too: sandwiches, crumpets and soups. Teas are served in individual pots, each of which comes with its own timer pre-set which counts down to alert you to the precise moment that your brew is appropriately infused. The whole experience is scrumptious.

5 ISLE OF WHITHORN

♠ The Steam Packet Inn (page 248)

Down at the southern tip of the Machars sits one of the most enticing fishing villages in Dumfries and Galloway, the Isle of Whithorn. A cluster of cottages with their backs to the sea nestles around the small harbour, creating a cosy enclave and the perfect retreat. Needless to say it can be busy, but even still, its charm is undeniable. Despite its name, this is no island but more of a peninsula, just about as far south in Scotland as you will find a village, rivalled only by Drummore on the Rhins (pages 240–1). Its history is one of trade, for it was from here that goods from the medieval Prior of Whithorn's estates were exported, but earlier than that it was the site of a tower house known as the **Cairn**, the remains of

THE CULT OF THE WICKER MAN 👆

Burrow Head, the most southerly point of the Machars, is just a couple of miles south of the Isle of Whithorn. Today it is a holiday village, but film buffs may know it as the location for the final scene in the cult film *The Wicker Man*, in which a young Edward Woodward is sacrificially burned alive inside the wicker man effigy. Released in 1973, the movie is set on a fictional island in northwest Scotland and tells of the plight of a policeman (Woodward) sent from the mainland to investigate the disappearance of a local girl. What he comes up against is a community of Pagan-type worshippers, intent on preventing him from disrupting their sinister traditions. Despite a cast of big names (Britt Ekland and Christopher Lee), the film never took off, although it has endured the years as a cult classic and also spawned the annual Wicker Man Festival which takes place each year in summer near Dundrennan (page 181) in the Stewartry.

which are still here today, standing at the end of the rocky promontory. Also still here are the remains of **St Ninian's Chapel** from around 1300, built on the site of an earlier chapel where pilgrims landing on the shore *en route* to Whithorn gave thanks for safe passage. From more recent times is the **Solway Harvester Seat**, just south of the chapel, a simple granite-hewn memorial to the seven local men who lost their lives when their boat, the *Solway Harvester*, sank in a storm off the Isle of Man in January 2000.

The Isle of Whithorn today is home to around 300 people and its harbour remains in use with regular landings from the Irish Sea shell fishing boats. The local fleet brings in lobster, which is served up at the **Steam Packet Inn** (Harbour Row, DG8 8LL), which occupies prime position on the quayside and has featured in the Campaign for Real Ale's National Pub of the Year competition. Further around the harbour are the light and airy **St Ninian's Hall Café and Shop**, making use of a newly extended space with picture windows overlooking the harbour.

If you fancy getting out on the water yourself, either for some fishing or simply for pleasure and wildlife spotting, trips are offered on the *Lauren Jade* through **Isle Adventures** (✆ 01988 500344, 07979 423584 🖮 https://isleadventures.co.uk).

STAIRHAVEN TO PORT WILLIAM

The west coast of the Machars is distinguished by its rolling hills from which there are superb views over Luce Bay to the Rhins and which drop down to several exquisite sandy beaches. At **Stairhaven**, no more than a handful of houses strung out along the edge of the sands, the Milton Burn marks the boundary between the Machars and the Rhins, according to Tom Stevenson, a native of these parts (see box, page 219). Just inland from here is the community-owned **Whitefield Loch**, one of numerous lochs which dot the interior of the northern Machars, home to otters, and a popular **fishing spot**. Permits are available from Keystone shop in Glenluce (✆ 07766 572266). Nearby to the southeast is **Castle Loch** (⚲ NX285536), in which are the remains of several crannogs. In his excellent book *The Wigtownshire Companion*, Haig Gordon talks of swimming out to the castle on the island at one end of the loch. We haven't tried it ourselves, but it's a lovely spot which on a warm summer's day may just entice determined outdoor types.

Gordon does warn, though, that you should remember to wear shoes as there are a lot of nettles on the island.

The countryside and views around here are terrific and we recommend exploring at will the network of roads which criss-cross the landscape from Bladnoch or Garlieston in the east over to the west coast. The route

A GALLOWAY LEGACY

Polly Pullar is a field naturalist, wildlife rehabilitator and guide, and freelance photo-journalist. She is currently the wildlife writer for *The Scottish Field* and contributes to a wide range of publications, including *The Scots Magazine, People's Friend* and *Tractor & Farming Heritage*. She has written five books, including *Dancing with Ospreys* and *Rural Portraits: Scottish Native Farm Animals, Characters and Landscapes*. We met her at the Wigtown Book Festival when she was talking about her lovely book, *Fauna Scotica: People and Animals in Scotland*. We are indebted to her for providing the text below about Galloway's native farm livestock. For more details about Polly and her work, see & www.pollypullar.com.

The Belted Galloway is formally recognised as a sub-species of the Galloway. It has its own separate breed society and a herd book that began registering animals in 1922. Though the Beltie has essentially the same origins as the Galloway, an infusion of Dutch blood from sheeted cattle in Holland during the 17th century is thought to be the reason for the distinctive white band. The black Beltie is the most common but there are also red and dun Belties as well as pure white animals attractively marked with clearly defined black etched around eyes, black hairy ears and a black nose. The riggit with a dark or red ground colour, and a white line and greyish markings down its back, was thought to be extinct. They had indeed almost died out, when years ago a white cow and bull produced a beautifully marked riggit bull. Soon after this the late Miss Flora Stuart of the Old Place of Mochrum (page 207), discovered that

several other cows had produced riggits too. They remain unusual and seldom seen.

The Stuart family have been famed for their Belties for generations, and theirs is one of the few herds left in the country that formed the foundation of the breed for the Belted Galloway Herd Book.

I had the fortune to meet the late Miss Flora Stuart on several occasions; she was without doubt one of the most dedicated and unusual people I have ever had the fortune to spend time with. She left her gentle mark on all who met her and she was a world authority on the breed, revered as such. Her father, Lord David Stuart, a son of the fourth Marquis of Bute, spent 15 years researching his book, *An Illustrated History of the Belted Galloway*.

Hidden in a wood of lichen-covered trees, parts of the Old Place of Mochrum date back to 1400. Mochrum is a hidden gem. The dense hedgerows are filled with berries and wildflowers and, as few agricultural pesticides via neighbouring **Mochrum Loch** from Kirkcowan is particularly lovely and passes the imposing **Old Place of Mochrum** (⊙ NX308541), dating in part from the 16th century, privately owned but visible from the road. Cyclists may wish to consider incorporating this quiet back road in a tour of the area, especially if hiring bikes from Kirkcowan (page 189).

are used, wild flowers and butterflies are abundant. Drive or bike along the narrow lanes on balmy spring and summer days and you may spy peacocks settling on bramble leaves or small tortoiseshells on purple spear thistle, while thistledown and rose-bay willow-herb fluff float along the ditches, back-lit by low rays of sun. The Galloway landscape is patterned with dry stone dykes, and as you travel nearer to the sea, the trees become shaped by the salt-laden winds driven in off the western seaboard. Knobbly hawthorns are laced with soft green lichens, and ivy grows in abundance, often forming a thick curled stem almost as dense as a small tree trunk. This part of Galloway has a timelessness, the pace of life appears slower. Though the fields are mostly small in size, the moorland around Mochrum stretches for miles, edged with scrub woodland, and fringed with bog cotton and flag iris. Kestrels hover by the grey dykes, and hen harriers are frequently seen quartering the heather-clad ground. A sparrowhawk may dash low over the road, while otters frequent the abundant watercourses. This is the childhood haunt of the well-known author Gavin Maxwell, and Elrig, his old family home close to the sea, is surrounded by wild landscapes that clearly inspired his beautiful writing. Flora Stuart knew him well.

Close to the farm, the Mochrum Lochs provide rich habitat for goosanders, mergansers, and golden-eye. Greylag geese, snipe and curlews nest on the moorland's raised blanket bogs; this is one of few inland-nesting sites for cormorants. Nicknamed the Mochrum Elders, due to their habit of perching with wings outstretched to dry themselves, they were amusingly thought to resemble the somewhat forbidding Presbyterian kirk elders that once presided over the area.

Flora Stuart bred Belties of all varieties. She knew every animal, its calving record, bloodlines and history, and explained their background to me as she took me round. She had a bovine family tree as an integral part of her psyche, and she was a highly skilled stockwoman. There was an unspoken rapport between her and her animals.

Having spent precious time in her company, and shared briefly a part of the Old Place of Mochrum, I know that the survival of the gorgeous Belted Galloway is largely down to Miss Flora Stuart and her family, for no-one could have been more truly dedicated to their survival.

Flora Stuart – 1941–2005. The Belted Galloway Society, ⊘ www.beltedgalloways.co.uk.

The Old Place of Mochrum was home to a Miss Flora Stuart up until her death in 2005, who we are informed by journalist Polly Pullar (see box, pages 206–7) devoted her entire life to Belted Galloway cattle (this is one of the best parts in Dumfries and Galloway to see them) and who, while living here: 'drew her water from a pump in the cobbled courtyard. She also kept an Ayrshire house cow for her own use and hand-milked her, and claimed that both the milk and water were of far purer quality being neither pasteurised nor filtered. Her passion for native breeds led to her keeping a small flock of coloured Shetland sheep, and she used their soft wool for spinning.'

Back on the coast, between Stairhaven and Auchenmalg are the remains of **Castle Sinniness** ($\mathcal{Q}$ NX215532), a name so intriguing that it demands investigation. Haig Gordon helps out again, for he writes that according to John MacQueen in his *Place-names in the Rhinns of Galloway and Luce Valley*, the etymology is Scandinavian and means 'castle of the promontory on which bladder serge grows.' South of here, beyond Auchenmalg, a long stretch of pristine **beach** is a perfect place for a picnic and a paddle, while a little further on still are the remains of Historic Scotland's **Chapel Finian**, humbling in its simplicity. This is another place where pilgrims on their way to Whithorn would have stopped. It was the Irish St Finnian [sic] who taught St Columba and today there is debate among some scholars as to whether he could actually be the historical figure who has come to be known as St Ninian (page 201).

"On the coast, between Stairhaven and Auchenmalg are the remains of Castle Sinniness, a name so intriguing that it demands investigation."

Continuing south, a mile or so inland lies the charming village of **Mochrum**, where the parish church of 1794 is built on the site of an older one from the 12th century. Mochrum parish extends over the western side of the Machars and is a region of moors and lochs, also incorporating the villages of Elrig to the north and Port William to the south. The tallest and most imposing of the crosses in the exhibition at Whithorn (page 202) once stood near the White Loch east of Port William.

A couple of miles north of Elrig, next to Elrig House (private), are the remains of **Barhobble Church** ($\mathcal{Q}$ NX311494; park at the barn on the entrance road to the house and walk up to the church site following the signs) 🖑, an intriguing example of modern detective work unearthing a historic site. The discovery in the northern part of Mochrum parish of fragments of a 10th-century building led to a search for the source and excavations in 1984–94 revealed a previously unknown religious site perhaps from AD700 to 1300. Some of the finds are on display in Whithorn (page 202). From here, make your way to **Elrig**, a timeless and picturesque hamlet, and then approach Mochrum from the small hill road to revel in the magnificent views from the top, looking out to the Rhins, the Mull of Galloway and Scare Rocks, and down to the Isle of Man.

PORT WILLIAM & MONREITH

Views westwards are the order of the day from the area around Port William, especially from the hill above the village itself. This particular part of the Machars coastline offers a mix of beaches, wildlife spotting, ancient monuments, and a glimpse into the early life of author Gavin Maxwell, who grew up here.

6 PORT WILLIAM

Port William huddles around the village square with a row of fisherman's cottages running out on each side and a small harbour tucked in to the hill. Fishing boats still head out from here lending an air of authenticity to this small community. In the 17th century Port William was something of a smuggler's village, with all manner of contraband being landed from the Isle of Man, where duty on imported goods had been slashed to encourage settlement by wealthy merchants.

A **bronze statue** of a man gazing out to sea, leaning on a post, stands at the waterfront. It's an evocative work and you can't help but go and stand next to him, lean on the post, and pause for a moment. On a clear day the Mountains of Mourne in Ireland can just be made out through the dip in the land at West and East Tarbet (page 240) at the southern end of the Rhins.

An inscription on a plaque in front of the statue reads 'What is this life if, full of care, We have no time to stand and stare', from W H Davies's poem 'Leisure'. We defy you not to slow down here! Otters are sometimes seen in the surrounding waters, so too are seals, basking sharks and dolphins. There's a large and varied bird population and adders can be found locally, so watch where you walk on warm sunny days. Picnic tables on the green are a good place to linger if you've brought your own food. If you haven't, a village shop and sandwich shop can be found on the village square, and there are also a couple of restaurants.

South of the village square, look for the house next to the burn, which for over a hundred years was the village butcher, piggery and abattoir. Today it is home to Clarabell, Moo Moo, Gary, Molly and others, **wooden sculptures** of pigs and sheep installed by the current owners and which can be identified from a sign in the front window. **Good beaches** can be found both north and south of the village where the road hugs the shoreline, and a couple of miles to the south is **Barsalloch Fort**, or at least the footprint of it, a fortified farming settlement accessed by a flight of steps up the hillside. The fort is believed to date from around 1000BC, but on the land below it, at Barsalloch Point, evidence of human settlement has been found dating from 6000BC, making it the oldest dated settlement in Galloway. All along here there is easy access to the rocky beach.

"Barsalloch Fort is believed to date from around 1000BC, but at Barsalloch Point, evidence of human settlement has been found dating from 6000BC."

7 MONREITH & AROUND

Monreith village, one mile further south, is a community-minded place of 70 or so souls, and was originally an estate and mill village serving nearby **Monreith House** (♀ NX356430; private, but grounds can be accessed) 🦶, home to the Maxwell family since the late 18th century, and the local grain mill. The grounds of Monreith House are described as a 'best-kept local secret' by those in the know and can be accessed (within reason) via either the north or south gates. A designated parking area for visitors is most easily reached from the South Gate. There are some fine trees, including old wych (or Scots) elm, English elm and some Japanese rarities, and wildlife is also abundant, including red squirrels. Fishing is offered but all equipment must be scrupulously cleaned to avoid contamination from signal crayfish. Permits can be bought on the bank or from ghillie-cum-handyman-cum-mechanical designer David Williams, who lives at the South Lodge. David combines his estate work with his membership of, and specialist interest in, the Mechanical Art and Design Museum in Stratford-upon-Avon and is happy to receive visitors who would like to see his work. Please call ahead on ✆ 01988 700667 or see 🖥 www.davidcwilliams.co.uk.

Also in this area, three miles to the south, is the **Galloway Astronomy Centre** (Craiglemine Cottage, Glasserton DG8 8NE ✆ 01988 500594 ✆ www.gallowayastro.com), where Mike and Helen Alexander have for the past 20 years been enjoying the lack of light pollution and offering courses on the night sky.

The area around Monreith House is known in part for the several groups of standing stones and cup and ring markings that can be found here. Near the north gate entrance to the Monreith Estate are the **Drumtroddan Stones** (♀ NX363447) ✋, three large stones in alignment, though only one remains standing, believed to have been erected at some time between 2000BC and 1000BC. Around 400 yards to the northwest, and most easily accessed via Drumtroddan Farm off the road to Whauphill (drive up the farm track and park where indicated), are associated cup and ring markings. Two sites, both fenced off in the middle of a field, consist of a series of markings on the bedrock. Their function and date remain a mystery, but they are definitely prehistoric.

Just south of Monreith, take the road to the right down to the golf club, at the end of which is easy parking and access to **sandy beaches** and bays in both directions. Halfway down this road a path goes off to the right, leading to Penny Wheatley's delightful **otter sculpture**, set atop a rock and gazing out at the mesmerising view, placed here to commemorate Gavin Maxwell, author of *Ring of Bright Water*, which told the story of his life with otters in the West Highlands of Scotland. A plaque pays tribute to Maxwell: 'This place he loved as a boy and made famous as a man'. Although Maxwell's life as an adult was based in northwest Scotland, when he returned to Monreith he could often be seen exercising his otter on the beach below. From here you also catch a glimpse below of **Kirkmaiden-in-Fernis churchyard** (♀ NX366399) ✋, associated with St Medan (page 239) and which can be accessed via a path opposite the parking area a little further down the road. Here stands the family mausoleum of the Maxwell family, with something of an enchanted, magic garden feel about it. This is also the resting place of the McCullochs of Myrton Castle, which once stood east of Port William. Legend tells of how the pulpit and bell from the church here were lost in Luce Bay while being transported to Kirkmaiden Church on the Rhins (page 239) following

"The area around Monreith House is known for several groups of standing stones and cup and ring markings."

the joining of the parishes of Kirkmaiden and Glasserton here on the Machars. Ever since then, it is said that every time a McCulloch's death approaches, a bell rings from the depths of Luce Bay.

Also buried in the graveyard is **François Thurot**, whose death in action off the Isle of Man on 28 February 1760 ended four years of terror against the British Navy and marked a pivotal moment in the Seven Years War between France and England (and many others besides, between 1756 and 1763). Defeated by one Captain Elliot, an eyewitness who later boarded Thurot's ship, the *Maréchal de Belleisle*, described the bloody carnage: 'turn which way I would, nothing but scattered limbs of dead and dying men presented themselves to my view, the decks and ship's sides could be compared to nothing but a slaughter-house'. In the chaotic aftermath of battle, Thurot's body was thrown by mistake off his ship and washed ashore here at Monreith. A memorial to him was erected by the ancient Order of Coldin, a secret society of mariners, which Thurot had introduced to Sweden.

Beyond the first parking area, carry on down the track and round the hill at the bottom to another, from where you can walk along the shore to the south to **Johnnie Logie's Cave**, where the raised beach meets the cliff. Originally a miner from Ayrshire, Johnnie Logie retreated from life to his cave here after being injured in an accident which left him half blind and deaf. Cultivating his own crops, he became almost self-sufficient and in 1960 was the only troglodyte recorded living in Scotland.

¶¶ FOOD & DRINK

The Clansman 11 The Square, Port William DG8 9SE ✆ 01988 700344. A small family-run restaurant in the central square at Port William offering a good range of well-reviewed food, from scampi to curry and omelettes to toasties, at reasonable prices.

St Medan Golf Course Clubhouse Monreith DG8 8NJ ✆ 01988 700358 ⌂ www. stmedangolfclub.com. Offers a small selection of food and refreshments in a course-side setting looking down to the shore.

UPDATES WEBSITE

You can post your comments and recommendations, and read the latest feedback and updates from other readers online at ⌂ www.slowbritain.co.uk and ⌂ www.facebook.com/slowbritain.

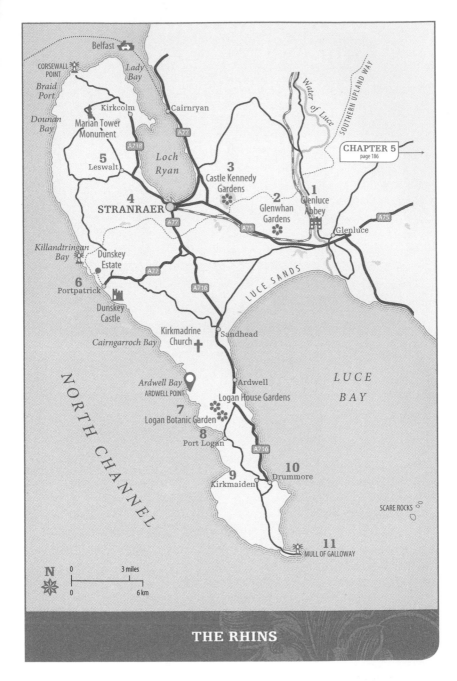

CORSEWALL POINT

Braid Port

Dounan Bay

Lady Bay

Belfast

Kirkcolm

Cairnryan

Marian Tower Monument

A718

A77

5
Leswalt

Loch Ryan

3
Castle Kennedy Gardens

2
Glenwhan Gardens

1
Glenluce Abbey

CHAPTER 5
page 186

4
STRANRAER

A77

A75

A75

Glenluce

Killandtringan Bay

Dunskey Estate

A77

A716

LUCE SANDS

6
Portpatrick

Dunskey Castle

Kirkmadrine Church

Sandhead

Cairngarroch Bay

LUCE

BAY

Ardwell Bay
ARDWELL POINT

Ardwell

Logan House Gardens

7
Logan Botanic Garden

NORTH CHANNEL

8
Port Logan

A716

10
Drummore

9
Kirkmaiden

SCARE ROCKS

11
MULL OF GALLOWAY

N

0   3 miles

0   6 km

THE RHINS

6

THE RHINS

For anyone who loves peace and isolation, arriving at the Rhins is like reaching the Promised Land. This narrow strip, less than 40 miles long and never more than five miles wide out on the peninsula itself, is almost completely surrounded by water, sparsely populated – a recluse's dream. It would be possible to hole up here in a cottage for a week and hardly see or speak to another soul. On a still day there is an intense calmness about the place that penetrates the consciousness and makes you wonder if you've been teleported to a lost land. On a blustery day, it is invigorating and life-affirming. We find the Rhins beguiling.

The beech hedgerows and copse woodlands of east and central Dumfries and Galloway grow ever-more scarce as you approach the Rhins, giving way to a landscape of undulating hills of lush green fields sprinkled with patches of scrub gorse and sedge. It is an open and stark place wrapped in a vast, uncompromising sky. The only wood to be seen is in the mile upon mile of fence posts and leaning telegraph poles linking isolated cottages and farmsteads. In the sun the Rhins is a place of vivid colours: lime green fields, shocking blue skies, dark blue seas, the sharp tangy yellow gorse of spring, startlingly white cottages, red-painted barns, and not forgetting the mixed black and white of both Friesian and Belted Galloway cattle.

The peninsula stretches from Corsewall Lighthouse, the most northerly point you can reach by road, down to the Mull of Galloway, Scotland's most southerly point. The name Rhins is derived from the Gaelic 'roinn' for 'nose' or 'promontory'. The west coast is etched by a line of cliffs, the east is gentler. Farming (dairy and beef) and tourism are the main industries. No matter which direction you travel, you soon hit a coastal road and you don't have to be here long before an island mentality sets in. The pace is just that little bit slower, pleasantly soporific in parts. The mobile library still does the rounds of the villages, country lanes wind through the middle of farmyards, and people you don't know wave as you pass in the car. And like any good 'island', the Rhins also boasts not just a super choice of **beaches** 🖐, most of which are covered throughout this chapter, but also a number of **lighthouses** 🖐.

But the Rhins is not just about grinding to a standstill. There is much here to see and do: walks and beaches, museums and monuments and, thanks to the mild climate, gardens galore. **Scotland's Garden Route** encompasses many of them and even if your gardening knowledge extends only to weeds, you'll find a garden here to stir your interest. Although the Rhins is in the direct line of the prevailing weather coming in from the Atlantic, its climate isn't as bad as you might expect due to the Gulf Stream or as it is known in this particular part of the world the North Atlantic Current. If you take a look on the UK Met Office website (⊘ www.metoffice.gov.uk) there's a handy interactive map which shows the averages – daily, monthly, seasonal and annual – of just about every weather condition you could want to know about. Suffice to say, don't be surprised to find palm trees in front gardens and herbaceous borders stuffed with a veritable plethora of southern hemisphere plants and shrubs. It's what many visitors come here for.

The people of the Rhins know well that they are custodians of a piece of Scotland that is unique and special, and there is a pride in the area among both established families and incomers, of whom there are a fair few.

SCOTLAND'S GARDEN ROUTE

At Logan Botanic Garden there is a display which describes the Rhins as the Tropic of Scotland, and it fits. Here in this southwest corner of the country is a cornucopia of gardens the collective likes of which exist nowhere else in Britain, except perhaps in Cornwall and the Scilly Isles. Scotland's Garden Route links six of these gardens: Dunskey, Castle Kennedy, Glenwhan, Ardwell, Logan Botanic Garden and Logan House Gardens. (Note: the last two are separate gardens, albeit located next door to each other, the former part of the Royal Botanic Garden in Edinburgh and the latter a private garden.) Each garden offers something different and all are worth visiting, but if six sounds like too many then check out ⊘ www.scotlandsgardenroute. co.uk or pick up a leaflet and decide which ones will be of most interest to you. Several of the gardens are located near to each other so it's possible to visit two or three in a day, and there is also a 'passport' scheme which entitles you to discounted entry to all of the gardens except Logan House Gardens which works on an automated ticketing system. The passport has to be validated at the first garden you visit, after which you are entitled to a 10% discount at subsequent gardens.

For some, leaving the Rhins even for a day or two is a wrench, such is the hold that this place can take. Nonetheless, day trips to Belfast are a popular jaunt for locals in need of some retail diversion. Ireland is only two hours away by ferry and the 'Galloway Irish' is a term which you will likely come across. There's a distinctive Irish twang to the local accent.

ONE 'N' OR TWO?

The chances are you will come across both 'Rhins' and 'Rhinns' in your travels around the area. Both are acceptable, but the single 'n' is the more common and is therefore what we have opted for in this guide. To supporters of the double 'n', therefore, we apologise.

GETTING AROUND

Driving around the Rhins is a pleasure and a challenge. Narrow country lanes make for sedate going, which is the pleasure, but they are also full of sharp corners, blind summits and junctions at which it can be almost impossible to distinguish between a farmhouse track and the public highway. Slow, leisurely, relaxed travel is the way to soak up the spirit of the Rhins and savour the views. No need to rush, just enjoy the experience of being here. It's not uncommon for roads to run through the middle of a farmyard either, with a row of cows stretching their necks out of the byre to feed on one side and the farmhouse on the other. And don't be surprised if you find livestock roaming the roads: sheep, cattle, deer, hares, pheasants ... any of them could make an appearance. Keep your wits about you and take it slowly. Remain conscious of potential oncoming traffic, especially larger vehicles such as tractors, delivery vans, a school bus and the mobile library.

There are relatively few A roads on the Rhins. Distances are not great but small roads can make timings longer than you may expect: Portpatrick to the Mull is just over 22 miles and takes around an hour to drive, Portpatrick to Corsewall Lighthouse is 15.9 miles and takes around 45 minutes, and Corsewall Lighthouse to the Mull of Galloway comes in at roughly 30 miles and takes around 1½ hours straight up the eastern edge of the Rhins.

One thing to note when driving is that there are very few road signs around the narrow lanes away from the main roads, rendering a good OS map essential.

***i* TOURIST INFORMATION**

VisitScotland Information Centre Stranraer 28 Harbour St, Stranraer DG9 7RA
✐ 01776 702595 ✉ www.visitdumfriesandgalloway.co.uk ◕ all year
Drummore Information Centre 21 Mill St, Drummore DG9 9PS ✐ 01776 840207
✉ www.visitkirkmaiden.co.uk ◕ Easter, & from mid May to end Sep Mon–Sat 10.00–16.00,
Sun 13.00–16.00. Volunteer-run centre located by the bus stop on Drummore's main street.
Often visited by people researching family history; public internet access available.

PUBLIC TRANSPORT

Despite its remote location, the Rhins benefits from direct **train service** connections from Stranraer up to Glasgow operated by Scotrail. In fact, in recent years this has been the best performing rural line in Scotland with a high jump in passenger numbers from one year to the next. However, at the time of writing the franchise is up for renewal and it's rumoured that in future the new operator will be under an obligation to run increased services only from Ayr and no longer to run a direct service from Stranraer. Changing at Ayr may therefore become necessary. The Stranraer to Ayr Line Support Association (✉ www. saylsa.org.uk) produces two good leaflets covering walks and sights to see from the rails.

There are regular **bus services** to Stranraer from Dumfries. Stagecoach Western services 500 and X75 between them offer seven departures daily Monday to Saturday from Dumfries railway station and Whitesands for a journey that takes between two hours and ten minutes and 2½ hours depending on the time of day. McCulloch Coaches also offers one service a day. On Sundays there are three service 500 departures. Return trips run as frequently. Once at the Rhins buses run with varying degrees of regularity from Stranraer to Stoneykirk, Sandhead, Ardwell, Port Logan and Drummore (Service 407 – James King Coaches) in the South Rhins; to Leswalt, Kirkcolm and Ervie (Service 408 – James King Coaches/ Wigtownshire Community Transport) in the north; and to Knock and Portpatrick (Service 411 – Wigtownshire Community Transport) in-between. Stagecoach Western also run service 416 from Stranraer down to Whithorn and back up to Newton Stewart on the Machars.

Local public transport information is provided by South West of Scotland Transport Partnership (✉ www.swestrans.org.uk), or alternatively the traveline (✐ 0871 200 22 33 ✉ www.traveline.org.uk).

RHINS COASTAL PATHS

This is fine walking country with routes to suit all ages and abilities, from gentle strolls to long-distance hikes, from an amble along a country lane to a steep cliffside path. The **Southern Upland Way** starts its 212-mile trajectory at Portpatrick and the first two days are entirely within the Rhins taking you around 20 miles to New Luce for an overnight stop.

The other official path is the **Mull of Galloway Trail**, which runs for 24 miles from the Mull up the east coast to Stranraer and then continues as the **Loch Ryan Coastal Path** to Glenapp in South Ayrshire. Both paths were developed and are maintained by the members of the Rotary Club of Stranraer, led by local force Tom Stevenson who has been instrumental in creating and publicising them. Together they are now part of a scheme instigated by Scottish Natural Heritage called 'Scotland's Great Trails' to form the southernmost end of a series of routes by which it is now possible to walk from Scotland's most southerly point at the Mull of Galloway to the most northwestern point

of mainland Britain at Cape Wrath. (If you're interested in the whole route, the paths in question beyond the Loch Ryan Coastal Path are the Ayrshire Coastal Path, the Clyde Coastal Path, the West Highland Way, and the Cape Wrath Trail.) The Rhins paths also form part of the International Appalachian Trail long-distance walking route.

Planning the walk route, Tom and his colleagues had to enlist the co-operation of local landowners and tenant farmers, as well as raising funds from a range of public and private sponsors. This they did with great success, managing to install 14 information boards along the Mull of Galloway Trail and ten along the Loch Ryan Coastal Path, all of them written by retired Stranraer butcher Archie Bell. There are also waymarks along the way so you can tell exactly where you are and see how many miles are left to go.

Every year there is a Trail and Sail event in late May or early June, involving a run from the Mull of Galloway up to Stranraer, followed by a sailing race up Loch Ryan.

FERRIES

The ferries to Northern Ireland no longer have their terminus at the foot of Loch Ryan in the centre of Stranraer, instead it is a few miles north up the eastern side of Loch Ryan at Cairnryan. P&O Ferries operates services to Larne, and Stena Line sails to Belfast.

CYCLING

From the Mull of Galloway in the south to Milleur Point at the north of Loch Ryan, the Rhins offers many miles of quieter lanes to be explored. A free *Cycling in Wigtownshire* leaflet, which covers the Rhins, has been produced by Dumfries and Galloway Council.

WALKING

Mile upon mile of rylock sheep fencing criss-crosses the area and can make roaming the hills a bit laborious as you concentrate on traversing the next barrier rather than taking in the fine views. Don't, however, let this put you off exploring on foot. The rolling fields complete with pockets of woodland and the fact you are almost completely surrounded by miles of fine coastline make walking very rewarding. There are plenty of walking leaflets and books available in Stranraer Information Centre (page 218) and local shops dotted across the district, and these offer a fine choice of clear routes. Dumfries and Galloway Council's free *Walking in and around the South Rhins* and *Stranraer & the North Rhins* leaflets are particularly good. For more on walking in the area, see the box on page 219.

GLENLUCE & THE EAST

This short stretch of Galloway from Glenluce up to Stranraer always seems to us to be a bit of a no-man's land. Although it's regarded as being part of the Rhins, it feels as if it falls between two camps: out of the Machars but not quite into the Rhins peninsula. Perhaps because of this people tend to pass through and not stop. However, there are several points of interest well worth seeking out.

1 GLENLUCE ABBEY
Glenluce DG8 0AF ♀ NX185587 ⊙ Apr–Sep; Historic Scotland

The ruined Cistercian monastery at Glenluce was built over 800 years ago and stands in a peaceful riverside setting by Luce Water. Founded by Roland, Lord of Galloway, it is thought that the monks who established the monastery and lived here would have come from Dundrennan Abbey near Kirkcudbright (page 181). Parts of the chapterhouse survive intact, including a fine entrance doorway, stone-vaulted ceiling and traceried windows. Monastic life continued here for around 400 years until the Protestant Reformation took hold.

"Parts of the chapterhouse survive intact, including a fine entrance doorway, stone-vaulted ceiling and traceried windows."

There's a small museum and visitor centre with artefacts discovered during preservation work which illustrate the daily lives of the monks. Note that the museum and shop are only open when staff are available.

2 GLENWHAN GARDENS

Dunragit DG9 8PH ♀ NX153586 (follow the signs from the main road at Dunragit & take off up into the hills) ✆ 01581 400222 ⊕ www.glenwhangardens.co.uk

Set 300 feet above sea level where hill meets moor, this is the only one of Galloway's many gardens to offer such a tremendous view. On a clear day you can see out over Luce Bay and right down the Rhins to the lighthouse at the Mull. The garden itself is a gem, and a fairly hidden one at that despite the brown tourist signs on the road announcing its presence. Over the years it has been the subject of much praise and inspiration. The story behind it is one of a restless farmer in search of pastures new, moving north from Herefordshire almost on a whim to a patch of land bought hastily in Dumfries and Galloway. In 1971, Bill and Tessa Knott decided they wanted a change of scene from farming and so they put in a very last-minute offer on 255 acres of land above Dunragit, part of an estate that was being split up and sold off by a disinterested landowner. To their delight and consternation, they found themselves the proud owners of a tract of Galloway hillside and moorland covered in bracken and gorse, with a couple of run-down houses thrown in to boot. It was a different time: they got it for a song and their solicitor told them they couldn't go wrong. He was right, too, for today at the heart of Glenwhan is a charming garden of 12 acres surrounding a delightful small country house which the Knotts renovated and extended from one of the original buildings. Make no mistake, though, the garden has come only with years of dedication and hard work. Take a look at the photographs in the tea room of how it was when the Knotts first arrived and you'll soon appreciate how much has gone in to making Glenwhan what it is today.

What is so appealing about this garden (apart from the red squirrels) is that it feels so domestic, albeit on a slightly grander scale than most of us are used to. It is with a slight sense of embarrassment at intruding into a private space that you realise you are actually walking in the Knott's back garden, where the lawn behind the house runs seamlessly into an array of shrubs, borders and trees arranged around a couple of lochans, laboriously dug out then filled with water piped down from the moor. Domestic details of family life punctuate the gardens: a diving board and bathing hut at the edge of the lochan, which the family use for swimming; a statue of Buddha and prayer flags in the trees positioned carefully by Tessa and Bill's son, Richard. A series of 'rooms' work their way up the hillside to a striking **slate sculpture** by local craftsman Joe

Smith, before leading you out into the 17 acres of moor where there are over 120 species of wildflower and a **circular walk** among the gorse and bracken for something a little wilder to finish off. Each section has a name. 'Choice Valley' is so called because it is full of choice plants. We particularly liked 'Thinking Rock', 'a good place to come and think' says Tessa Knott.

"We particularly liked 'Thinking Rock', 'a good place to come and think' says Tessa Knott."

It would be so easy to overlook Glenwhan on a visit to this area. Don't. It's quite special. Dogs are allowed on leads, and there's a cosy tea room. What makes the whole thing even more impressive is that Tessa, who has been the driving force behind Glenwhan, never considered herself a gardener. 'I was a cordon bleu cook first and a bit of a gardener', she says. Everything she has learned has been on the job, resulting in a Visit Scotland four-star rating plus partner garden status with the Royal Horticultural Society. For more details of the gardens, take a look at the website. The seasonal notes have a good slideshow.

3 CASTLE KENNEDY GARDENS

Castle Kennedy DG9 8SJ ♀ NX111608 (for sat nav) ⊘ www.castlekennedygardens.co.uk
⊙ Apr–Oct

The original Castle Kennedy was the home of the Kennedy family but it then passed to the current owners, the Dalrymples and Earls of Stair. It is known to have been standing in the 14th century but was destroyed by fire in 1716, though the ruins can still be seen in the grounds today. The story goes that on hearing of the imminent return of the second Earl of Stair, the staff aired his bedding in front of an open fire, with disastrous results.

Today's castle is known as **Lochinch Castle** and is home to Jamie Dalrymple, 14th Earl of Stair, who sits as a Crossbench member in the House of Lords. 'Inch' means spit (as in a spit of land) and the castle gardens are situated on a peninsula between two lochs: Loch Crindle, which is known as the Black Loch because of its peaty water, and Loch Inch, which is known as the White Loch.

There is something of Balmoral about Lochinch Castle, albeit on a smaller scale, which is not necessarily surprising given that the royal household in the north of Scotland was opened just eight years before work began here. Both buildings are every inch Scottish Baronial (or at least, 19th-century Gothic revival), with a wealth of turrets and crow-stepped gables. There's also a royal family connection, for the current Countess Dowager of Stair is a cousin of the Queen. Her father, the Honourable David Bowes-Lyon, was the Queen Mother's younger brother. He also happened to be president of the Royal Horticultural Society, which is fitting given the incredibly impressive gardens that are the main attraction here (the castle itself is not open to the public), 75 acres of them which have been nurtured and curated by successive generations.

It was the second Earl of Stair who was so inspired by the gardens at Versailles that he resolved to develop his own. He was a military man, having attained the rank of Field Marshal, and this is reflected in parts of the gardens which are named after battles in which he took part, thus Mount Marlborough and Dettingen Avenue. He also enlisted the help of the Royal Scots Greys and Inniskilling Fusiliers in developing the gardens, and it is said that the distinctive embankments were created by his own private army. By the 19th century the gardens had become neglected and overgrown, but a bundle of plans was found in a gardener's cottage showing how they had once been and the eighth earl took it upon himself to restore them to their former glory.

THE CLAN CHIEF & HEAD GARDENER

The gardens at Castle Kennedy boast the unusual distinction of being in the care of one of the 120 or so clan chiefs in the Standing Council of Scottish Chiefs. **John MacArthur of that Ilk** is head of the clan Arthur (Mac means 'son of', thus MacArthur is 'son of Arthur') and has been Head Gardener at Castle Kennedy Gardens for the past 27 years. John's father started the search for the chief of the clan Arthur, a task in which John became involved and during which he began to realise that the chiefly line might actually run through his family. John worked with Hugh Peskett, specialist genealogist and Scottish editor of *Burke's Peerage*, and after extensive research was successful in matriculating the

Arthur coat of arms through the Court of the Lord Lyon in Edinburgh (the Lord Lyon is the 'sole King of Arms in Scotland, Head of the Heraldic Executive and the Judge of the Court of the Lord Lyon which has jurisdiction over all heraldic business in Scotland').

When not attending to the gardens, John is kept busy in his role as clan chief. He sees his role as one of promoting Scotland to the diaspora. He's passionate about his home country and is a regular bagpipe player with the Cairnsmore Pipers, who you might catch playing at one of the local festivals. A highlight for them in recent years was playing at the Wicker Man Festival in front of 20,000 people.

As with most gardens in the Rhins, one of the chief attractions is the **rhododendrons**, which come in every size and colour and attract enthusiasts from all over the world. Between March and July the rhododendrons are in flower, from the early large-leafed variety to the later, wild *Rhododendron ponticum* (the one that gets all the bad press for being so invasive). The 12th earl was a great rhododendron fan and would compete in shows in London. To get there he would book two sleeper compartments: one for the gardener and one for the exhibits!

. There are plenty of other plants and wildlife, too, including a splendid 1,000-foot avenue of monkey puzzle trees, a perfectly circular mirror pond with stunning reflections on a still day, giant redwoods and several Scottish champion trees, and an impressive walled garden, originally the kitchen garden, which for the past 35 years has been the project of Davina, Countess Dowager of Stair, aided by Head Gardener John MacArthur of that Ilk (see box, page 223). But while the gardens offer one of the finest collections of plants in the area, the main delight is their architecture – the long vistas along the terraces, the avenues of trees radiating from the old castle, and the gentle stretch of the old canal linking the two lochs and spanned by a lovely formal bridge.

4 STRANRAER

Stranraer has all the ingredients of a good old-fashioned seaside town: a superlative setting at the head of Loch Ryan, some fine old buildings, enticing narrow lanes and alleys, a quirky old harbour office on the seafront and brightly painted houses. There's even a castle in the middle of the main street. It's a town worth visiting but it's also a town that's suffered from loss of industry and investment, most recently with the relocation of the ferry terminal to Cairnryan, and in parts it shows. There are plans to redevelop the harbour front and if they go ahead they will make a significant difference, the potential is terrific if only the funding can be found.

"Discover Stranraer through a mix of the town trail and a visit to the local museum."

The best way to discover Stranraer is through a mix of the **town trail** and a visit to the local museum. Start off at the **VisitScotland Information Centre** on Harbour Street (page 218) and pick up a town trail leaflet. There are plaques all around the town with information about specific points of interest and the trail makes for an easy and interesting walk of a couple of hours. Along the way the story of Stranraer from the 16th century onwards will emerge, from the **The Castle of St John**, built around 1510 for the Adairs, a powerful local family, through to the prosperity of the late 18th century and an economy based on tanning, fishing, boat building and weaving. Extant from the 19th century is a range of buildings, including **North West Castle**, which was built in 1820 as the home of Arctic explorer Admiral Sir John Ross, who was born in nearby Kirkcolm in 1777. It's now a hotel with the curious distinction of being

"North West Castle was built in 1820 as the home of Arctic explorer Admiral Sir John Ross, who was born in nearby Kirkcolm in 1777."

the first hotel in the world to have its own indoor curling rink. The trail also passes the **Princess Victoria Monument**, which commemorates one of the three transport disasters for which Dumfries and Galloway is known, the sinking in the North Channel (the strait that separates northeast Ireland from southwest Scotland) of the Stranraer to Larne car ferry MV *Princess Victoria* in 1953 with the loss of 135 lives. (The other two disasters are the Lockerbie bombing, page 42, and the Quintinshill rail disaster, see box, page 53.)

One building which isn't mentioned as part of the town trail is **32 Charlotte Street** in the centre of Stranraer. This was once the town house of the Maxwell family, whose coat of arms can still be seen above the front door. The most famous member of the family was **Gavin Maxwell**, who grew up at the family home near Monreith on the Machars (page 211) and whose tales of rearing and living with otters made him a household name.

For a more in-depth look at not just Stranraer but the Rhins in general and the Machars, too, spend some time at the excellent **Stranraer Museum** (The Old Town Hall, 55 George St, DG9 7JP ✐ 01776 705088 ☉ closed Sun) 🖑, which explains the history of the region, from the first settlers in 7000–4000BC, nomads who travelled inland to the Galloway Hills in the summer, through to the present. It houses the unique **Chilcarroch Plough**, which is the only remaining example in the country of the old Scotch Plough. This particular one was first used in the area in 1793 but lay in a barn for many years from around 1870 before being discovered in the 1950s.

It's a fearsome looking thing, heavy and cumbersome, and it would have taken a strong animal to pull it and stamina to walk behind it.

Agriculture and beef and dairy farming in particular have long been important to the Rhins. Galloway cattle are renowned for their hardiness and quality of beef and in addition to local stocks, by the late 18th century 15,000 head of Irish cattle were passing along the droving route from Portpatrick, where they arrived from Ireland, to Dumfries. Here they were fattened up before being driven south on foot to the Norfolk Cattle Fair. (There are still signs in the centre of Dumfries today which show the droving distances; see page 112.)

The mid 18th to mid 19th centuries were also a time of shipbuilding, notably at Stranraer, Portpatrick and Drummore on the Rhins, and also at Port William, the Isle of Whithorn, Garlieston and Bladnoch on the Machars. The largest ships were built at Stranraer, with smaller boats coming out of local yards. The Stranraer crest shows a full-masted sailing ship in a shield, with the Latin motto *Tutissima Statio* or 'Safest Harbour'. As bigger and faster ships were built, though, beef farming became less and less viable since droving was being fast outpaced and cattle could be transported to their destination far quicker than was previously possible. Thus the early 19th century saw the advent of commercial dairy farming with the first large-scale dairy farm going into operation at Kirkcolm in 1802. Farming on the Rhins today remains more dairy than beef, and many farms are tied in to supplying manufacturers in Stranraer and further up the coast at Girvan in South Ayrshire. Stranraer is the home of the Seriously Strong Cheddar brand that you'll find in supermarkets, as well as the Galloway cheddar: 'Scotland's favourite' as they say.

FOOD & DRINK

Henry's Bay House Restaurant Cairnryan Rd, DG9 8AT ℰ 01776 707388 ⓖ www. bayhouserestaurant.co.uk. A new addition to Stranraer's eateries. John Henry and his wife Jane took over the restaurant in September 2014 and now offer diners a prime setting, with views and an outdoor terrace looking straight up Loch Ryan. Prices are reasonable, ingredients sourced locally and the menu changes regularly. Starters might include black pudding and bacon salad or smoked mackerel pâté, mains seafood pancake or strips of fillet. Grills, sides and indulgent desserts are also offered.

Stir-it 99 George St, DG9 7JP ℰ 01776 700099. A popular local café with a reputation for good homemade soups, sandwiches and cakes, and friendly staff.

THE NORTH RHINS: EAST OF LOCH RYAN

The east side of Loch Ryan is dominated by the hills that mark the boundary between coast and moor beyond. The A77 hugs the shoreline for the six miles to Cairnryan and then continues up into South Ayrshire. Other than the views across the loch, which are good, the main reason people come this way is for the ferry terminals. **Cairnryan** itself consists of not much more than a village shop and a row of waterfront cottages, its low-key presence giving little away of its maritime history. It was here during World War II, when Cairnryan was designated 'No.2 Military Port' and operated as a secret base for troopships, that parts of the floating Mulberry Harbour were built for testing.

> "It was here during World War II, when Cairnryan was designated 'No.2 Military Port', that parts of the floating Mulberry Harbour were built for testing."

There's a parking area near the Stena Line terminal for anyone who wants to come and ferry spot, but the best general views are from further up in the hills. Opposite the roadside parking area a single-track road takes off up a steep hill. This used to be the main coach road between Stranraer and Ayrshire, and it's difficult to imagine anything other than more modern vehicles conquering the gradient. You can only drive so far these days before reaching a stretch of private road closed to all but walkers (this is also the route of the **Loch Ryan Coastal Path**), but the views are splendid.

For a detour completely off the beaten track and a taste of the moors described in *Chapter 5* (pages 192–3), head northwards on the small road just north of where the A751 meets the A77. From here you can loop around and back down to New Luce (pages 193–4) to the east on a route which is mostly single-track road with passing places and cattle grids, where sheep roam the hills, buzzards perch on top of telegraph poles and in August the landscape turns purple with heather. It's a glorious area of desolate moorland, where the landscape is rife with signs of ancient history. The remains of farms and fields, burial places and ritual monuments have survived relatively well because the uplands have not been altered by modern agriculture, and there's a small patch of mixed woodland still standing shortly before the road runs beneath the railway viaduct into New Luce.

THE NORTH RHINS: WEST OF LOCH RYAN

🏠 **Corsewall Lighthouse Hotel** (page 249)

Travel north from Stranraer up the west side of Loch Ryan and you find yourself in a sparsely populated landscape of undulating hills with views to water on three sides, especially at the northernmost reaches of the peninsula. Pottering around this area is an enjoyable way to spend a day or two, soaking up a bit of history, taking in the sea views and stopping off here and there for a cup of coffee or a bite to eat. This is not a place to rush but an area to be savoured and somewhere to enjoy the peace and quiet. Small roads mean that progress is leisurely.

5 LESWALT

Just a few miles outside Stranraer is Leswalt, where there are the remains of a medieval church. This is where some of the Agnew family, whose hereditary ancestral home was in nearby Lochnaw Castle, are buried. The Agnews no longer occupy Lochnaw, but their descendants can still be found in Dumfries and Galloway.

Just north of Leswalt stands the **Agnew Monument** (♀ NX008646) at the top of Tor of Craigoch, from where there are good views in all directions taking in Loch Ryan and the Irish Sea. As for **Lochnaw Castle** itself, it's not open to the public but it does run a restored fishery for coarse anglers in its 48-acre Lochnaw Loch.

THE NORTHERN TIP OF THE PENINSULA

Beyond Leswalt is Ervie and just beyond Ervie heading north are the remains of Balsarroch House, once the home of the Ross family. **Sir John Ross** (1777–1856), son of the minister at Balsarroch, was known for his expeditions to the Arctic and for his explorations to try to establish the route of the Northwest Passage. His nephew, Sir James Clark Ross (1800–62), accompanied him on several expeditions, one of which saw them become the first Europeans to reach the North Magnetic Pole. If you come up this way, keep an eye open on the right-hand side for the white-painted **Marian Tower monument** on the top of Craigengerroch Hill above Drumdow Farmhouse, from where there are views out to the distinct volcanic rock of Ailsa Craig in the Firth of Clyde. A plaque on the monument states simply

ALDOURAN WETLAND GARDEN

DG9 0LJ ♀ NX015637 (watch for roadside signs on entering Leswalt village ♿ www.
leswaltwetlandgarden.org.uk; free entry, although donations are welcomed via a box at
the entrance gateway; parking at Leswalt Village Hall, & for Blue Badge holders at the
entrance gateway; dogs allowed on leads in the garden & wetland, & off the lead in the
neighbouring woodland

*Aldouran is a community-based garden at Leswalt. Jane Sloan, Chair of Aldouran, kindly
agreed to write the following report of the work that has gone on since 2005.*

Aldouran Wetland Garden at Leswalt near Stranraer is variously described by visitors as a 'magical', 'peaceful', 'fantastic gem of a place', and combines a community garden, wetland habitat and woodland walk with an adjoining bird hide.

The community garden features raised dry stone wall flowerbeds nurturing both native and non-native plants and trees, bug hotels, a willow bower, a picnic boat particularly popular with children, and picnic tables and benches, whilst the wetland area supports one large pond and several smaller ones plus a large reedbed all linked by good paths and a boardwalk. From the bird hide you can observe the wildlife both in the wetland and the woodland. As well as many species of birds, red squirrels can be seen at the feeding station by the hide and roe deer frequent the wood. The pond has a huge diversity of invertebrate life and also provides a home for mallard ducks and greylag geese.

The most amazing thing about Aldouran, however, is that it is entirely managed by volunteers from the local Leswalt community. In 2005 they rose to the challenge set them by Scottish Natural Heritage and the Woodland Trust to take over the project which had been instigated by a charity and quickly abandoned, threatening to turn the area into an inaccessible wilderness. In the intervening years they have, by sheer hard work and community spirit, transformed the area into an environmental and educational haven.

Today around 20 adult volunteers and 28 children come together to weed, plant, clean the ponds, deal with maintenance issues and applications for funding whilst always focusing on improving the project for the benefit both of the resident wildlife and for the 5,000 plus visitors who use the site annually. Activity Days are organised during the year where volunteers who are experts in several wildlife fields lead activities such as pond dipping, moth trapping, species identification, etc for enthusiastic groups of children.

'Marian Hill 1818', giving rise to two different tales about its origins. One is that it was built as a memorial to one of the ladies of the Ross family, while the other is that it commemorates a local girl killed by a bull.

At **Corsewall Point** (9 NW981727), the most northerly spot on the Rhins that can be reached by car, stands one of the three lighthouses on the peninsula and, like its southern counterpart at the Mull, this one is still in operation (although it has been automated since 1994), its light helping to guide boats to the mouth of Loch Ryan. The surrounding buildings now form the Corsewall Lighthouse Hotel (open to non-residents; page 249). On a clear day the views from here are tremendous, taking in Ireland, Ailsa Craig, the island of Arran, the Kintyre Peninsula and the Firth of Clyde, and this is a beautiful spot to come and sit and watch the birds and the passing ferries. It's also particularly atmospheric in the fog.

Just south of Corsewall Point on the west coast are a couple of less well-known but worthwhile beaches. First, **Genoch Rocks** at **Braid Port** (9 NW968708) is a secluded spot where there's a good chance of seeing seals. It's a tricky one to reach as you'll need to drive the narrow lanes to reach the deserted farmhouse and then, unless you're in a 4x4, get out and walk the track. This was also the site of an old RAF chain radar station about which notoriously little is known. The old bunkers are still here, open to the elements. A little further south again, **Dounan Bay** (9 NW966688) should also be visited just for the bay, the beach and the walks along the shore. Again, you need to make a point of heading here. And again, you'll probably need to leave the car at the top of the track and walk down unless you're in a 4x4.

For easier access to a quiet beach, head to the opposite side of the North Rhins, to **Lady Bay** (9 NX026717). The track down to it is manageable even in a small car if you take it easy; alternatively leave the car at the top and walk down. The bay is sandy, a good length, and stretches along the northwest shore of Loch Ryan, giving great views to the hills on the opposite side (at this point you're looking across to the boundary between Dumfries and Galloway and South Ayrshire). It's a good spot for birdwatching and wildlife: we saw eider, cormorants and goosander during our last visit, as well as a roe deer on the track right in front of us. There's also a lovely display of wild daffodils on the lower slopes of the hill in spring.

Kirkcolm, roughly halfway down the North Rhins on the east coast, is an attractive village with a main street lined by cottages. There's a good pub here (see opposite) and in the churchyard a curious 10th-century stone cross, the **Kilmorie Stone**. Kirkcolm has long had Christian associations, the name itself means church of St Columba, and one interpretation of the cross is that it illustrates the triumph of Christianity over Paganism, with Christ on the cross appearing above a figure who is believed to be a hero from Viking mythology. The carvings on each side appear to be by different hands revealing both Celtic and Scandinavian influences.

¶¶ FOOD & DRINK

The Blue Peter Hotel 23 Main St, Kirkcolm DG9 0NL ✆ 01776 853221. Offers a convivial welcome and serves up hearty, wholesome and tasty home-cooked food. It's said to have the best fish (beer-battered) and chips in the area, and the Lancashire hot pot's pretty good, too. Food is served in the cosy bar (log fire in winter) and also outside in the summer. The spacious rear garden is a good place for spotting red squirrels. If you're staying nearby, they will wrap up your dinner for take-away.

6 PORTPATRICK

🏠 **Kirklauchline Holiday Cottage** (page 249), **Knockinaam Lodge** (page 249), **Rickwood House Hotel** (page 249)

Portpatrick's luck has waxed and waned over the years as much as the Atlantic tides which batter its harbour, and it's those very tides that have been at the root of the town's fluctuating fortunes. From the 17th to 19th centuries came a succession of entrepreneurs and statesmen who were convinced that Portpatrick should and could be the official port for all boats coming from Ireland. With just 21 miles separating its harbour from that at Donaghadee, it was an obvious but ill-advised choice. Sir Hugh Montgomery from neighbouring Ayrshire – one of the founding fathers of the Ulster Scots – was to blame. He acquired both harbours and capitalised on a Royal Warrant of 1616 which restricted travel between the Irish Ards Peninsula and the Rhins of Galloway to Donaghadee and Portpatrick. Thus started 150 years of engineering folly in which successive attempts to build, strengthen and enlarge the harbour at Portpatrick were destined to end in calamity. The 18th-century engineer John Smeaton had a go, followed in the 19th century by John Rennie Senior and, subsequently, his son John Rennie younger. No-one heeded the warnings of renowned engineer Thomas Telford (see box, page 68), who in 1802 passed judgement that Portpatrick remained 'destitute of the advantages requisite for a perfect harbour'. Finally in 1839, a newly constructed pier was destroyed by storms and the authorities accepted it was time to throw in the towel.

That would have been it had it not been for the mail boats, or at least the promise of the mail boats, and for the perceived need for ease of access for both mail and cattle from Ireland through to Stranraer. The idea of the Portpatrick Railway to link with Stranraer as part of a bigger trunk route between London and Belfast was too tempting to resist, and inherent with it was the need to develop the harbour at Portpatrick. Yet again the scheme was doomed. Just as the advent of faster ships brought an end to the cattle route from Ireland (page 226), so too did it spell the end for the mail route, which the government had transferred south bypassing Dumfries and Galloway – and Portpatrick – altogether. And so when Portpatrick Harbour Railway Station was opened on 11 September 1868 it must have been something of an anti-climax and with a sense of futility, for there was no longer a requirement for it. Alas, it closed two months later.

"Portpatrick Trust was formed in May 2004 'to secure community ownership of the harbour'."

Despite such fluctuations, Portpatrick did find favour for a period as the 'Gretna of Ireland' following the introduction of the Marriage Act in Ireland (and England) in 1754, the same act that transformed the fortunes of Gretna Green in the east of Dumfries and Galloway (pages 50–2). Eloping couples could cross the sea to wed in Portpatrick, where it is said that the minister was known to relax the requirement for a period of residence so that not much more than hour might pass between an unwed couple disembarking their boat and re-boarding for the journey home as a married couple.

Portpatrick Harbour is now in the care of the Portpatrick Trust which was formed in May 2004 'to secure community ownership of the harbour', a purchase that was completed in September 2012 thanks in part to a sizeable donation from the North Rhins Wind Farm. The trust's website ⊘ www.portpatrickharbour.org is worth a visit for its information and some good historical pictures showing the harbour through the ages.

As for Portpatrick itself, reconciled to the fact that it was destined never to become a major port it resolved to make the most of its attractive location and associated leisure opportunities. Step forward C L Orr Ewing, MP, who owned (and whose descendants still own) the Dunskey estates, who saw the potential and who in April 1903 opened the Dunskey Golf Club (now the Portpatrick Dunskey Golf Club) on

100 acres of land on the north cliff behind the imposing Portpatrick Hotel (opened 1905). It was a smart move and heralded the start of Portpatrick's success as a popular seaside town.

Portpatrick today is as pretty as a picture, of which there are many to be found, and boasts the highest sunshine record in Dumfries and Galloway. It has all the charm of a quaint fishing village and in summer all the crowds that go with it, too. Come at the end of July/start of August when it's Lifeboat Week, and there is a range of activities taking place. Traditional cottages are strung around the harbour and a mix of cafés, gift shops, hotels, restaurants and pubs are dotted along the waterfront and up the adjoining streets. Further up the hill in the residential area elegant villas enjoy sea views, including a number of guesthouses. If you want to visit by public transport, buses 367 and 411 come here from Stranraer.

A WANDER AROUND PORTPATRICK

At the northern end of the harbour it's impossible to resist the urge to walk out on to **McCook's Craig** and **Dorn Rock** and feel as if you're on an island. From here, you may see some of the **black guillemots** (or tysties) that return to nest here each year in the nooks and crannies of the harbour walls. Passing the **Lifeboat Station and Museum** you'll find first of all a sign marking the start of the **Southern Upland Way**, and then beyond, further around the seafront northwards, the **Princess Victoria Memorial** on the cliff face commemorating the Portpatrick lifeboat men involved in the attempts to rescue the MV *Princess Victoria* on 31 January 1953 (page 225).

Further round the harbour, behind North Crescent and overlooking the putting green, is a smart row of black-and-white terraced houses on **Blair Terrace** that might have been lifted straight from the English Riviera, an unexpected sight in this very Scottish setting. Carrying on round to the southern side of the waterfront, at low tide there's a small sandy **beach**, and above it, next to Campbell's Restaurant you can see the remains of a 19th-century **lime kiln**, a series of arches dropping down to ground level and now filled in, which was built for use during one of the drives to develop the harbour. **St Andrews Kirk**, built in the 17th century, stands a short way back from the harbour off St Patrick Street. The round tower is thought to be older, possibly medieval, and is believed to have acted as a landmark for sailors. In the cemetery are maritime monuments to sailors, sea captains, customs officers and even to shipwrecks.

DUNSKEY CASTLE & ESTATE 🖐

A popular walk from Portpatrick is to wander south of the harbour for half a mile or so along the coastal path to **Dunskey Castle** (♀ NX004534), an impressive ruin gazing out to sea from its clifftop vantage point and which is only accessible on foot. It's an easy walk but there are steep steps to start with. For a **circular walk**, carry on past the castle and then drop down to the right to the disused railway line, which can be followed back into Portpatrick. In total, the walk is about 1¼ miles.

"Dunskey is well known for its snowdrops and opens in February each year as part of Scotland's Gardens Scheme for the Snowdrop Festival."

Between Portpatrick and Killantringan to the north is the **Dunskey Estate** (DG9 8TJ ⊘ www.dunskey.com), home to the Orr Ewing family. The house itself isn't open to the public, but the **gardens** are (☉ seasonal; admission charged for walled and woodland gardens; part of Scotland's Garden Route, see box, page 216) and feature an engaging, recently restored walled garden and a fine range of 19th-century glasshouses which are used to grow peaches, nectarines and grapes. There's also a **maze** to entertain kids and adults alike based on the one at Hampton Court but with a few tweaks. What is particularly impressive about the gardens here is that up until the late 1990s they had been neglected for many years, so what you see today is the result of only just over a decade's work. Dunskey is particularly well known for its snowdrops and opens in February each year as part of Scotland's Gardens Scheme for the Snowdrop Festival. Later on in the year it has a fine display of bluebells and rhododendrons in the woodland garden. There's a tea room and the estate also has a number of holiday cottages available.

KILLANTRINGAN

About a mile further north on the B738 from Portpatrick, a small road goes off to the left down to **Killantringan Lighthouse** and **Killantringan Bay** (♀ NW983566). The lighthouse has been decommissioned and is now privately owned and divided into holiday lets (on the market for sale at the time of writing, but still taking bookings) so it is not generally accessible. Next to it, though, is the wonderful bay, easiest to get down to at low tide and a great spot to come whatever the weather, either to enjoy the beach in the sunshine or to blow away the cobwebs in a blustery breeze.

¶¶ FOOD & DRINK

The Waterfront (7 North Crescent, DG9 8SX ☎ 01776 810800 ⌂ www.waterfronthotel. co.uk) and **The Crown** (9 North Crescent, DG9 8SX ☎ 01776 810261 ⌂ https:// crownportpatrick.com) next door are both good for meals, the latter has a welcoming fire in the winter and allows dogs too. Both also offer accommodation and enjoy prime locations on the waterfront with outside tables.

Campbell's Restaurant 1 South Crescent, DG9 8JR ☎ 01776 810314 ⌂ www. campbellsrestaurant.co.uk. A smart, family-run business with a fine menu of seafood and meat dishes, all locally sourced as much as possible. Everything from light lunches to full dinners is on offer, generally at the pricier end of the Portpatrick eating out scale. Conveniently located next to the car park on the waterfront.

Knockinaam Lodge Portpatrick, DG9 9AD ☎ 01776 810471 ⌂ www.knockinaamlodge. com. Definitely one for special occasions, the elegant restaurant at Knockinaam has held a Michelin star for over 20 years and is still wowing diners under the expert direction of head chef Tony Pierce. A range of stylish Scottish-based dishes is on offer, making good use of local produce, especially fish. Even if you don't come for dinner, splash out on a traditional afternoon tea. Reservations recommended for both.

Port Pantry 24 Main St, DG9 8JL ☎ 01776 810655 ⌂ www.theportpantry.co.uk ☉ café & gift shop are only open during the day, the bistro only in the evening at weekends. A cosy mix of café, bistro and gift shop. Food is a mix of café fare and more inventive and exotic dishes from around the world and there's a changing menu. The jalapeno quesadilla hits the spot on a winter's day. Check online or call ahead for opening times and to make reservations, as there are limited tables.

THE SOUTH RHINS

The southern half of the peninsula is a maze of winding lanes and rolling hills edged by cliffs and a rocky shore to the west and (on the whole) a fringe of beaches and gentler drops to the east. Heading down the Rhins there is a choice of either following the more westerly roads, which generally run inland from the coast itself, or the main A716 in the east which pretty much hugs the shoreline all the way to Drummore. Alternatively, a mix of both east and west can work depending on what you want to see and where you're aiming for; it doesn't take long to cross from one side of the peninsula to the other. The further south you go the more remote it feels until eventually the hills slope down to the dramatic clifftop lighthouse at **the Mull of Galloway**, Scotland's most southerly point.

SANDHEAD TO LOGAN HOUSE GARDENS

À New England Bay Caravan Club Site (page 250)

From Sandhead southwards there are splendid views across Luce Bay to the Machars and easy access to rocky beaches. Neat cottages and a grand house here and there dot the countryside, crow-stepped gables and Scottish baronial flourishes in evidence. Even in perfect weather you can see how harsh conditions can sometimes be here: the tops of the trees have been flattened by the prevailing winds.

The beach at **Sandhead** is a popular place to while away a few hours. The village is strung out along the road and the **beach** on the edge of Luce Bay stretches for a mile, seemingly endless when the tide is out.

In the middle of the peninsula stands pretty little **Kirkmadrine Church** (♀ NX080484; Historic Scotland) on or near the site of what would have been an important early Christian cemetery in this area. The present church is 19th century having been rebuilt from the ruins of an earlier medieval one by Lady MacTaggart Stewart of nearby Ardwell (see below) and based on the Romanesque church at Cruggleton (pages 197–8) near Garlieston on the Machars. The main attractions here are the three early Christian stones from the mid to late 6th century, some of the oldest monuments in Scotland outside Whithorn (pages 200–4).

From here it's a short hop down to **Ardwell**, an estate village of whitewashed cottages on the shoreline, and neighbouring **Ardwell Gardens** (DG9 9LX ✐ 01776 860227 ☉ seasonal), part of the Garden Route scheme and also in the Historic Houses Association (free to members). The gardens surround an imposing 18th-century estate house (private) and are noted for their daffodils and bluebell woodland walks. Azaleas, camellias and rhododendrons thrive and there is a relaxing walk around the pond with good views over Luce Bay. If you come at the right time in the summer there's an irresistible choice of fresh produce available from the walled garden.

Not to be confused with Ardwell House, **Ardwell Bay** is a few miles away on the western side of the peninsula and makes for a nice combination when visiting the eponymous gardens. It has a fine beach and there's a good walk from here, too (see box, opposite).

Logan House Gardens (DG9 9ND ☉ Mar–Sep, other times by appointment) are just a few miles south of Ardwell. A very long tree-lined drive replete with snowdrops and daffodils in spring gives way to

Ardwell Bay

❀ OS Landranger map 82, OS Explorer map 309; start: bay-side parking area, ♀ NX071449 (see below for details); 2 miles/1 hour; moderate (couple of steeper sections).

To access the car park from Sandhead, follow the A716 south and then turn right at the sign for Kirkmadrine Stones. Continue straight ahead and the road turns into an uneven track before dropping down to a small parking area right next to the bay. Note: there is no public transport to the bay and no refreshments are available.

From the 1 **bay-side car park** continue on the track past the small slipway and follow the waymarkers towards Ardwell Point, passing 2 **Doon Broch** (♀ NX066446), a once fortified dwelling built between 100bc and ad200, but now little more than a pile of stones, although with a bit of imagination you can make out the rooms.

Continue around the headland taking in the rugged cliffs and sea views. Grey seals can

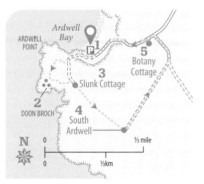

often be seen bobbing around in the water and, on our visit, we saw a magnificent nest of driftwood on a cliff ledge, likely belonging to a bird of prey. If you have a dog, we would pop it on a lead at this point as there are various caves, gullies and steep drops.

At 3 **Slunk Cottage** pass around to the right and then follow the track inland. Turn left at 4 **South Ardwell** (♀ NX073443) and follow the quiet track back past 5 **Botany Cottage** and down to **Ardwell Bay**. The sand dunes are a fragile ecosystem held together by plants such as marram grass, so please avoid trampling on this area and keep to the paths.

an avenue of rhododendrons which leads to the house. Press the yellow button to pass through the gate, which opens automatically, enticing you in. There is a small charge for entry/parking, and tickets are available from the machine in the parking area. The Queen Anne House (private) is surrounded by sweeping lawns and splendid Victorian woodland gardens. Logan House has seven UK champion and 14 Scottish champion trees, contributing to the description they use of 'forty shades of green' representing trees from all over the world.

7 LOGAN BOTANIC GARDEN ☝

DG9 9ND ✆ 01776 860231 ⊘ www.rbge.org.uk ⊙ Mar–Oct

Right next door to Logan House is Logan Botanic Garden, one of several outposts of the Royal Botanic Garden in Edinburgh and the only garden in Dumfries and Galloway to achieve a 5-star rating from VisitScotland, a fact of which they are justifiably proud.

Originally part of the grounds of Logan House owned by the MacDouall family, the gardens were developed initially by Agnes MacDouall in the 1870s. Today, curator Richard Baines looks after the gardens with a team of just five helpers. The range of trees, plants and shrubs is extraordinary, from the Australian collection to the woodland pond, via the Chilean collection, the biggest fuchsia we've ever seen, Gunnera bog, walled garden and a whole lot more in-between. There's also a Discovery Centre for kids, as well as a children's audio tour.

Twenty different species of palm and 20 of eucalyptus now grow here, and some of the tree ferns were originally part of the Great Exhibition at Crystal Palace in 1851. Other plants include a strawberry tree native to Portugal, a whopper of a giant ornamental rhubarb species from Brazil that grows to 14 feet tall, and a Tasmanian creek full of plants from the Anitpodes. Streuth! We particularly like the area known as the 'Bamboozling', with lots of different types of bamboo to walk through.

If you want to visit Logan by public transport, the 407 Stranraer–Drummore bus runs past the bottom of the garden drive from Monday to Saturday and will drop you off or pick you up. There are several services a day in each direction.

8 PORT LOGAN

The MacDoualls of Logan House are also to be thanked for the estate village of Port Logan on the west coast. It's a sleepy place with cottages set around a sandy bay with an old lighthouse, and yachts and boats bobbing inside the breakwater. On a calm, quiet day, this is the stuff of holiday snaps. It's said that on a stormy day, though, when the Atlantic pounds the beach, the sound of the breakers can be heard on the other side of the peninsula, which at this point is less than two miles away. This little village became known for an aquatic eccentricity, the questionable brainchild of Colonel MacDouall who was so keen on a spot of fish for his dinner that he fashioned a living larder out of a naturally occurring blowhole in the rocks where fish caught at sea could be kept until wanted for the table. **Logan Fish Pond** (DG9 9NF ✆ 01776 860300 ⌂ www.loganfishpond.org.uk ☉ seasonal) is still there today and usually has around 50 fish in it of various species, from cod and turbot to bull huss, conger eels and wrasse.

9 KIRKMAIDEN

Continuing south on the B7041, Kirkmaiden (the kirk of St Medan) stands proud atop a hill with a commanding view out to Luce Bay and across to the Machars, both associated with the church's eponymous saint. Medan arrived from Ireland in the 8th century, settling in a cave near East Tarbet (page 240) where she established a church. Her past caught up with her though when her former lover arrived from across the sea. She fled to a rock in Luce Bay, but the gods were against her for the rock moved of its own accord, transporting her to Monreith Bay (page 211) on the Machars. Undeterred, her lover followed and, when challenged by Medan as to why he pursued her with such ardour, proclaimed that it was her eyes that captured him. Desperate for an end to her torment, Medan gouged out her own eyes and her suitor retreated back to Ireland. That wasn't the end of it though, for Medan then bathed her eyes in a nearby well and her sight was restored. (The site of St Medan's Well is believed to lie near Kirkmaiden-in-Fernis on the Machars; page 211.) She spent the rest of her life founding churches all over Scotland.

THE LIGHTHOUSE GRAVESTONE

The graveyard at Kirkmaiden has an impressive range of 18th- and 19th-century funerary monuments and memorials, many topped with urns and shrouds. Particularly touching is a gravestone in the form of a lighthouse erected by James B Scott, principal lighthouse keeper at the Mull of Galloway (pages 241–3) in the mid 19th century, in memory of his son James. Maureen Chand of the Mull of Galloway Trust has looked into the history of this and tells us that Scott and his fellow lighthouse keepers were working on a gantry outside the tower at the Mull when his son sneaked up to help but fell off. He was killed immediately. The memorial is based not on the lighthouse at the Mull but on the one at Skerryvore off the south end of the island of Tiree, the most westerly isle of the Inner Hebrides. After leaving the Mull, Scott went on to Oban where the ships of the Northern Lighthouse Board are based. While there his wife died and so Scott made her gravestone in the shape of one of the lightships.

10 DRUMMORE

Scotland's most southerly village, Drummore is as far as you can get by public transport. If you're heading for the Mull, this is frustrating as it leaves you five miles short. From here you have no choice but to walk unless you happen to be staying in one of the cottages at the Mull itself (page 250), in which case a lift can be organised. Alternatively, if you're cycling or if you have a bike with you, there's a good route taking in the Mull and Kirkmaiden (details available from the information centre at Drummore; see page 218). Or, for a different view of the Mull, you can take a **boat ride** from Drummore just for the scenery, or to go fishing, seal spotting or birdwatching. Ian Burrett runs trips and can be contacted through his website *⊘* www.onyermarks.

"Scotland's most southerly village, Drummore is as far as you can get by public transport."

co.uk or by phone on *⊘* 01776 840346.

Drummore sits around and above its harbour, from which the main street runs uphill at right angles. It's a friendly place with a hotel, coffee shop, post office, **tourist office** run by volunteers, and general store.

Despite the discovery of gold here in the 1870s, Drummore has remained relatively isolated. Long ago it was said that the sheep of Drummore 'have all their teeth very yellow, aye, and their skin and wool are yellower than any other sheep in the country' because of the presence of gold; however, only thin flakes of the precious metal were ever found.

DRUMMORE TO THE MULL OF GALLOWAY

Between Drummore and the Mull of Galloway the peninsula narrows to not much more than the width of the road where it's nipped between the two bays of **West** and **East Tarbet**. Here in ancient times boats were rolled on logs between the bays, to avoid having to navigate around the Mull with its dangerous currents. North of East Tarbet about half a mile is **St Medan's Cove**, where Medan came ashore and fashioned her first chapel out of a natural rock formations before fleeing from her pursuing lover (page 239). Nearby are **Chapel Wells**, also referred to as The Well of the Co', of which it was recorded in the mid 19th century: 'To bathe in the well as the sun rose on the first Sunday in May, was considered as an infallible cure for almost any disease'. It was customary to leave a gift at the well, and coins of Charles I and II and William and Mary farthings have been found here.

From the Tarbets the road snakes ahead, crossing the **Double Dykes** that were thought to be the last line of defence of the Picts against the Scots. The road climbs upwards to the top of the 260-foot cliffs and the majestic vantage point of **the Mull of Galloway**, Scotland's most southerly point (latitude 54.6351°N) and actually further south than Penrith and Hartlepool. This is an awesome and inspiring place. One guidebook writer in the 1950s described it as: 'grand, high and frightening. A great point of headland thrust down in to the southern seas, a fortress whose stacks of cliffs bristle with knives and spears of rock, buttresses and crenelated and corbelled'. Nothing has changed.

11 THE MULL OF GALLOWAY 🖐

🏠 **Lighthouse Holiday Cottages** (page 250)

🖰 www.mull-of-galloway.co.uk. Note: the nearest petrol station is at Stranraer, so make sure you have plenty of fuel before heading down here.

The **Mull of Galloway Experience** (♀ NX155165) includes the lighthouse and associated buildings run by the Mull of Galloway Trust, adjoining RSPB reserve, and the superbly positioned Gaille Craig Coffee House (page 243), built on the very edge of the cliffs with a grass roof and vertiginous drop from the terrace. At the lighthouse itself is the main tower (small charge) and lighthouse keeper's cottages, which are now run as holiday lets (page 250), plus an exhibition (small charge) in the engine room.

From the bottom of the lighthouse tower up to the first gallery you climb 93 steps, after which there are two ladders, one to reach the outside viewing platform and another from there up to the light itself. The views are worth it: to Ireland and the Mountains of Mourne in County Down, and to the Isle of Man, just 19 miles away (and yet so far if you want to go there; the nearest ferry from the mainland departs from Heysham, just under 200 miles away). On a clear day you can see to Cumbria, too, and of course

"Gaille Craig Coffee House is built on the very edge of the cliffs with a grass roof and vertiginous drop from the terrace."

eastwards across to the Machars and north back up the Rhins. (There's no disabled access to the tower, but it's planned to build a disabled viewing platform at ground level.)

'I loved the place ... you can see ... Scotland, Ireland, Man, and the Kingdom of Heaven' is the famous quote from Bill Frazer, Principal Keeper 1971–75, and it pretty much sums up the feeling you get when standing on the clifftops or gazing out from the top of the lighthouse.

"Minke whales, porpoise and dolphins, puffins and guillemots are all visitors to the area."

This is a good place to bring the kids with lots to see and do. The **exhibition** is fun: huge red tanks that were once full of compressed air for the fog horn, an explanation of semaphore and a chance to try out your Morse code, a display on lighthouse keepers past, and there's always the story of James Birnie, the ghost of the lighthouse, who was the only keeper who actually died here.

In front of the lighthouse is a walled garden where once the lighthouse keepers grew their vegetables. It's now disused but the heather here and in the surrounding area comes out each August to provide a vibrant foreground for photographers. Tales of the Mull have long featured heather, or more specifically heather ale, the first ale brewed in the British Isles, for it is said that this is where the recipe for it was lost forever, a story that was immortalised by Robert Louis Stevenson in his poem 'Heather Ale: A Galloway Legend'.

Minke whales, porpoise and dolphins, puffins and guillemots are all visitors to the area, and adjoining the Mull lighthouse is the 30-acre **RSPB Mull of Galloway Reserve** (⊙ Mar–Oct). The main display is housed in a cottage which was home to the workers who built the lighthouse. The reserve consists mostly of maritime heath and cliffs, but also includes the **Scare Rocks** six miles out to sea, and a wide range of birds can be spotted here. A seasonal ranger runs the reserve and can point out other wildlife, including voles, mice, roe deer, a quite spectacularly iridescent beetle (the rose chafer beetle), and, controversially, weasels, which pose a threat to ground- and low-nesting birds. It's a bit too blustery and exposed for butterflies, but one or two day-flying moths might be spotted, notably the brightly coloured cinabar moth and similar five-spot burnet. Entertainment for kids is usually on offer, too, including colouring desks, films and webcams, and the chance of an activity tour looking for specific species and items. There are recordings of bird sounds and, for the ghoulish, bird skulls to try and identify. And if you fancy getting a closer look at the wildlife, there's always the option of a boat trip from Drummore (page 240).

⁋ FOOD & DRINK

Gaille Craig Coffee House The Mull of Galloway DG9 9HP ✆ 01776 840558 ⊘ www.
galliecraig.co.uk ⊙ Feb–Nov, but on reduced hours at either end of the season. Angela and
Harvey Sloan have been farming at the Mull of Galloway for many years; theirs is the last
farm you pass before reaching the lighthouse. Harvey still farms beef and sheep, but around
ten years ago he had a vision for creating an environmentally sensitive visitor facility and so
he set about designing and building a café that would fit in with the landscape and provide
a refreshment spot at Scotland's most southerly point. The result – a grass-roofed, glass- and
stone-encased shed with spectacular views and a cliff-edge terrace which makes the most
of its unique location – was so successful that it won the Green Apple Award from The Green
Organisation. What's really impressive about this building is that Harvey built a lot of it
himself and it's still owned and run by the family. It's a great place to come for teas or for a
fuller lunch (the chicken and bacon pie hits the spot). On a sunny day, the terrace at the end
can be a suntrap. And the name? Well that comes from the rocks far below that mark the
exact spot of Scotland's most southerly point.

Tigh Na Mara Main St, Sandhead DG9 9JF ✆ 01776 830210 ⊘ www.tighnamarahotel.
co.uk. Popular restaurant on the waterfront at Sandhead, serving traditional favourites from
local produce under head chef Duncan Mackay.

SEND US YOUR SNAPS!

We'd love to follow your adventures using our Slow Travel Dumfries & Galloway guide – why
not send us your photos and stories via Twitter (@BradtGuides) and Instagram (@bradtguides)
using the hashtag #dumfries&galloway. Alternatively, you can upload your photos directly
to the gallery on the Dumfries & Galloway destination page via our website (⊘ www.
bradtguides.com/D&G).

ACCOMMODATION

Below we offer a selection of accommodation options from across the area. Naturally this is far from exhaustive. These are hand-selected places that we have visited ourselves and which we feel fit the Slow ethos of the guide. None has paid to appear in these listings.

The hotels, B&Bs and self-catering options included here are indicated in the main body of the book by 🏠 under the heading for the town or village in which they are located. Campsites and caravan parks are indicated by ▲.

Due to space restrictions, descriptions here are necessarily limited to short entries.

👆 For further details and additional listings, go to ⟨ www. bradtguides.com/D&Gsleeps.

For the more intrepid traveller wanting to get right off the beaten path, there are a number of remote bothies across the southern region, details of which can be found at ⟨ www.mountainbothies.org.uk.

1 ANNANDALE & ESKDALE

Hotels

Annandale Arms High St, Moffat DG10 9HF ⟨ 01683 220013 ⟨ www. annandalearmshotel.co.uk. Comfortable and historic coaching inn in the centre of town with 16 en-suite rooms. Pets allowed in rear ground floor rooms next to the parking area.

Eskdale Hotel Market Pl, Langholm DG13 0JH ⟨ 01387 380357 ⟨ www.eskdalehotel. co.uk. Ideally located in the centre of Langholm, friendly and welcoming traditional hotel with spacious, well-turned-out rooms.

B&Bs & self-catering

Byreburnfoot Country House B&B and Cottages Canonbie DG14 0XB ⟨ 01387 371209 ⟨ www.byreburnfoot.co.uk. Three luxurious en-suite rooms and two self-catering cottages in a tranquil location on the River Esk with delightful views. Fishing on the river can be arranged from April to October. See advert in fourth colour section.

Cauldholm B&B Beattock, Moffat DG10 9QA ℘ 01683 300466 ◊ www.
moffatcountrysidebedandbreakfast.co.uk. Farmhouse comfort on the Annandale Way above
Moffat, with one en-suite room in the house, and an adjoining 'bothy' that sleeps four. Very
cosy, well finished with some nice touches.

Limetree House Guest House Eastgate, Moffat DG10 9AE ℘ 01683 220001 ◊ www.
limetreehouse.co.uk. Traditional Georgian townhouse with six spacious en-suite rooms,
including a family suite on the top floor. Comfortable guest lounge with wood-burning
stove. Convenient location just off Moffat High Street.

Nether Boreland B&B Boreland, Lockerbie DG11 2LL ℘ 01576 610248 ◊ www.chariots.
org.uk/BandB.html. Two en-suite rooms in the farmhouse at Chariots of Fire Driving/Horse
and Carriage Centre in a rural location near Lockerbie.

No. 29 Well Street Moffat DG10 9DP ℘ 01683 221905 ◊ www.moffatbandb.co.uk.
Contemporary and homey B&B right in the centre of town with four en-suite rooms, one of
which allows pets. Friendly and welcoming.

Waterside Rooms Dornock Brow House, Dornock, Annan DG12 6SX ℘ 01461 40232
◊ www.thewatersiderooms.co.uk. Cosy guest suite in a coastal cottage in a memorable
location with great views at the eastern end of the Solway. Quirky and friendly.

Campsites & caravans

Hoddom Castle Caravan Park Hoddom, near Lockerbie DG11 1AS ℘ 01576 300251
◊ www.hoddomcastle.co.uk. Caravans, 'Chill Pods' and a traditional Finnish Kota in the
grounds of a 16th-century castle in southern Annandale.

Moffat Camping and Caravan Site Hammerlands Moffat DG10 9QL ℘ 01683 220436
◊ www.campingandcaravanningclub.co.uk. Conveniently located 180-pitch site with good
facilities in a scenic setting.

2 NITHSDALE

Hotels

Blackaddie Country House Hotel Blackaddie Rd, Sanquhar DG4 6JJ ℘ 01659 50270
◊ www.blackaddiehotel.co.uk. Fine dining and luxury accommodation in a country house
that dates in part from the 16th century. Two self-catering cottages also in the grounds. See
advert in fourth colour section.

Buccleuch & Queensberry Arms Hotel 112 Drumlanrig St, Thornhill DG3 5LU ℘ 01848
323101 ◊ www.buccleuchhotel.co.uk. Historic hotel in the centre of Thornhill with 12
mostly spacious en-suite rooms. Lots of attention to detail, very comfortable.

Trigony House Hotel Closeburn, Thornhill DG3 5EZ ℘ 01848 331211 ◊ www.
trigonyhotel.co.uk. Originally a shooting lodge, now a hotel offering ten comfortable
en-suite rooms. Special deals often available; check the website.

B&Bs

Auchencheyne B&B Moniaive DG3 4EW ✆ 01848 200589 ⊘ www.auchencheyne.co.uk.
More than just a B&B, accommodation is in an 18th-century farmhouse annexe, plus there's
a walled vegetable garden and eco-conscious hosts.

Scaurbridge House Penpont, Thornhill DG3 4LX ✆ 01848 330152 ⊘ www.
scaurbridgehouse.co.uk. Characterful accommodation in a gracious former manse next to
Scaur Water in a popular village. Charming host who bakes delicious cakes. See advert in
fourth colour section.

Self-catering

See **Blackaddie Country House Hotel** under *Hotels* page 245.

See **Glenmidge Camping and Self-catering** under *Campsite* below.

Three Glens House Moniaive DG3 4EG ✆ 01848 200589 ⊘ www.3glens.com. Top-of-the-
range eco-lodge that's luxurious and innovative, complete with live-in cook. Very impressive
but requires deep pockets.

Campsites & caravans

Barnsoul Caravan Park Shawhead, Dumfries DG2 9SQ ✆ 01557 814351 ⊘ www.
barnsoulcaravanpark.co.uk. Caravans, camping, pods and mini-lodges in a lovely hillside
setting west of Dumfries.

Glenmidge Camping and Self-catering (The Old Smithy) Auldgirth DG2 0SW ✆ 01387
740328 ⊘ no website but details can be found on various general camping websites.
Popular site in a charming location in the hills.

3 DUMFRIES & THE NITH ESTUARY

B&Bs

Barr Farmhouse The Barr, Amisfield, Dumfries DG1 3LJ ✆ 01387 711384 ⊘ www.
barrfarmhouse.co.uk. Great location close to Dumfries but hidden away up a track. Two
rooms, scrumptious home baking and impressive breakfasts.

Glenaldor House 5 Victoria Terrace, Dumfries DG1 1NL ✆ 01387 264248 ⊘ www.
glenaldorhouse.co.uk. Central location overlooking private gardens in a mid 19th-century
terrace with four large en-suite rooms.

Self-catering

Wildfowl and Wetlands Trust Caerlaverock Eastpark Farm, Caerlaverock DG1 4RS
✆ 01387 770200 ⊘ www.wwt.org.uk (Caerlaverock section). The perfect choice for
birdwatchers, a traditional farmhouse renovated for communal living, though you
could potentially also have it to yourself. Great location actually within the boundaries

of the reserve, which you could also have to yourself after the gates close and everyone goes home.

4 THE STEWARTRY

Hotels

Cally Palace Hotel Gatehouse of Fleet DG7 2DL ✆ 01557 814341 ⏚ www.mcmillanhotels. co.uk/cally-palace-hotel. A historic country mansion with 56 en-suite rooms and opulent public spaces surrounded by parkland and a golf course.

The Selkirk Arms Hotel High St, Kirkcudbright DG6 4JG ✆ 01557 330402 ⏚ www. selkirkarmshotel.co.uk. Strong historical and literary connections in a traditional, recently refurbished hotel with 17 en-suite rooms on the old High Street. A good base for immersing yourself in the delights of Kirkcudbright and the surrounding area.

The Ship Inn 1 Fleet St, Gatehouse of Fleet DG7 2HU ✆ 01557 814217 ⏚ www. theshipinngatehouse.co.uk. A pleasant, recently refurbished hotel with historic literary connections located towards the southern end of the main street with ten comfortable en-suite rooms.

B&Bs

Craigadam Country House Hotel and B&B near Kirkpatrick Durham, Castle Douglas DG7 3HU ✆ 01556 650233 ⏚ www.craigadam.com. Impressive country farmhouse B&B in a scenic and convenient location with seven en-suite rooms set around a courtyard. Comfortable, hospitable and with great food. See advert in fourth colour section.

Douglas House 63 Queen St, Castle Douglas DG7 1HS ✆ 01556 503262 ⏚ www.douglas-house.com. Smartly turned-out B&B in a central location offering four tastefully decorated en-suite rooms and an award-winning breakfast.

Self-catering

Galloway Activity Centre Loch Ken, Parton DG7 3NQ ✆ 01556 502011 ⏚ www.lochken. co.uk. Wide range of accommodation, from cabins to the bunkhouse, plus two innovative lochside 'eco-bothies', compact but perfectly formed, cosy and with great views over the loch.

Gelston Castle Holidays Gelston, Castle Douglas DG7 1SW ✆ 01556 502211 ⏚ www.gelstoncastle.com. Four delightful courtyard cottages plus one other on the estate in a private setting, complete with communal tennis court and outdoor heated pool. See advert in fourth colour section.

Glenlee Holiday Houses Glenlee, New Galloway DG7 3SF ✆ 01644 430212 ⏚ www.glenlee-holidays.co.uk. A conversion of the old home farm into five c ourtyard cottages on a country estate. Traditional feel, more basic than some but comfortable and scenic.

Orroland Holiday Cottages Orroland, Dundrennan, Kirkcudbright DG6 4QS ✆ 01557 607707 🖰 www.orroland.com. Three elegant and cosy cottages sleeping two to 14 people on a private coastal estate. Whitewashed stone buildings, log fires and comfortable furnishings. Everything you could wish for from a country retreat with immaculate attention to detail.
The Grange Kirkcudbright DG6 4XG ✆ 01557 330519 🖰 www.cottageguide.co.uk/gallovidia. Two suites of rooms sleeping four and six in a Victorian country house with a more traditional – even old-fashioned – feel than many, but replete with old-world charm and boasting gorgeous coastal views.

Campsites & caravans
Loch Ken Holiday Park Parton, Castle Douglas DG7 3NE ✆ 01644 470282 🖰 www. lochkenholidaypark.co.uk. Static caravans and 100 camping pitches on a family-owned site on the shores of Loch Ken, plus kayak and pedalo hire.
Lochside Caravan and Camping Lochside Park, Castle Douglas DG7 1EZ ✆ 01556 503806 🖰 www.dumgal.gov.uk (click on 'Leisure Facilities' and then 'Tourism and Visitor Attractions'). Touring caravan and camping site next to Carlingwark Loch.
Sandgreen Caravan Park Sandgreen, Gatehouse of Fleet DG7 2DU ✆ 01557 814351 🖰 www.sandgreencaravanpark.co.uk. Long-standing and popular static caravan park. Most of the caravans are privately owned but two are available for hire, both located next to a lovely beach.

5 THE MACHARS & THE MOORS
Hotels
House o' Hill Hotel Bargrennan DG8 6RN ✆ 01671 840243 🖰 http://houseohill.co.uk. The only hotel within Galloway Forest Park (located on the western edge north of Newton Stewart), with two comfortable and stylishly refurbished guest rooms, plus a self-catering cottage that sleeps three (pets welcome).
Kirroughtree House Newton Stewart DG8 6AN ✆ 01671 402141 🖰 www. kirroughtreehousehotel.co.uk. Imposing country house with 17 traditionally decorated en-suite rooms and impressive public spaces. Scenic location above Newton Stewart.
The Steam Packet Inn Harbour Row, Isle of Whithorn DG8 8LL ✆ 01988 500334 🖰 www. thesteampacketinn.biz. Superbly located, very popular inn in a harbourside setting. Seven rooms, five overlooking the harbour.
Whithorn House Hotel St Johns St, Whithorn DG8 8PE ✆ 01988 501081 🖰 www. whithornhouse.com. Stylish small hotel with nine good-sized en-suite bedrooms, lots of attention to decorative detail. Popular tea room and a whisky lounge. See advert in fourth colour section.

B&Bs

Glaisnock Café and Guest House 20 South Main St, Wigtown DG8 9EH ✆ 01988 402249
🖰 www.glaisnock.co.uk. Small B&B with two en-suite rooms above this popular café in the
heart of Wigtown. Cosy and friendly.
Hillcrest House Maidland Pl, Station Rd, Wigtown DG8 9EU ✆ 01988 402018 🖰 www.
hillcrest-wigtown.co.uk. Welcoming hosts in a Victorian villa offering six large en-suite
rooms. Good food and a guest sitting room with wood-burning stove.

Self-catering

Cairnharrow Cairnhouse Farm, Newton Stewart DG8 9TH ✆ 01988 403217 🖰 www.
cottageguide.co.uk/8914. Very comfortable, spacious and well-presented modern cottage in
a convenient and scenic location with great views. Sleeps six.
The Pend George St, Whithorn DG8 8NS. Privately owned with the bookings handled
by National Trust for Scotland ✆ 0131 458 0305 🖰 www.pend-house.com. Historic and
beautifully furnished former monastery gatehouse in the centre of Whithorn. Sleeps four.
See advert in fourth colour section.

6 THE RHINS

Hotels

Corsewall Lighthouse Hotel Corsewall Point, Kirkcolm, Stranraer DG9 0QG ✆ 01776
853220 🖰 www.lighthousehotel.co.uk. Superbly located lighthouse hotel offering six
en-suite rooms and three suites. A tempting characterful retreat.
Knockinaam Lodge Portpatrick DG9 9AD ✆ 01776 810471 🖰 www.knockinaamlodge.
com. Luxurious and historic Victorian country house hotel in a superb setting with its own
beach just south of Portpatrick. Ten rooms, all ensuite. An altogether very special place
to stay.

B&B

Rickwood House Hotel Heugh Rd, Portpatrick DG9 8TD ✆ 01776 810270 🖰 www.
portpatrick.me.uk. Delightful B&B and charming hosts offering six en-suite rooms in an
Edwardian house. At the time of writing, there are plans to install a hot tub. See advert in
fourth colour section.

Self-catering

Kirklauchline Holiday Cottage Stoneykirk, Portpatrick DG9 9EE ✆ 07824 770968
🖰 www.portpatrickholidaycottage.co.uk. Charming renovated cottage with wood-burning
stove in a tranquil coastal location a few miles south of Portpatrick. Perfect for an escape and
as a base to explore the area. See advert in fourth colour section.

Lighthouse Holiday Cottages The Mull of Galloway Trust, The Mull of Galloway Lighthouse, Drummore, Stranraer DG9 9HP ℘ 01776 980090 ℘ www. lighthouseholidaycottages.co.uk. Converted lighthouse keeper's cottages at Scotland's most southerly point. Comfortable and cosy, with spectacular views. See advert in fourth colour section.

Campsites & caravans
New England Bay Caravan Club Site Port Logan, Drummore DG9 9NX ℘ 01776 860275 ℘ www.caravanclub.co.uk. Beautifully located caravan site with 155 pitches on the east coast of the Rhins. Sea views and direct access to the beach.

INDEX

Entries in **bold** refer to major entries; those in *italic* indicate maps.

INDEX OF ADVERTISERS

All adverts to be found in the 4th colour section at the back of this guide.

Blackaddie Country House Hotel
Byreburnfoot Country House B&B and Cottages
Craigadam Country House Hotel and B&B
Gelston Castle Holidays
Kirklauchline Holiday Cottage
Lighthouse Holiday Cottages
Pend, The
Rickwood House Hotel
Scaurbridge House
Whithorn House Hotel

BLACKADDIE HOUSE HOTEL

A romantic retreat with great food and attentive service, ideal for a relaxing break.

Of Scotland's many hidden treasures few are as precious as Sanquhar's Blackaddie. This beautiful and comfortable 16th-century country house hotel on the Southern Upland Way is set amidst the rolling hills in its own gardens on the banks of the Nith. Home to one of Britain's most celebrated chefs, it's perfect for family holidays and celebrations, for outdoor enthusiasts, business meetings, romantic breaks and weddings. Owner Ian McAndrew also offers the opportunity to join him in the kitchen to be 'Chef for a Day'.

Blackaddie House Hotel
Blackaddie Road
Sanquhar DG4 6JJ

Blackaddie
COUNTRY HOUSE HOTEL

www.blackaddiehotel.co.uk
Tel: 01659 50270
Email: ian@blackaddiehotel.co.uk

GELSTON CASTLE HOLIDAYS

'One of God's holiday destinations.'
(Guest's verdict)

- 'We never want to leave.' That's why so many of our guests are regulars.
- Idyllic 4,500-acre estate running down to the Solway coast.
- 'Better than home!' Comfortable, characterful self-catering houses.
- Log fires, big baths, trees and gardens, tennis, steam room, pool, lots more.
- Christmas special: turkey, tree, decorations, bottle of Port. Escape!
- A quirky and informative website (below) gives the full picture.

GELSTONCASTLE
holidays

www.gelstoncastle.com

Gelston   Tel: 01556 502211

Castle Douglas DG7 1SW   Email: holidays@gelstoncastle.com